Kohn Pedersen Fox
Architecture and Urbanism
1986–1992

Kohn Pedersen Fox
Architecture and Urbanism
1986–1992

Edited by
Warren A. James

KPF

Introduction by
Christian Norberg-Schulz

Essays by
Joseph Giovannini
Thomas L. Schumacher
William Pedersen
Warren A. James

Postscript by
Judith Turner

RIZZOLI
NEW YORK

To Warren, Magda, and Helen James
W. A. J.

First published in the United States of America in 1993 by
Rizzoli International Publications, Inc.
300 Park Avenue South, New York, New York 10010

Copyright © 1993 Kohn Pedersen Fox

"Introduction: The High-Rise City"
copyright © 1993 Christian Norberg-Schulz
"Kohn Pedersen Fox: Transition and Development"
copyright © 1993 Joseph Giovannini
"The Facades of KPF: Abstraction and the Limits of Figuration"
copyright © 1993 Thomas L. Schumacher
"The Circle and the Square"
copyright © 1993 Warren A. James
"Postscript"
copyright © 1993 Judith Turner

Library of Congress Cataloging-in-Publication Data
Kohn Pedersen Fox : architecture and urbanism, 1986–1992 / preface, A.
Eugene Kohn, William Pedersen, and Sheldon Fox ; introduction by Christian
Norberg-Schulz ; essays by Joseph Giovannini ... [et al.] ; postscript by Judith
Turner ; edited by Warren A. James.
p.   cm.
Includes bibliographical references.
ISBN 0-8478-1486-6.—ISBN 0-8478-1487-4 (pbk).
1. Kohn Pedersen Fox (Firm). 2. Architecture, Modern—20th century—United
States. 3. Architectural practice, International. I. James, Warren A., 1960– .
II. Giovannini, Joseph.
NA737.K65K59 1993
720'.92'2—dc20   92-33347
                                        CIP

Designed by Massimo Vignelli
Design Coordinator: Abigail Sturges
Printed and bound in Hong Kong

Revised, 1994

Contents

Preface

In 1976 we founded our firm with the intention of creating architecture that would make positive and sensitive contributions to the environments of cities throughout the world. We wanted to make our buildings active and engaging participants in their sites, buildings that are not only part of the fabric but also works of architecture that redefine and transform their context. That was our vision.

Since then, we have worked in different cultures with people from around the world. From Canada to the United Kingdom and from Germany to Cyprus in the Western Hemisphere, and from Japan to Australia and from Indonesia to Singapore in the Eastern Hemisphere, we strove to enrich the fabric of cities. We have worked in a variety of building types and scales. Not only have we designed and built skyscrapers, hotels, residential buildings, and corporate headquarters, but also a convention center, an art museum, private residences, and a major mixed-use transportation center. We have had wonderful experiences. We have learned and grown with our work.

Today, we still believe that our vision is unique. This book is a window into some of our recent efforts to fulfill that vision. The collection of buildings and projects represents our convictions and dreams. We hope our work speaks for itself. That is our aspiration.

A. Eugene Kohn
William Pedersen
Sheldon Fox

Introduction:
The High-Rise City

Christian Norberg-Schulz

Like no other architectural firm, Kohn Pedersen Fox has dedicated its attention to the development of the most characteristic and significant American building type, the skyscraper. For about one hundred years the American scene has been distinguished by high-rise buildings, and since the end of World War II the type has spread to other parts of the world as well. We have good reason to believe that the skyscraper will constitute a basic element in the city of the future, an assumption that implies that the modern city and the high-rise structure belong together. The work of Kohn Pedersen Fox is based on this very assumption and therefore represents an important contribution to the growth of the new city. In order to corroborate this assertion, we must take a look at the history of the skyscraper.

The rise of the skyscraper in Chicago after the Great Fire of 1871[1] was due in part to an understanding of the urban infrastructure as an open network or grid and of its vertical dimension as open to unrestricted growth. In the past, on the contrary, the vertical as a rule represented the sacred, and the tower acted as a landmark symbolizing the presence of forces and meanings that transcended everyday life. In other words, daily life did not take place in the tower but was provided with a spiritual component through the presence of the vertical element. In the American city, however, the role of the tower is fundamentally different, and accordingly the city as a whole takes on a new appearance. For a long time this was exemplified by the view of lower Manhattan for those arriving in New York by sea; today most American cities present themselves as a cluster of high-rise buildings of varying size and shape.

William LeBaron Jenney's invention of what is known as "Chicago construction" also contributed to the rise of the skyscraper.[2] But its origin lies further back in time and may be connected to the introduction of the gridiron plan during the seventeenth century. When William Penn planned Philadelphia as an extended grid in 1682, he transformed the city from a hierarchical structure around a dominant square into a neutral network focused on nodes of activity.[3] That is, the city was no longer the expression of a closed, integrated society but was an open framework where individuals could make their success manifest as buildings of varying height. Thus in the American city, the achievements of the individual are presented in terms of architecture, and the city becomes a forum for freedom of choice.

In general, the structure of the American city represents a development of its original form: an open street lined by rows of separate houses. This demonstrates the essentially democratic origin of the open city as an expression of the equal rights and opportunities of the individual. In the American city, urban freedom appears total but still remains within the grid. The new cityscape is thus constituted by individual structures standing and rising within the grid. Growth happens spontaneously and everywhere, and the nodes of activity that come and go evince the environment's dynamism.

Does this mean, then, that the American city is an amorphous non-place? Such a conclusion is implied by Lewis Mumford:

"In the gridiron plan, as applied in the commercial city, no section or precinct was suitably planned for its specific function: instead the only function considered was the progressive intensification of use. . . . Now the fact is that in urban planning, such bare surface order is no order at all."[4] In the American city, in fact, we do not arrive at any particular goal but find ourselves within an indeterminate pattern. Still, an order exists, an order that in a new way reflects the human activities that take place between earth and sky. In general, the order is a novel interpretation of the horizontal and vertical dimensions, as already suggested.

It is important to note that the new meaning of horizontality and verticality is common to the American house as well as to the American city. Frank Lloyd Wright's understanding of the horizontal as unlimited expanse and the vertical as manifestation of the human foothold in infinity is echoed by the general openness of the grid and the nodal function of the skyscraper. Hence, Alberti's dictum—that the house is a small city, and the city a large house—still holds true. But horizontal expanse only becomes meaningful if it is related to the rhythms inherent in the local environment. The early American street made clear such an order. For instance, a view of Philadelphia's Chestnut Street from 1879 seems to say: "You all had the same chance, and you may demonstrate your success by getting up in the high, but you cannot step out of the system, because then freedom would turn into its opposite and become a destructive mutual fight."[5]

Vertical rise also possesses its order, derived from the basic relationship between earth and sky. In his famous essay of 1896, "The Tall Office Building Artistically Considered," Louis Sullivan gave an early interpretation of the meaning of the skyscraper. First he stated the problem: "How shall we impart to this sterile pile, this crude, harsh, brutal agglomeration, this stark, staring exclamation of eternal strife, the graciousness of those higher forms of sensibility and culture that rest on the lower and fiercer passions?" His answer was simple: a very tall building also has to relate to the earth with "a great freedom of access" and terminate toward the sky with an attic of "dominating weight and character." In between, the world of the individual is expressed as "an indefinite number of stories of offices piled tier upon tier, one tier just like another tier, one office just like all the other offices." Hence Sullivan envisages a new vertical openness: human achievement is expressed not only by a distinguished street front but also by the height of a building. Implicit in Sullivan's concept is the elaboration of the termination with a symbolic "top" that adds an iconographic presence to the urban skyline.

This formation of the skyline—which also characterizes the new city—is the primary role of the skyscraper. A number of great contributions to this theme were realized between 1900 and 1940, such as the Woolworth Building in New York by Cass Gilbert (1913), the Chicago Tribune Tower by John Mead Howells and Raymond Hood (1922), and the Chrysler Building by William Van Alen (1929) and the Empire State Building by Shreve, Lamb and Harmon (1931), both in New York. The Chrysler Building, in particular, has become one of the city's

best-remembered landmarks, thanks to its distinct image. It shows us how architecture may assure human orientation and identification in an open city.

The development of the urban structure entered another phase with New York's Rockefeller Center (1928–1941), by a team of architects including Raymond Hood. Here, "almost everything that a city . . . should be comes together: skyscrapers, plazas, movement, detail, views, stores, cafés," Paul Goldberger writes. "It is all of a piece, yet it is able to appear possessed of infinite variety at the same time."[6] It is all of a piece because it respects the grid and the street and at the same time activates the space within the block. Thus Rockefeller Center constitutes an island of meaning within the indeterminate grid and suggests what may become one of the open city's basic structural qualities.

Unfortunately, this crucial lesson of the early skyscrapers was forgotten after World War II, and high-rise building degenerated into the monotonous repetition of inarticulate curtain-wall architecture. Although some of the executed works possessed true artistic value, such as Mies van der Rohe and Philip Johnson's Seagram Building (1958), they did not represent any real contribution to the further development of the high-rise city. Instead, the most important achievements of the postwar years were the structural innovations of Fazlur Khan, notably in the impressive John Hancock Center (1970) and Sears Tower (1974), both in Chicago.

What was lost after the war, first of all, was the expressive skyline, a loss that in 1983 prompted the Chicago Architectural Club to sponsor a public design competition entitled "Tops." This was intended to "revive the richly symbolic iconography and articulately ornamental monumentality of the urban tower."[7] Shortly thereafter, Philip Johnson and John Burgee completed the AT&T Corporate Headquarters in New York. AT&T chairman John deButts was from the beginning opposed to a "glass box," a form he felt would not distinguish AT&T from its neighbors. To meet this demand, the architects sought to revive the great architectural traditions of the first half of the century. The result is a building that we recognize and remember, because of its active relationship to the street and its expressive silhouette. As a part of the cityscape, the AT&T Building stands forth with a characteristic identity.

It is in this context of the open city and the related development of the skyscraper that we must consider the works of Kohn Pedersen Fox. Already by 1979 William Pedersen had designed the seminal 333 Wacker Drive in Chicago, a building in which the basic aims of the firm are set forth. Located where the urban grid meets the bend in the Chicago River, the building had to resolve two conflicting situations: the orthogonal geometry of the grid and the topology of the river. Accordingly, the volume was split into two segments, a curved front facing the waterway and a faceted series of steps in the back. At the top, the segments interpenetrate, becoming a significant part of the urban skyline.

An analogous interpretation determined Pedersen's grandiose project for Houston Office Tower–Block 265, from 1981. Here the building comprises a park side and a city side. The former consists of a low pavilionlike structure opening on the green with a tall curved wall of reflecting glass above, whereas the city side is composed of solid granite elevations. Again the two sides interpenetrate in a collagelike manner in order to express the role of the building in the total context.

Equally important is the competition entry for the Bank of the Southwest in Houston (1982). Here, wrote Pedersen, "the base establishes a facade providing a continuity and cohesion to the public realm. The tower asserts its individuality as an object in the sky." In an interview in November 1985, he elaborated on his intentions: "The tall building must begin at its lower levels by acting as a facade that can join with other facades to create the urban walls that define a street. Once it meets that need, the tall building can rise as a freestanding object to fulfill the demands of its own program. We do this by treating the tall building initially as facade and then as object."[8]

In a rich and varied series of projects and buildings, Kohn Pedersen Fox has realized these aims. Many stylistic references have been used, and the classical language has served as a general compositional aid. It cannot be denied, however, that a certain stagnation set in during the mid-to-late 1980s. In projects such as 125 East 57th Street (1983–1986) in New York, National Bank of Commerce (1984) in San Antonio, and 125 Summer Street (1985–1990) in Boston, the modern, collagelike freedom of the earlier works was replaced with an additive and over-articulated mode of composition, and the new and the old failed to enter into a convincing dialogue.

It is therefore with great pleasure that we recognize the exceptional quality of Pedersen's recent projects. Starting with Three Bellevue Center (1988–1994) in Bellevue, Washington, he returns to compositional methods that are more in tune with our time. Thus he reinterprets his environmentally determined structures from about 1980 in a truly creative manner, and at the same time he preserves the classical control he employed in the late 1980s. The result is a convincing alternative to the more superficial fashions of the present, such as deconstructivism. Among the new projects, we may single out One Fountain Place (1985–1988) in Cincinnati, where the original concept of the high-rise structure has found a new and fascinating interpretation. The same holds true for Mainzer Landstrasse 58 (1986–1993) in Frankfurt am Main, Germany; St. Paul Companies Headquarters (1987–1991) in St. Paul, Minnesota; Chifley Tower (1987–1992) in Sydney, Australia; and the Ameritrust Center (1988–1995) in Cleveland. However, 311 South Wacker Drive (1985–1990) in Chicago still represents a phase of transition. Pedersen's recent development culminates in the splendid Rockefeller Plaza West (1987–1991) in New York.

Regarding this last project, William Pedersen writes: "The contrasting models of modernism, Rockefeller Center and Times Square, form the context of the project and inform its design. The lessons offered by these fantasies of the city have allowed for a consideration of the buildings as an assemblage, the pieces of which resolve the various site conditions, while the whole is both monumental and dynamic, embodying the energy of the modern city." Thus the project truly expresses the new open world of memories and possibilities. Ada Louise Huxtable evaluates the design, saying: "Rockefeller Plaza West is a skilled exercise in the historical continuum of humanistic architecture that can give both service and pleasure, even at today's superscale."[9]

With rare perseverance Kohn Pedersen Fox has offered ever novel contributions to the development of the high-rise city. The idea of simultaneously adapting to the horizontally extended environment and creating an individual object in space grasps the problem of the new urban pattern at its core, and the results show that independence and interdependence are qualities that may be reconciled. Hence the proximate street is preserved as a basic environmental fact at the same time that the distant skyline expresses the new pluralism.

To make the open city truly alive, what is needed above all is architectural quality. Fortunately the Americans have always given quality pride of place. It is a basic misunderstanding to reject American architecture as arbitrary manifestations of the "melting pot." Early on Thomas Jefferson wanted to revive "the first principles of the art," and in our century Louis Kahn advocated a return to the beginnings.[10] American architecture in fact proves that a new start is not necessarily a start from zero. The works of Kohn Pedersen Fox belong to the American tradition of first principles and teach us that the high-rise city, in addition to offering service and pleasure, is a meaningful expression of the new world.

Notes

1. See Carl W. Condit, *The Rise of the Skyscraper* (Chicago: University of Chicago Press, 1952).
2. Condit, *Skyscraper*, pp. 6, 9.
3. John L. Stilgoe, *Common Landscape of America 1580–1845* (New Haven: Yale University Press, 1982), pp. 94–96, 97–99.
4. Lewis Mumford, *The City in History* (New York: Harcourt, Brace & World, 1961), p. 424.
5. Christian Norberg-Schulz, *New World Architecture* (New York: Princeton Architectural Press, 1988), p. 31.
6. Paul Goldberger, *The City Observed: New York* (New York: Random House, 1979), p. 168.
7. "Introduction to Tops," *The Chicago Architectural Journal* 3 (1983): p. 11.
8. Sonia R. Cháo and Trevor D. Abramson, eds., *Kohn Pedersen Fox: Buildings and Projects 1976–1986* (New York: Rizzoli International Publications, 1987), p. 305.
9. Ada Louise Huxtable, "Rockefeller Plaza West," *Center: The Magazine of Rockefeller Center*, March/April 1991, p. 9.
10. Norberg-Schulz, *New World*, p. 15.

Kohn Pedersen Fox:
Transition and Development

Joseph Giovannini

In 1989, at an American Institute of Architects convention in Orlando, Gene Kohn attended a business seminar in which a nationally known economist told his audience that unless they soon started to work internationally, half of their firms would be out of business within five years. Kohn took the prediction seriously and launched a campaign to target clients abroad. Within months, Kohn—who had long since blanketed the primary and secondary cities in the United States—was flying across the Pacific Ocean and introducing KPF to Asia, Southeast Asia, Australia, and New Zealand; recently he has been heading to South America. The travels would have serious impact not only on KPF's livelihood but also on its design.

In corporate America in the 1980s, KPF earned its reputation as a high-service firm creating contextually sensitive, classically styled office buildings that performed a socializing role in their neighborhoods and cities. The dominantly horizontal classical podiums supporting the towers acted like urban hyphens, linking surrounding buildings, while the richly patterned figural towers became logos and beacons on the skyline. The architects reconceived the high-rise building, which is insular by nature, as a messianic arrival with connective powers that could again make cities whole. Taking the Chrysler Building rather than the Seagram Building as a model for the towers, the architects voted for spirit over Cartesian reason, and the architectural charisma of their designs helped rescue the American high-rise from bottom-line banality and reclaim the American city from the drift typical of cities during the country's long postwar romance with the suburbs. KPF buildings helped recharge downtowns with the energy they had prior to World War II, when exuberant skyscrapers idealistically symbolized the promise and greatness of cities. The firm's designs captured the nature of the white-collar urban renaissance taking place across America.

The best of their buildings—such as the 1983 Brancusi-esque 333 Wacker Drive in Chicago, with its bowed front turning along a bend in the Chicago River—managed to preserve both the order of the building and the order of the city. The newly established but very successful firm brought postmodernism out of the arena of the rarefied domestic and institutional commission and into the marketplace. In 1985, even John Burgee, of rival firm John Burgee Architects with Philip Johnson, proclaimed it "the best commercial firm now practicing in the U.S."

But by the late 1980s, doubt settled on what risked becoming a formulaic practice. Bill Pedersen, whose designs set the firm's direction, came to realize that the continuity and harmony of the traditional European city, which KPF's classicized buildings overtly espoused, was an ideal that rarely existed. Furthermore, the ideal might not even be desirable: disjunction, he stated, was the dominant characteristic of most cities and the factor that energized them. And if buildings are, in some way, a mirror of the city, then buildings without disjunction lack energy.

Seriously compounding this doubt about the desirability of traditional European urbanism was the fruit of Gene Kohn's business trips: an increasing number of commissions came from cities *un*like Paris, London, Philadelphia, Boston, and New

11

1

2

York. In 1986, with its design for 1000 Wilshire Boulevard, KPF had already learned that setting a classicized building next to a freeway in downtown Los Angeles made dubious urban sense. When the firm pushed into Japan and designed for Tokyo, Osaka, Makuhari, and Nagoya, it encountered concerns of urbanism and scale (along with a Japanese sense of space) that made traditional European planning obsolete, as did commissions in Jakarta, Singapore, Taiwan, Bali, Seoul, and Kuala Lumpur. In Honolulu, KPF architects encountered an urbanism based on a different premise, one that related to nature and the climate rather than to streets and squares shaped by walls of buildings. A traditional European approach was proving misplaced—even anticontextual —in towns typified by discontinuity or organized as garden cities and autopias. In KPF's increasingly multinational and multicultural practice, Eurocentric urbanism was often wrongheaded.

Even in Europe it was ringing false: the context for the new Warsaw Bank Center (fig. 1) in Poland was not a friendly, street-oriented traditional neighborhood but a forlorn, antipedestrian district exploded in scale and populated by alienating megablocks dating from the Communist regime, dominated by a monumental Stalinist palace of culture done in the style of official state classicism. A classicized KPF building hardly had the power to precipitate a more humane urbanism in this isolating context, and the authoritarian connotation of the style would strike the wrong note. The new building could not be saddled with the classicist symbolism of axial, centered, hierarchically organized design that implied that capitalism was simply another authoritarianism.

And so by the late 1980s, even though their buildings were not broken, KPF architects were fixing them. Despite its success, the firm substantially redefined its design practice with a new generation of buildings. Pedersen critiqued the authoritarian nature of the earlier projects: "The scale and presence of the buildings we were generating was somewhat autocratic, so centralized and hierarchical that every part pointed to a larger whole that didn't contribute to a city with so many conflicting forces at work."[1] Some of the buildings, though good citizens, had simply become boringly polite, the surface development of the skins excessively and obsessively formal; a few of the more self-conscious verged on the decadent. It was indeed becoming clear in KPF's increasingly elaborate classicized buildings that the idiom could no longer contain the metabolic rate of change in the office and that the language was bottling the search and the need to change. A break was coming. The classically replete 125 Summer Street (fig. 2) in Boston, completed in 1990, was overwhelmed by its obeisance to a perceived traditional context that was itself problematic; it emerged looking like a sculptural antimacassar. Not all contexts, even old ones, need be perpetuated; some might even be challenged. Accelerating and intensifying the change within KPF was an accompanying sea change in the sensibility of the field. The energy and force of the work of such architects as Zaha Hadid, Coop Himmelblau, and Frank O. Gehry attracted considerable attention by the 1980s, shifting the intellectual and formal terrain of architectural practice.

12

3. Kohn Pedersen Fox, Mainzer Landstrasse 58 (1986–1993), Frankfurt. Model.

The pivotal project for KPF was Mainzer Landstrasse 58, an office tower designed in early 1987 for Frankfurt (fig. 3). Although this old German banking city on the Main would seem to be the appropriate place for a postmodernist effort, saturation bombings during the war had wiped out almost everything but the street patterns. Historical buildings were scant; postwar growth was dominantly modernist or in a simple commercial vernacular; any expectation of responding to a traditional context was predicated on a nonexistent condition. The Westend site for the tower was itself conflicted. It lay at a transitional edge between business and residential districts, among buildings of varying types and heights, from villas to high-rises. Rather than proposing a characteristic high-rise with a clearly defined figural tower and an articulated top and base, Bill Pedersen sensed that it was necessary to respond to the more diverse elements in the context: "We had been looking to the past, not the present or future—I was not acknowledging the full set of forces in a modern city." The recognition of greater complexity started to dissolve the tower as a unified figure, and a new type of building began to emerge that not only acknowledged a richer context but also started to transcend it, asserting its own presence and defining its own context.

To acknowledge the nearby low, medium, and tall buildings, Pedersen broke the building down into parts that corresponded to the heights and character of surrounding buildings. The mixed-use program itself encouraged short perimeter structures at the base, also varied in height and material. These low-rise structures, as diverse as buildings in a local townscape, wrap around a winter garden, front the streets, and interlock with a complexity reminiscent of Richard Meier's Museum for the Decorative Arts on the other side of the Main. No longer did a formulaic base, shaft, and top constitute the building; rather its fragments registered the site's urban complexities, with the parts loosely gathered around the (stabilizing) elevator core—known in the office as the "stick in the Popsicle."

Frankfurt, a city that wanted to manifest its "Manhattan-ness" as a banking capital, has been one of the few old European cities to encourage the high-rise, and the controversial pro-skyscraper stance begged alternatives to the numbingly monotonous towers that had deadened too many downtowns. KPF's building was among the first to collage and collapse the surrounding urban characteristics volumetrically within the body of the building rather than just graphically on the curtain wall as a sign. In plan, the high-rise lost its usual symmetries, even in the tower. Pedersen was breaking the high-rise box, but he was not prescribing another, "better" form; instead, he was proposing a strategy for inventing responsive shape and organization in the tall building. A single building might now be able to initiate multiple dialogues with its near and distant neighbors or to accommodate conflicting programmatic demands, because the figural whole did not demand conformity. The individual parts were freer to refer to contexts outside the object. For Pedersen, a combination of the formal and informal was possible; he felt his work in the high-rise had graduated to a more mature phase. For the rest of the firm, Mainzer Landstrasse 58 opened new possibilities beyond the self-referential, self-containing

3

*4. Kohn Pedersen Fox, Chifley
Tower (1987–1992), Sydney.
View.
5. Kohn Pedersen Fox, One
Fountain Place (1985–1988),
Cincinnati. Photomontage.*

4

classicism of buildings subordinated to a single dominant idea. Just as KPF had brought postmodernism into the commercial marketplace, it was bringing strategies of fragmentation to the high-rise—even if corporate patrons remained the very symbols of hierarchical organization.

The Frankfurt tower was not immediately built, but it fathered a new generation of buildings, including One Fountain Place in Cincinnati, Rockefeller Plaza West in New York, 1250 Boulevard René-Lévesque in Montreal, and Chifley Tower in Sydney (fig. 4). The towers eschew the monolithic figure in favor of simultaneously informal and formal designs that respond to the push and pull of internal and external pressures. The sculpturally multivalent Chifley Tower, for example, relates so strongly to surrounding buildings that it seems to exceed its own boundaries and compose the skyline into a collage. The new addition refigures the cluster so that the skyscrapers no longer form a patch of stand-alone asparagus stalks.

Designed a short time after Frankfurt, One Fountain Place (fig. 5) takes Frankfurt's design strategies to a heroic scale and, in its boldness and originality, supersedes the context that it consciously acknowledges. A fifty-story mixed-use building with huge retail, hotel, parking, office, and observatory components, it is an assemblage of architectural types—arcade, court, rotunda, gallery—as well as skin patterns, all of which sustain an intelligible human scale. A dramatic hat-truss, which stabilizes the building against the overturning force of wind, consummates the structure and crowns the skyline. A tall planar wall rising from the body of the building separates the more public face from the more private and endows the front with the civic presence of a campanile. With a bowed facade that acknowledges Fountain Square and a body that locks into the grid of the surrounding blocks, the building honors its context while erupting in a spirited and independent cadenza in its upper reaches where a multiplicity of forms breaks up the single figure. One Fountain Place not only confirms its context, but changes it, maintaining its own order and the order of the city without being mimetic.

The designs for both One Fountain Place and the Frankfurt tower were achieving what Robert Venturi calls the "difficult whole," but not just as a patterned figure. In each case, parts of the building were acquiring separate, though not independent, identities, and the presence of the entire structure, though huge, was less authoritarian and more benign. This new family of buildings pointed to a direction that soon eclipsed KPF's postmodernist efforts, the last of which would be the United States Courthouse at Foley Square in Manhattan.

These inventions, however, were not acts of contrition by repentant postmodernists. When viewed in the larger context of KPF's work, the new complexity was consonant with a firm whose work, even from its beginning modernist phases in the late 1970s, was characterized by the urge to elaborate rather than reduce. Very early the firm had designed the shape and skin of a building as the record and result of the internal forces of its program as well as the external forces of the city. In the late 1980s, a building like Cleveland's Ameritrust Center (fig. 6)—

5

6. Kohn Pedersen Fox,
Ameritrust Center (1988–
1995), Cleveland. Model.
7. Kohn Pedersen Fox, Canary
Wharf Tower (1986–1987),
London. Model.

8. Kohn Pedersen Fox,
Rockefeller Plaza West (1987–
1991), New York. Model.

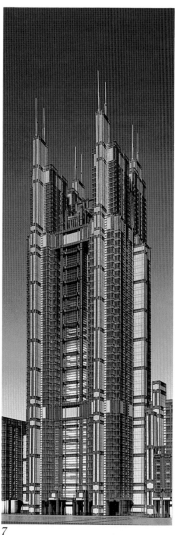

6

7

8

fragmented and divided into volumetric parts—recalled such projects as the Tampa Financial Center of 1980, where the facades, responding to different views and exposures, became a large-scale collage.

But while Frankfurt, One Fountain Place, and Ameritrust Center alluded to the earliest work, they also took advantage of KPF's sophisticated development of their often elaborate postmodern curtain wall. The classicized work had led to textural and material weaves and to intimations of spatial depth in shallow curtain walls—as in the highly literate, even witty wall of ABC Phase II (1984–1986), with its surprising scale jumps and dropped panels. The skin of the Canary Wharf Tower (fig. 7) became so articulated and spatial that it emerged from the surface as an exoskeleton: Pedersen's highly wrought curtain wall of brushed metal and metalized-stone infill panels transformed the building into a high-tech, Gothic cathedral of industry.

By the time KPF embarked on the Frankfurt project and a new generation of buildings, then, the architects were able to support a multiplicity of shapes in a fragmented high-rise with a multiplicity of surfaces from their repertory. The architects could easily turn the surface volume up or down, but they were not always aware of one important implication: the curtain walls developed in the earlier period had the unexpected ability to carry early ideas over into late buildings, mixing the messages.

KPF buildings, whatever their ideology, have always been civilized and elegant neighbors, and Rockefeller Plaza West (fig. 8) is a paradigm of diplomacy in a context that spans the worlds of Fifth, Sixth, and Seventh avenues. Through mixed allusions of shape, surface, and material, the complex design makes an architectural transition between the RCA (now GE) and Exxon buildings and the luminous headwaters of Times Square. Breaks in massing and shifts in scale correspond to changes of program inside. The facade maps the surrounding context: to the south it wraps the elevator core in an asymmetrical de Stijl or constructivist composition referring to neighboring structures; to the north it recalls the slabbed massing of RCA; the base is a frieze of electronic billboards.

The graphically active surfaces provoke the eye to roam freely over their cross-patterns and floating planes. In its ambidirectionality, the building ignores gravity and denies the visual accumulation of weight that characterized the firm's postmodernist designs. The loss of weight equates with a loss of mass and allies the building with the modernist rather than the classical tradition. The horizontals lighten the tower and through a hyphenating effect carry the lightness over to surrounding skyscrapers.

Compositional strategies of fragmentation also helped resolve pressing issues of gigantism in the forty-seven-story, 1.6-million-square-foot 1250 Boulevard René-Lévesque for IBM/Canada in Montreal (fig. 9), where the subtle, individually distinct responses to the cityscape and landscape reduce the bulkiness of the hefty 28,000-square-foot floor plates. The abstraction of the language also avoids the difficulty of applying a classical vocabulary to the high-rise, in which architects grapple with an essentially horizontal idiom in an overwhelmingly vertical context.

Loosely organized into a base, middle, and top, the IBM/Canada building has one facade layered in thin, mostly granite slabs that refer to nearby buildings and another tensely bowed, mostly glass facade with a horizontal sweep centering on the dome of the cathedral opposite. The horizontal spandrels of the bow front weave through the gridded pattern of the more solid parts, uniting rather than colliding the parts. Its asymmetrical massing gives the building the sculptural *contrapposto* of a *David* and is most intense around the building's mast, where the skin breaks into an architectural equivalent of constructivist counter-reliefs—an abstract and very spatial composition of interpenetrating metal-and-glass elements. IBM/Canada represents a paradigm different from the cruciform Place Ville Marie tower by I. M. Pei several blocks east, which in the late 1950s and early 1960s heralded the coming age of the developer building in North American cities.

The evolution of KPF's work has hardly been linear. The firm is structured so that there are several design partners and a pluralistic voice; one partner will even pursue different directions simultaneously. The constructivist leanings of Rockefeller Plaza West and IBM simply represent one strong current. More closely related to the postmodernist work, yet also affected by the new sensibility, is the Goldman Sachs European Headquarters (1987–1991) in London, a statically massed office building in the center of London where the density of the city, along with implicit height limitations, has compressed independent pavilions into a dense composite structure. A different context obtains in St. Paul, Minnesota, where—in the St. Paul Companies Headquarters (1987–1991)—midwestern space has instead released the pavilions, which emerge as almost independent of the main body of the building, breathing more freely. The several shapes—a cylinder, pyramidal tower, and rectangular base—are designed in contradistinction to one another and in response to their urban roles. Rather than integration, the architects were positing that systems of difference—the opposition of forms, textures, scales—breed formal tension, unlike the systems of agreement in classicized buildings, where the parts add up to a balanced and settled whole.

Differentiation was achieved not by shape but by abrupt changes in surface patterns in KPF's design of the World Bank Headquarters in Washington, D.C. (fig. 10). Again, the technical virtuosity coming out of KPF's complex curtain walls of the 1980s, where patterns were manipulated to look inlaid, woven, or assembled, allowed the architects to summon patterns that can stabilize, destabilize, stop, stretch, center, or even jump scales. In this two-phase addition to the bank's headquarters, the architects pinwheeled two office blocks around two existing structures, patterning one in sweepingly horizontal lines and the other in verticals that arrest the eye. Patterning the facades gave the building an active surface and a design that could easily be adapted to the circumstances of the varied perimeter.

9

10

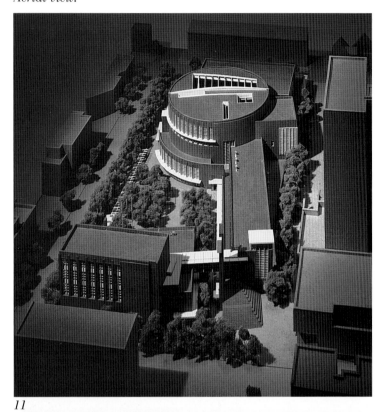

11

12

KPF rarely accepts commissions for single-family houses, but the first scheme Bill Pedersen produced in 1988 for the Carwill house, on a hilltop in Stratton Mountain, Vermont, proved pivotal for the generation of high-rise structures that was to follow the generation of works fostered by Mainzer Landstrasse 58. This house and the international commissions Gene Kohn was bringing into the office for buildings other than high-rises were to diversify KPF's typical commissions and expand the firm's formal range.

Though hardly located in an exotic culture, the house was one of the first buildings for which KPF took its design cues from nature rather than from the city, and the commission helped open KPF buildings to a broader definition of context. The commission provided a welcome escape from corporate culture and an escape from the issue of repetition as a determinant of form, so pressing in the high-rise. Pedersen took full advantage of the new liberties.

The initial (unbuilt) design for the Carwill house was by far the more interesting and influential of the two designs. The design handily survived the local requirements of sloping roofs and vernacular materials: wings of the house, on top of a hill, wheeled around the site, capturing certain views and exposures. The angles hardly constituted any vernacular typology known in Vermont. The wings remained tethered at points, stabilizing the whole.

The house had an especially strong effect on three projects in Hawaii, where views of the ocean and mountains, like the views in Vermont, exert a strong formal attraction on the building. Tugged by the ocean in one direction, the mountains in another, and acknowledging road axes and local street conditions, the buildings lose their usual geometric rigidity and obeisance to the right angle. In Honolulu, as in Vermont's landscapes, there is little contextual reason for a classical building. Hawaii, so unexpected a venue for a KPF skyscraper, presented conditions that challenged KPF's scope of concerns in the high-rise.

Prominently located on the water in Honolulu, Waterfront Place is made up of two pairs of clustered apartment towers variously angled to the ocean, mountains, and city streets. The architects have shaped a waterfront signature, monumentalizing a typological form whose breakdown into apartment units usually resists monumentality. Seeking the sculptural impact of the Sydney Opera House, the architects shaped the brise-soleils of balconies into a gestural sail of metal and glass and were especially attentive to the base and top, which, as terminal points, are freer than the repetitive shaft. The roofscape strongly resembles the freewheeling, view-oriented plan of the Carwill house (though the roof shapes in Hawaii are more contoured and dynamic). Unfortunately, the freedom of the roofscape and groundscape and the unfolding orientation of the two pairs of towers do not penetrate to the floor plans of the apartment units, which are locked into a strict orthogonal organization. Still, KPF again has managed to introduce into a large-scale developer commission ideas generated in the far more precious environment of a design for a private house.

KPF has a very long formal and ideological memory and, rather than shedding expertise and ideas as it evolves, tends to fold them into a cumulative repertoire. The single longest common thread around which KPF has built its practice has always been a response to context, though the understanding of context has changed. It was first perceived as the forces from within and without the building, then as the given surroundings of the site, and most recently as a complex of conditions including views and nature which together act as a field of forces. Over a decade ago, when KPF architects spoke of buildings designed to respond to forces, force was used largely as a design metaphor to shape buildings. What has changed is that the force metaphor has settled into the building as an idea in the same way that weight settled into classical columns to create entasis: form became ideated. In the firm's 1991 design for the mixed-use Platz der Akademie/Block 30 building in Berlin, the plan of the entire building is occupied by the notion of force: at the back corner the memory of the seventeenth-century military ramparts that once existed there pushes the building forward into the dominant court.

In Beaux Arts urbanism, buildings were planned as simple static figures to receive and complete axes; KPF buildings in Hawaii, on the contrary, not only receive but exert force, sending it along transformed. The building has now become an actor in the force field: the building is broken into parts, and the parts become dynamic. The design preserves the order of the building and the order of the city, but the orders of both are now differently conceived.

Contradictions naturally exist in a formal and ideological memory that spans several periods. In the Concert Tower, another Honolulu project, the shearing forces generated by opposing views to the mountains and sea are clearly mapped in the plans. On the other hand, the graphics of the curtain walls—horizontal toward the ocean and vertical toward the mountain, where the elevator shaft is situated and exposed—remain those of a handsome but still conventionally extruded skin. Plan and elevation express a different body language. The elevation does not yet acknowledge the physics of the site.

The unresolved contradictions of KPF's periods are perhaps most visible in the Revlon Campus Center (fig. 11), a student center on the University of Pennsylvania campus in Philadelphia. The plan, whose interruptive geometries recall Pedersen's Aid Association for Lutherans Headquarters (fig. 12) of the mid-1970s,[2] could easily be the architectural development of a study of interpenetrating geometries in energy fields by Malevich or Lissitzky. The suprematist composition stems from KPF's interest in fields of interactive urban forces. As with so many of their projects, the architects have tried to sense and intensify the urban context with their building and, in this design, seem to gather the surrounding campus with wings that pivot the focus toward the center. There, a circular drum collects the student body in a large terraced room. It is not a perimeter building with a courtyard: the center is not a void but a positive presence that activates the interior of the site, inverting KPF's postmodernist urbanism, which had always emphasized the boundaries.

The plan has generated descriptives that allude to its apparent accidentalism—the "train-wreck scheme," "the jack-knife"—but the elevations, rendered in brick and patterned in regularly centered bays to refer to the campus context, do not match the expectations set up by the plan, with its abstract pedigree and asymmetrical disposition of parts. If the plan is the generator and represents the dominant idea, the architects have not carried its ideas into the elevation, where the patterns of the brick facade (as well as the material) are by and large static rather than dynamic and do not accord with the energy diagram of the plan.

The result is a strong tension between the perception of the building as an abstract object and as a classical piece, a hybrid of purely formal composition and old-fashioned humanism. The Revlon Campus Center concretized the contradictions of the firm during a moment of transition. It was perhaps an inherently problematic commission because the client had strong attachments to KPF's earlier designs, while the architects themselves had moved on to a new design philosophy. The transitional nature of the design is an attempt to bridge the lag between the client's perception of KPF and its current interests.

Participating in a limited invited competition in Southeast Asia for the huge Singapore Arts Center, KPF proposed in 1992 a building without such identity problems—one in which the plan and elevation interact with the urban forces as an integrated three-dimensional piece. The design emerged with a consistent identity—a dynamic composition whose fluid gestures respond to the sweeping site along the waterfront, while engaging in more detailed ways the immediate urban context. With this design, KPF seems to have moved beyond a transitional stage. The architects have resolved the tension between KPF's design past and future in a refined but powerful project that convincingly redefines the firm.

Notes
1. This quote and others throughout the essay are drawn from a continuing series of conversations with William Pedersen.
2. This building was designed by Pedersen while he worked for John Carl Warnecke and Associates.

Kohn Pedersen Fox, 712 Fifth Avenue (1985–1991), New York. View.

The Facades of KPF: Abstraction and the Limits of Figuration[1]

Thomas L. Schumacher

Craft without imagination provides us with useful objects like wicker picnic baskets; imagination without craft gives us modern art. Tom Stoppard

The architect's ever diminishing power and his growing ineffectualness in shaping the whole environment can perhaps be reversed, ironically, by narrowing his concerns and concentrating on his own job. Robert Venturi[2]

Kohn Pedersen Fox is something of an anomaly in recent architecture: a firm that is highly respected and appreciated by a wide spectrum of the profession, from academics to practitioners, but is not part of a vocal avant-garde. Not since before the advent of the modern movement, when offices like those of McKim, Mead & White and Richard Morris Hunt were in ascendancy, have the professionals, the intellectuals, and the public been so appreciative of a large firm responsible for commercial work. In the recent past in particular, individual art-stars have dominated the architectural press with their polemics and monographs. These same architects have exercised an extraordinary influence over architectural style and form. Today, KPF finds itself among them. But many an avant-garde architect has concentrated on the imagination part of the architectural puzzle, leaving craft to the yeoman practitioner. Few architects since Mies have built so well and been so aesthetically influential.

KPF came into being at the height of the postmodern reaction to mature modernism. The partnership was created by a small group of architects who had previously worked in high-style modernist offices. Influences from both mainstream modernism and more traditional architectural sources were seen early in the firm's work, but unlike many architects who came into prominence in the 1970s, KPF's chronology cannot be read simply as an architectural history film run in reverse. Rather, the KPF style seems to proceed from late modernism to postmodernism, and then back toward the modernist vocabulary. But identification of style is the least important thing in an analysis of significant architectural works, even in these zeitgeist-crazed times. Embracing both the modern and the traditional, KPF has developed a distinctive yet adaptable style, and this essay will focus on some of its particulars.

Most of KPF's buildings are skyscrapers. Architects' approaches to the tall building have varied over the hundred years of its existence, some conceiving the skyscraper as a singular sculptural object, others as an assembly of smaller parts. Some have sought a unified repetitive surface; others have pursued a hierarchy of volumes as well as a hierarchy within the surfaces themselves. But since World War II, a simple mass covered by a unified curtain wall has been the norm, and the results have been uneven, particularly in relation to the street. KPF's response to the problem of the tall building has been to humanize it via a more contextual approach.

Skyscrapers of the 1930s, such as the RCA (now GE) Building at Rockefeller Center (fig. 1), reduced the problem of expression to a game between complex massing and a totally repetitive window system articulated in vertical, structurelike bands. When

21

1. *Associated Architects, RCA (now GE) Building (1933), New York. View.*
2. *Ludwig Mies van der Rohe, Glass Skyscraper Project (1922). Model.*
3. *Ludwig Mies van der Rohe, 860 Lake Shore Drive (1949–1951), Chicago. View.*
4. *Ludwig Mies van der Rohe, 900 Lake Shore Drive (1953–1956), Chicago. View.*

1

2

3

4

5. I. M. Pei & Partners,
Canadian Imperial Bank of
Commerce (1969–1973),
Toronto. View.
6. Kevin Roche John Dinkeloo
and Associates, United Nations
Plaza Hotel (1969–1975,
1979–1983), New York. View.

functionalist aesthetics triumphed over art deco–influenced
design in the postwar period, skyscraper design oscillated
between the articulation of the important parts—generally the
structural bay—and a kind of streamlining that subsumed the
structural articulation under modules and rhythms based on
window dimensions or some other small-scale division. On the
one hand, a machine aesthetic of articulated parts recalled
Renaissance urban architecture, with its applied structure
employed to embellish an otherwise smooth surface. On the
other, we find skyscrapers with a ground-smooth seamlessness
like "the airships of Jules Verne,"[3] recalling Renaissance rural
rusticity. (Compare Palladio's palazzos to his villas).

Mies has been credited with developing the postwar skyscraper
as an exercise in bay design, and his process was a long and
arduous one. The seamless curtain wall was unveiled in Mies's
skyscraper project of 1922 (fig. 2). This exercise in less-is-more
displayed a curtain wall stretched, like plastic wrap, around a
form that had been structurally neutralized by its apparently
arbitrary curvaceous perimeter. None of the details actually
needed to hold together such a curtain wall (in 1922, at least)
were included on Mies's model. During the 1950s Mies
continued the task of ironing out the frills. 860 Lake Shore Drive
(fig. 3) was one of the first attempts at resolution, but a curious
compromise between the structural bay and the window division
is evident there. If the column were separated from the wall,
evenly spaced windows could ride behind or in front of the
structure; but because the column is coplanar with the curtain
wall, Mies was forced to decide whether the mullions would be
equidistant or the windows would be the same size. He opted for
equal mullion divisions, thereby making the windows adjacent to
the columns narrower than those in the middle of the structural
bay. At 900 Lake Shore Drive (fig. 4), Mies solved the problem
by setting the column slightly back from the curtain wall, thereby
allowing the glazing partially to overlap the column. The
mullions are all equidistant and the windows are all the same
width. The consistent repetition and relative lack of hierarchy in
the window divisions of 900 Lake Shore Drive would become the
preferred model for curtain walls in the 1960s and 1970s (at least
in metal-and-glass-clad buildings).

Architects from I. M. Pei to Kevin Roche used details to suppress
any inconsistencies and irregularities between the structural bay
and the curtain-wall divisions. At the Canadian Imperial Bank of
Commerce in Toronto (fig. 5), Pei designed 54-foot-wide spandrel
panels (the structural module) without seams, a feat of
streamlining well recognized in the contemporary press. At the
United Nations Plaza Hotel (fig. 6), Roche hid the structure,
including the floors, behind a curtain wall which was so neutral
that neither window nor solid spandrel could be discerned, much
less slabs or columns. Streamlining was the name of the game,
but in the emerging postmodernist avant-garde of the 1970s, the
"ligaments of construction," as Kenneth Frampton has called
such details, were making a comeback. Articulation was the new
name of the new game.

333 Wacker Drive in Chicago (1979–1983) was among KPF's
first inroads into such articulation, with its upper curtain wall (far

5

6

7

8

from the viewer's reach and close perception) smooth and flattened behind its gentle curve and with a base resembling a baroque arcade in Turin or Paris. Having begun to attack the problem of how to enliven the curtain wall without being overly decorative or arbitrary, KPF then produced numerous projects, from the Procter & Gamble General Offices Complex (1982–1985) to the St. Paul Companies Headquarters (1987–1991), where a three-way dialogue among the window, the structural bay, and the overall massing became the primary design theme.

Since Sullivan, one of the crucial compositional problems of the exterior surface has been the relationship between the structural bay and the window, the large module versus the small module, whether or not massing came into the picture. Sullivan's buildings pose the problem of the expression of reality in terms of the location of important vertical lines on the facade. In the Guaranty (later Prudential) Building in Buffalo (fig. 7), completed just before the turn of the century, for example, all the verticals are treated equally and are of the same width, yet only every other vertical corresponds to a structural bay. In addition, Sullivan arcuates the piers, further destroying the reality of the reading. Sullivan's mezzanines and attics, as well, were even less functional than those of the Renaissance; his mezzanine floors were virtually identical with those above, the attic floors identical with those below. (These facts might very well scandalize certain "fundamentalist functionalist" modernists.) Having cast off a straightforward vertical extension of neo-Renaissance palazzo forms (with their insistent tripartition), Chicago-influenced designers began to exercise more independence from classical forms, while they maintained much of the interest in the individual bay and its extensions and variations within a closed composition.

KPF's adherence to classical and Renaissance goals and compositional techniques has been well known and well publicized for some time and is related to early-twentieth-century skyscraper design. In his lectures, William Pedersen has consistently alluded to the classical tripartitioning of the vertical compositions of KPF skyscrapers, the overlap of elements, and the divisions of all descending members into groups of three. He also cites a specific interest in Renaissance themes through what he has labeled "the Cornell connection."[4] This Cornell connection refers to the theories and influences of Colin Rowe, teacher to numerous associates and designers who have worked at KPF over the past fifteen years.

The connection is best understood through the structural bay. The bay is the key to Renaissance palace facade design, according to James Ackerman. Ackerman has explained how, in domestic architecture, Renaissance architects tended to draw a single bay within which were concentrated the tectonic ideas of the entire composition. Builders would then build three, five, seven, or however many bays would fit the context, and would then alter the entrance bay and finish off the corners and other components. Ackerman concluded that "the average palace or church was built from rough plans and a batch of details."[5] The bay was king.

10. Sir John Soane, Soane House at Lincoln's Inn Fields (1812–1813), London. Drawing of facade.
11. Giulio Romano, Palazzo Maccarani (c. 1520–1524), Rome. Detail of mezzanine windows.
12. Kohn Pedersen Fox, ABC Phase II (1984–1986), New York. Detail of facade.
13. Kohn Pedersen Fox, St. Paul Companies Headquarters (1987–1991), St. Paul. Detail of facade.

The bay begins its life in Renaissance domestic architecture (having been the germ of the whole composition in numerous Gothic and early Renaissance churches) as a simple imitation of the three-over-four tiered composition of the Colosseum in Rome (like Palazzo Rucellai by Alberti), but it soon becomes a complex composition of overlaps, scale shifts, and subtle modulations of surface and volume. The structural members of the palazzo bay also begin as simple versions of the orders, but they are transformed by architects of the sixteenth, seventeenth, and eighteenth centuries into more abstract elements. In this regard the works of Giulio Romano, particularly the Palazzo Maccarani of the early 1520s, comprise an important inspiration for the KPF facade.[6] It is with Giulio and the Maccarani (fig. 8) that we see the beginning of the difficult trip from the literal adaptation of classical orders of the early and high Renaissance to the mannerist and baroque abstraction of those orders into elements that never lose their constructive syntax—but do lose their literality. They gain flexibility and therefore utility for ensuing generations, including twentieth-century architects. The pilaster strips and paneling of numerous KPF facades, such as 500 E Street S.W. in Washington, D.C., show this influence. At 500 E Street (fig. 9), the paneling operates like pilasters without capitals but with a structural function for the horizontal, not unlike the pilasters on Sir John Soane's house in London (fig. 10).

A particular detail of Palazzo Maccarani is germane to this discussion: the absence of the rustication around the windows of the mezzanine floor (fig. 11), which has the effect of breaking up the solidity and continuity of the rustication and, more importantly, allows the mezzanine to belong equally to the base and the piano nobile. The detailing around the windows further connects the mezzanine to the piano nobile. The Maccarani motif gets an early KPF iteration at ABC Phase II in New York, where the so-called KPF window (a wide central window flanked by receding narrow side lights) is employed to create an ambiguous mezzanine floor (fig. 12). In KPF's St. Paul Companies Headquarters, the repetitive long facade shows the same characteristics (fig. 13). The strong horizontal of the steel beam over the lower window is the equivalent of the travertine strip-molding at the Maccarani.

Despite the specific connection to Giulio Romano, of all the Renaissance architects with whom a connection to KPF might be made, Vignola is the best parallel. Not Palladio, although the KPF system, like Palladio's, is eminently adaptable. Not Giulio, although some of Giulio's less manneristic devices (as noted above) are similar to KPF's. Not Michelangelo, although some of the complexities of Michelangelo's San Lorenzo facade are imitated by KPF (especially in ABC Phase II). Vignola is important for three reasons. First, his flatness; he is the least plastic and least robust of the sixteenth-century architects and is often the brunt of criticism for his lack of plasticity. Second, his utility: the ease with which his system was disseminated throughout Europe and later America. Third, and most important, the way he (like Giulio) began to abstract the literal forms of the classical vocabulary into more generic, decorative, nonspecific elements. We see this in the paneling and stripping of the elements of the rear facade of the Palazzo Farnese at

9

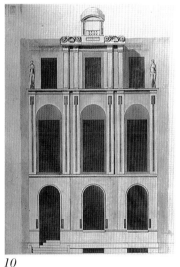

10

11

12

13

25

14. *Giacomo Barozzi da Vignola, Palazzo Farnese (1559–1573), Caprarola. View.*

14

Caprarola (fig. 14), in the interior of the little church of Sant'Andrea in Via Flaminia in Rome, and in the facade of the Portico dei Banchi in Bologna (published as a supplementary illustration in the first KPF monograph of 1987).

Throughout this discussion one might get the impression that for KPF the International Style might not have existed, and as regards surface—but not massing—one might be tempted to assert so. The "white architecture of the twenties," as Reyner Banham referred to it, was produced without the articulations of the surface that other modernist styles, from art nouveau to art deco, had embraced. Other twentieth-century modernists, from Berlage and Horta to the later works of Cret and Perret, are closer to KPF's style than are Gropius, Le Corbusier, and Rietveld, at least in their approach to surface.

In massing, however, recent KPF buildings have returned to the asymmetrical interlocking massing of 1920s and 1930s modernism. They have also been influenced by the outrigger style of the recent deconstructivist avant-garde. Buildings like Rockefeller Plaza West (1987–1991) in New York, Three Bellevue Center (1988–1994) in Bellevue, Washington, Mainzer Landstrasse 58 (1986–1993) in Frankfurt, and 1250 Boulevard René-Lévesque Ouest in Montreal (fig. 15) display these tendencies. The asymmetries, however, are primarily responses to the context; at the bottom of the buildings, where the pedestrian is in direct contact with the base, symmetry most often reigns. 550 South Hope Street in Los Angeles follows this pattern as well (fig. 16).

It would be a mistake to argue the supremacy of the above influences on KPF over a myriad of other models, precedents, and sources. KPF is an eclectic practice in the most complete sense of the term, absorbing influences from the entire spectrum of architectural production in the tradition of many of the masters of modernism. These influences range from the high-style modernism of van Doesburg and Rietveld to lesser known, but just as talented, Dutch modernists. The interlocking volumetric massing of Dudok's de Bijenkorf Department Store in Rotterdam (fig. 17) is reinterpreted in KPF's World Bank Headquarters (fig. 18). We find similar Dutch themes of interlock in William Pedersen's early volumetric elevation sketches for 1250 Boulevard René-Lévesque (fig. 19).

Closer to home, on the northeast corner of East 57th Street and Lexington Avenue in New York, once stood a building by Thompson & Churchill (fig. 20). A KPF building now stands on this site, 125 East 57th Street (1983–1986). The original building was illustrated in Henry-Russell Hitchcock and Philip Johnson's International Style exhibition catalogue of 1932. While this new KPF building does not in the least resemble the former occupant of the site, two KPF buildings in other cities do. The lower, street-related volumes of both 1250 Boulevard René-Lévesque and 550 South Hope Street (fig. 21) are curiously related to the Thompson & Churchill building, almost as if the ghost of 137 East 57th were now haunting Montreal and Los Angeles. 137 East 57th Street was quite innovative in its structural and expressive dynamics, so much so that its exclusion

15. Kohn Pedersen Fox, 1250 Boulevard René-Lévesque Ouest (1988–1992), Montreal. Detail of model.
16. Kohn Pedersen Fox, 550 South Hope Street (1988–1992), Los Angeles. Model.
17. W. M. Dudok, de Bijenkorf Department Store (1929), Rotterdam. View.
18. Kohn Pedersen Fox, World Bank Headquarters (1989–1996), Washington, D.C. Model.
19. Kohn Pedersen Fox, 1250 Boulevard René-Lévesque Ouest (1988–1992), Montreal. Sketches.

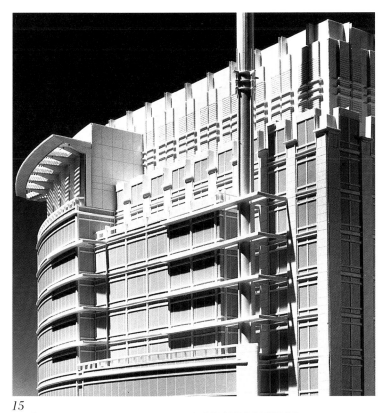

15

16

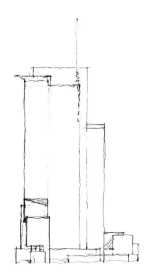

17

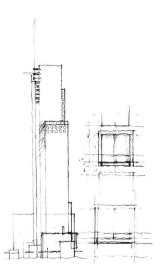

18

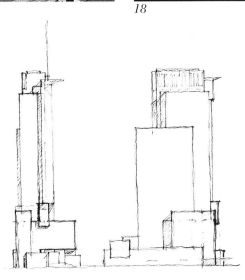

19

20. *Thompson & Churchill, 137 East 57th Street (1930), New York. View from the southeast.*
21. *Kohn Pedersen Fox, 550 South Hope Street (1988–1992), Los Angeles. Perspective at eye level.*

20

21

from the actual International Style exhibition has been viewed by at least one observer as ideologically motivated.[7] Whatever the inspiration for Thompson & Churchill, the effect of this elegant facade was a tour de force in its display of a hanging structure.

But we are far from KPF's palette. In Los Angeles and Montreal, KPF used the corner cantilever and slender verticals to bring the eye as well as the weight of the members directly to the ground. Here is KPF's direct refutation of the Hitchcock and Johnson principle that the expression of volume rather than mass is one of the important directives of modernism. Other KPF buildings, such as Procter & Gamble (fig. 22), have reestablished mass (or better, thickness and depth) without the assertive plasticity of the concrete bunker style of the 1960s. In other words, thickness and depth are achieved without sacrificing surface tension (recalling Vignola again). Among International Style architects, the Italians were the most interested in retaining massive readings of their materials and surfaces, as Terragni's Casa del Fascio in Como (fig. 23) so eloquently portrays. The affinity between Procter & Gamble and the Casa del Fascio goes beyond the high-contrast photos shown here.[8]

We see another important difference between the 1930s model of 137 East 57th Street and the 550 South Hope Street adaptation: the respective architects' attitudes toward the surface itself. Behind the strong verticals of the Thompson & Churchill building hangs a neutral curtain wall which slightly emphasizes the horizontal; it is pure and it is simple. At 550 South Hope Street, the bay (fig. 24) is developed as a complex set of rhythms using the horizontal and the vertical equally and employing a secondary reading of a prominent vertical in the center of the bay. This element connects to an intermediate horizontal band intersecting the open ground floor. Ambiguities, overlaps, and counterpoint emerge; not so pure and simple.

Where the lines of force of the verticals are dissolved into the surfaces, KPF's facades still maintain a modernity through an insistent shallow overlap of the surfaces, as in ABC Phase II, 70 East 55th Street, and 712 Fifth Avenue (fig. 25), all in New York City. At 712 Fifth Avenue, the design process divulges a tendency to imbue the vertical surface with more ambiguities as the project develops. A comparison between the scheme for the 56th Street facade and the built version illustrates this point. The first version (fig. 26) relies on a local symmetry produced by a simple (albeit not dimensionally equal) A-B-A-B rhythm. Pilasters are overlaid onto a plain wall, thereby giving the otherwise equal window dimensions varying segments of wall to inhabit. The hierarchy is further enhanced by fluted pilasters over the entrance; this figure dominates a relatively neutral and repetitive facade. In the project as built the pilasters are gone; panels of wafer-thin stone take their place. The general effect is an amplified gradation; the concatenation of the early facade is now replaced by a more integrated composition, without the artifice of the pilasters. A scaffold of figurative pieces gives way to a more abstract holistic composition.

Like Vignola, Soane, or Cret, Kohn Pedersen Fox is an architectural studio imbedded in a tradition rather than at the

*22. Kohn Pedersen Fox, Procter
& Gamble General Offices
Complex (1982–1985),
Cincinnati. Photograph by
Judith Turner.
23. Giuseppe Terragni, Casa
del Fascio (1932–1936),
Como. Photo of south facade.*

22

23

24. Kohn Pedersen Fox, 550 South Hope Street (1988–1992), Los Angeles. Detail of model.

25. Kohn Pedersen Fox, 712 Fifth Avenue (1985–1991), New York. Photo of lower facade.

26. Kohn Pedersen Fox, 712 Fifth Avenue (1985–1991), New York. Early scheme.

24

25

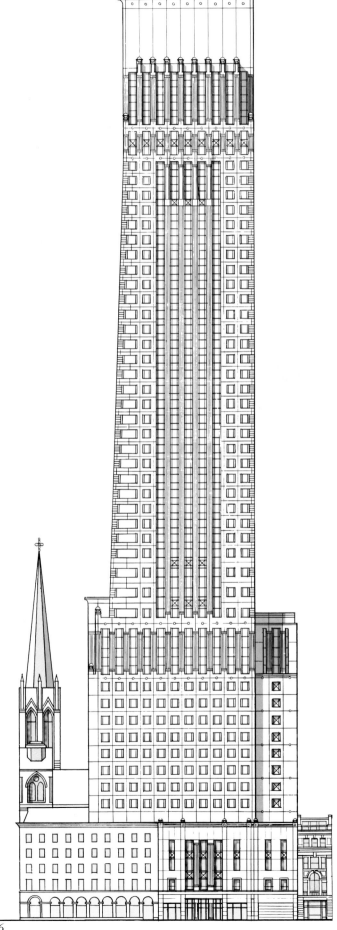

26

beginning of one. Using the forms and elements of those who have come before, these architects have furthered our understanding of the act of building in an urban context. Theirs is a quiet, deliberate development, without bells and whistles, representing excellence in normal architecture rather than revolutionary architecture.[9] Our era expects a kind of trickle-down architecture, whereby paradigms are created by a few high-style avant-garde architects. Trickle-up architecture comes to us via anonymous and vernacular building and from the industrial landscape. KPF has given us innovation from the middle, almost unheard of in our century and often maligned for being a mere shadow of real style. But the commercial buildings of late-twentieth-century America, like those of Chicago a century ago, must be well built, not just photogenic enough for a full-color magazine spread.

Notes

1. Two definitions of "figuration" are important here: Webster 3: "an act or instance of representation in figures and shapes" and 4: "ornamentation of a musical passage by using decorative and usu. repetitive figures." I am also dependent on Alan Colquhoun's distinction between "form" and "figure." See his "Form and Figure," in *Essays in Architectural Criticism* (Cambridge: MIT Press, 1981), pp. 190–202.
2. Robert Venturi, *Complexity and Contradiction in Architecture* (New York: Museum of Modern Art, 1966), p. 20.
3. Roland Barthes, "The New DS," *Mythologies* (New York: Hill and Wang, 1972), p. 88.
4. Sonia R. Cháo and Trevor D. Abramson, eds., *Kohn Pedersen Fox: Buildings and Projects 1976–1986* (New York: Rizzoli International Publications, 1987), p. 306.
5. James Ackerman, "Architectural Practice in the Italian Renaissance," *Journal of the Society of Architectural Historians* 13, no. 3 (October 1954): pp. 3–11.
6. Colin Rowe, "Grid/Frame/Lattice/Web: Giulio Romano's Palazzo Maccarani and the Sixteenth Century," *The Cornell Journal of Architecture* 4 (1991): pp. 6–21.
7. "[137 East 57th Street] . . . was not included in Hitchcock and Johnson's compilation, perhaps in part because its stripped forms and structural innovations were the product of a utilitarian functionalism rather than an artistic intention, the unusual structural system being a response to the site's difficult subsurface conditions." Robert A. M. Stern, Gregory Gilmartin, and Thomas Mellins, *New York 1930* (New York: Rizzoli International Publications, 1987), p. 367.
8. In this regard, the details of Procter & Gamble are surely dependent in part on the work of Michael Graves, who, according to Vincent Scully, is one of the innovators in the restoration of mass. See Vincent Scully, "Michael Graves' Allusive Architecture," in Karen Wheeler, Peter Arnell, and Ted Bickford, eds., *Michael Graves: Buildings and Projects 1966–1981* (New York: Rizzoli International Publications, 1982), pp. 289–98. See also K. Nichols, P. Burke, and C. Hancock, eds., *Michael Graves: Buildings and Projects 1982–1989* (New York: Princeton Architectural Press, 1990).
9. "Normal" versus "revolutionary" architecture is here taken to parallel the differences between "normal" and "revolutionary" science, as described by Thomas Kuhn in *The Structure of Scientific Revolutions* (Chicago: University of Chicago Press, 1962).

The Bow and the Lyre

William Pedersen

Several years ago I was invited to watch a "rehearsal-practice" of traditional Japanese archery. The solemnity of the protracted, yet eloquently simple, ritual leading to an explosive release of the arrow had an effect upon my senses that still remains strong. I refer to the event as a "rehearsal-practice" with intended meaning. If the word "rehearsal" is appropriate, then the event can be thought of as a performance art. However, if "practice" is the suitable word, it is then, by implication, a sport. Obviously, its power to command my senses lies in the ambiguity of its position between art and sport, as both share aspects of ritual and the attempt to transcend worldly constraints.

Architecture, too, holds such a relative position. Undeniably it can be an art; too often it remains only a commodity. Today, when expectations are highest for architecture to be an art, it frequently becomes a commodity. Sometimes it does become an art, often when only those involved in its creation hold such expectations. Our contemporary society places great pressure upon artist-architects to create works that are willful expressions of personal originality. The context within which these works are most often experienced (and consumed) is not the human and physical context of a specific place but rather the artificial context of journalistic documentation. Architects who ignore this human and physical context encourage an architecture of mere self-indulgence. Our architecture holds as its premise that this condition must be resisted.

I have great admiration for an architect who is centered by a core of meaningful architectural principles early in life and allows those principles to guide a lifetime of artistic production. If the principles are sufficiently deep to allow for an architecture that embraces the full spectrum of human experience, few alterations to one's artistic course are needed. However, for those not adequately endowed with such initial perception, the pursuit of a meaningful personal architecture requires a long process of experimentation and discovery. Along the way much needs to be discarded, but some must be retained. Gradually, that which is retained gathers mass, like layers of coral upon a reef, to represent a mature body of intentions.

Over time serious architects reveal, through their work, a number of central themes that form the basis of their artistic sensibility. While the form and expression of these themes may vary over a long period, their importance is, to some extent, measured by the frequency of their appearance. For my work these dominant themes can best be illustrated by two important symbols in Greek mythology: the bow and the lyre. The bow is a system of conflicting forces; the greater the tension of the polarity, the better the bow. But the cord of the bow can become the string of the lyre. The lyre is built upon the principle of the bow. It is a many-stringed bow, a transformed, sublimated bow. With it we can see and hear how, from conflict, the finest harmony arises. For the Greeks, the bow and the lyre represented a symbolic expression of one of life's central themes: duality. For them duality lay behind all forms of existence, whether expressed as good and evil, light and dark, birth and death, male and female. Duality was at the source of their consciousness. For me, these symbols, the bow and the lyre, have a similar significance, although perhaps more through the meaning of their physical form than through the products of their action. For the Greeks, the products of their action—conflict and harmony—were in themselves a duality that, in turn, came to represent all dualities.

I, on the other hand, think of these instruments primarily as representations of my architectural sensibility. Many years ago, when my two daughters were beginning the study of the cello and the violin, they were asked to choose the sound, between the two instruments, that most appealed to them. Their sensibilities led one to choose the cello and the other the violin. For me, a choice between the bow and the lyre reveals my visual sensibility. I much prefer the bow. Its physical form has come to represent much of what I seek to express through my architecture. Above all, the bow achieves a level of aesthetic simplicity that is satisfactory to the mind because it is derived from an intensive inner complexity. The elegance of its shape is achieved through the interaction of only two dominant parts. Furthermore, these two parts are, in themselves, contradictory. The cord is elementary, linear, of constant sectional form, and exists in tension. The shaft is of complex curvature, of changing sectional form, and exists under compression. In such an equivocal relationship, one contradictory meaning usually dominates another. In the bow, neither part prevails. During the process of drawing the bow and releasing the arrow the parts play fluctuating roles. Interchangeably, each dominates, or is subordinate to, the other. The bow is what Robert Venturi would call a "difficult unity." It symbolizes, as he has quoted Samuel Johnson, "the most heterogeneous ideas yoked together by violence." Equilibrium is achieved through a dialogue of the static and the dynamic, the linear and the curvilinear, and the complex and the elementary. Above all, the bow combines abstraction (like a great work of Brancusi) and representation. Its form exemplifies Leibniz's definition of perfection and is an ideal example of "extreme integration of extreme differentiation" or of "the greatest unity of the greatest diversity." The whole is achieved without loss of identity to the parts. The bow has become symbolic of my most significant artistic strategy. This is a strategy that attempts to unveil the inherent diversities within an architectural problem. Once they are revealed, my primary artistic challenge is to bring a balanced unity to them.

Years ago I attended a master's class given by the great cellist Mstislav Rostropovich. During his lesson he said that all significant music is written with both standard and exceptional parts, and, in performance, the dialogue between the two needs to be exploited. Architecture, I believe, should be composed similarly. Generally, the context of a building will encourage responses that require different levels of visual intensity from one part to another. This is particularly true of urban contexts. An architecture that encourages a coexistence of the standard and the exceptional is more capable of being an architecture of inclusion. It is an architecture that is potentially less reductive regarding the scope of its intent and more reflective of the totality of human experience. It is also an architecture that can be directed, according to Venturi, to the "evolutionary as well as the revolutionary." As an art it can acknowledge "what is and what ought to be," the immediate and the speculative. It allows for a

generous portion of pragmatism, hopefully combined with an equal degree of idealism. While it can be an architecture that never breaks totally with convention, it may be one whose innovations are appreciated and understood in reference to convention. Additionally, it can be an architecture whose form is achieved from the internal pressures of intended use and the external pressures of place and context. Moreover, it should show a concern for context that leads to linking a building to its site in a fundamental and meaningful way, where its existence attempts more to explain and, therefore, to transform the site rather than merely to mimic obvious features of it.

Currently our North American cities, and in general the cities of the Western Hemisphere, are structured by two parallel themes that address each other in fluctuating opposition. The first of these is represented by the weighty, traditional artifacts that acknowledge a significant past. The second is formed by the less substantial products of the more recent modern tradition, which can now be referred to as the current past. The discord caused by the juxtaposition of these two contending conditions is the reality of our times. The unstable equilibrium formed by this conflict can be decried for its inhuman tendencies, yet it shapes the condition we are required to resolve. An architecture that predominantly addresses only one side of this temporal equation will ultimately be unable to create the synthesis necessary for it to enter a new phase. This synthesis must recognize the past, be rooted in the present, and be directed toward the future. For a period of time my work ignored the spirit of this obligation. It is a fact that I have come to regret deeply. For the last seven years we have sought to redress this situation, and much of the work represented in this book documents our progress toward that goal of equilibrium. Works such as Mainzer Landstrasse 58 in Frankfurt, Rockefeller Plaza West in New York, 1250 Boulevard René-Lévesque in Montreal, Goldman Sachs in London, the World Bank in Washington, and the Arts Center in Singapore each represent an architecture that acknowledges not only the past, but also the present and the future. They are an architecture that attempts to combine simultaneously the formal with the informal, the figural with the abstract, the monumental with the human, and the modern with the traditional. They accomplish these objectives by employing strategies that center upon the unification of differentiation. They each use abstraction, representation, ambiguity, contradiction, and juxtaposition to create the tension inherent in works aimed at a "difficult unity."

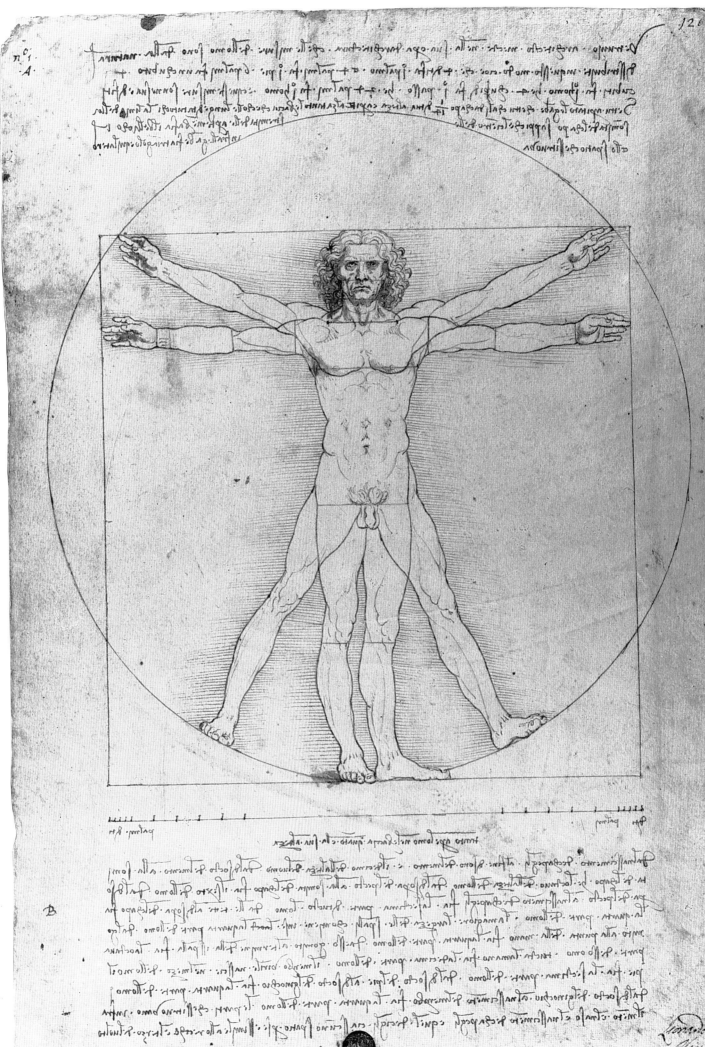

The Circle and the Square

Warren A. James

A work of art is that which elicits a prolonged suspension of disbelief.   Colin Rowe[1]

Architecture, as opposed to construction, is distinguished by a single element: the dimension of the mind, that is to say, aesthetics. Left to our own devices we usually build and construct for practicality and functionality. But we can also rise to the occasion and make architecture. As Le Corbusier stated, "you employ stone, wood, and concrete, and with these materials you build houses and palaces. That is construction. Ingenuity is at work. But suddenly you touch my heart, you do me good, I am happy and I say: 'This is beautiful.' That is Architecture. Art enters in."[2] It is within this realm of the artistic that we may be able to understand the skyscraper as architecture and thus as a work of art.

Modern works of art depend a great deal on their ability to generate metaphors for their strength and meaning, their importance, their resonance. Skyscrapers too may be seen as capable of sustaining such a response—the number of powerful metaphors they can generate is apparently endless.[3] Within the last two decades the American skyscraper has reemerged as a work of art, in part due to its revitalization within a culture that makes these buildings possible—and builds them more frequently—but also due to the numerous works of Kohn Pedersen Fox. The work of William Pedersen, a founding partner and the principal design partner at KPF, holds a most prominent position, not only within the production of the firm itself but also within the scope of American skyscraper production made possible by the favorable economic conditions of the past three decades.

Meaning in the buildings designed by Pedersen arises from their strength as autonomous works of art: their ability to generate multiple readings. These may be divided into three broad categories: sculptural form, expressionistic gesture, and geometric composition. (These terms have been borrowed from the field of art to enlarge the discussion within our own field.) The specific complexity found in these works, in which technique is more often than not subservient to form and meaning, represents a significant advancement of the American skyscraper.

Almost one hundred years ago, Louis Sullivan wrote his prophetic essay, "The Tall Office Building Artistically Considered," in which he longed for architecture to be "on the high-road to a natural and satisfying art, an architecture that will soon become a fine art in the true, best sense of the word."[4] In early American skyscraper development, internal conditions often prevailed as a shaping force. The evolution of the skeletal support structure, vertical transportation core, and other technical components highly influenced the resulting form from within. The architect reacted to these advances, integrated them, and put them to good use. This, as Le Corbusier would say, was mostly construction.

This progression of constructive knowledge took place in large part in Chicago, rendering the skyscraper as a vertical frame, a

1. *Sol LeWitt,* 21B *(1989).*
Courtesy Barbara Mathes
Gallery, New York.
2. *Claes Oldenburg,* Lipstick in
Piccadilly Circus *(1966),*
London. Collection of The Tate
Gallery, London.

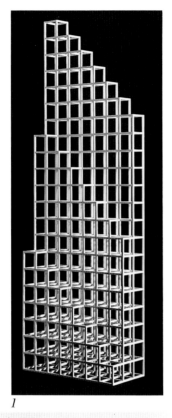

1

2

grid projected up. The early evolution of the Chicago skyscraper suggests the sculpture of Sol LeWitt, such as his *21B* of 1989 (fig. 1). The earliest of Chicago's tall buildings were simple grids just like the archetypal American city plan seen vertically.[5]

On the other hand, the development of the skyscraper in New York followed a path that was profoundly and conceptually different from that of Chicago. In New York, the skyscraper was most often designed as a symbolic form, an icon; it was conceived as a whole, from the outside in. In sharp contrast to Chicago, external conditions were more related to historical style and prevailing fashion. The architect was the shaper, the sculptor—creating architecture in which art entered in, as Le Corbusier might say.

The work of Claes Oldenburg, in which he enlarges the scale of everyday objects into gigantic sculptural forms, has profound architectural implications and is an apt parallel to the New York skyscraper, particularly his *Lipstick in Piccadilly Circus* of 1966 (fig. 2). The tall office building in New York, like Oldenburg's sculpture, is first and foremost an icon, and then a building. These two concepts, the internally driven Chicago skyscraper and the externally shaped New York high-rise,[6] one all structure and the other all symbol, define the possibilities of the skyscraper as a potential work of sculpture. For as we begin to see sculptures as skyscrapers and skyscrapers as sculptures, the work of William Pedersen becomes more easily understood.

However, before the emergence of KPF, there had been a vast loss of interest in the external sculptural possibilities of the skyscraper following World War II. Technique once again dominated meaning; curtain-wall detailing became more worthy of study than overall form. This shift had severe detrimental implications for the American city, and in the process the skyscraper lost its ability to suspend disbelief. By the time Pedersen's first, seminal work, 333 Wacker Drive, was completed, this building type was beginning to be advanced once again as a work of art that could embody the aspirations and convictions of the late twentieth century.[7]

Paradoxically, it has been the artists, not the architects, who have been stretching the possibilities of skyscraper design beyond minimalist sculpture (fig. 3). It is this continued and persistent oscillation between internal and external influences, between technique and meaning, that seems to be the common denominator of the American skyscraper throughout its hundred years of development. This paradox may also be illustrated by two pivotal skyscrapers built only twenty-seven years apart, Mies van der Rohe and Philip Johnson's Seagram Building (1958) and Johnson and Burgee's AT&T Building (1984), both in New York. If we were to remove their outer layer of skin, the two would appear identical in form. Nothing had changed in those two decades, despite common assertions to the contrary. With their skins on, however, the first can be seen as being generated internally by modular rigor (like LeWitt's sculpture) and the second as externally by stylistic conviction (like Oldenburg's work). One is a quintessential Chicago skyscraper and the other a quintessential New York skyscraper. What remains constant is that the form of the skyscraper is inevitably dependent on the depth of the architect's artistic vision.

The three characteristics (sculptural form, expressionistic gesture, and geometric composition) that identify Pedersen's work as uniquely his are subsumed by a concept of greater significance: all of Pedersen's work is about *juxtaposition*.[8] He understands a project in relation to his ability to sculpt, express, and draw his buildings with juxtaposition, or duality, in mind. Pedersen often expresses scale, form, and intention by juxtaposing opposing qualities: formal and informal, masculine and feminine, classical and modern, innovative and traditional. The work thus accommodates both the ideal and the circumstantial. Pedersen is in this regard very much an artist whose sculptures happen to be like buildings.

Pedersen's capacity to render tall buildings as plastic *sculptural form* is best seen in one of his earliest tall buildings, 333 Wacker Drive, which has been likened, in this book and elsewhere, to a Brancusi sculpture,[9] specifically his *Bird in Space* of 1928 (fig. 4), a singular dynamic form. But the metaphor is also appropriate regarding the tautness of the cladding of the building and the smooth finish of the sculpture, the juxtapositions of straight and curved and of movement and rest, and the unity and seamlessness of both forms—what Sullivan alluded to when he said the skyscraper "must be tall; every inch of it tall. The force and power of altitude must be in it, the glory and pride of exalting must be in it. It must be every inch a proud and soaring thing, rising in sheer exultation that from bottom to the top it is a unit without a single dissenting line."[10]

Another example of Pedersen's mastery at sculptural form-making can be seen in a more recent skyscraper, Rockefeller Plaza West in New York. In *Development of a Bottle in Space* of 1912 (fig. 5), Boccioni proposes some fundamental questions: What is the *essence* of the bottle? Is it the glass or the space contained within? Yet the essence of the bottle is the external space and forces that act upon it, the spiraling forces made visible by form.[11] At Rockefeller Center a similar proposition is made. What is the *essence* of the skyscraper? Identically, it is the external space and forces that act upon it.

More recent work explores this movement of form via the metaphor of the sailboat (fig. 7). In the abstract, a sailboat is a pure and simple composition of three principal elements: horizontal hull, vertical mast, curved sail. The economy of means, the intimate relationship between sailboat, wind, and water, and the equilibrium between vertical and horizontal is too tempting for Pedersen to resist. At 1250 Boulevard René-Lévesque in Montreal, the building's curved curtain wall is deployed like a sail and held in place by a vertical mast, all anchored by a horizontal, hull-like base. In this building and other recent projects, inspiration is transformed into sculptural form through metaphor. If movement can be best represented through static means by the juxtaposition of straight and curved lines and forms, as in Boccioni's *Unique Forms of Continuity in Space* of 1913 (fig. 6), then these skyscrapers can be said to express such conditions as a dominant theme.

3

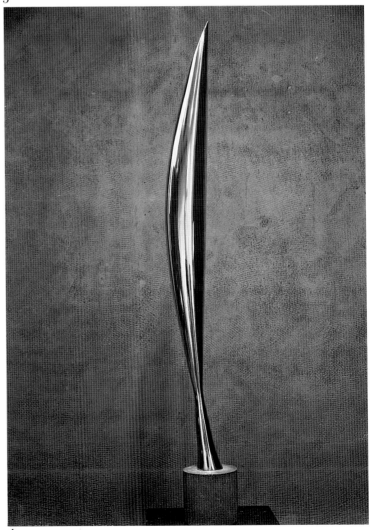

4

5. *Umberto Boccioni,* Development of a Bottle in Space *(1912). Collection of The Museum of Modern Art, New York.*

6. *Umberto Boccioni,* Unique Forms of Continuity in Space *(1913). Collection of The Museum of Modern Art, New York.*

5

6

Pedersen's second strategy, the *expressionistic gesture,* is found in both small- and large-scale works. Two small-scale schemes for the same site, Carwill House I and Carwill House II (built), and the large-scale St. Paul Companies Headquarters show this. These examples occur in fractured contexts, in irregular, non-ordered, preexisting physical conditions, as in the case of the Vermont houses (irregular topography, competing exigencies, and programmatic elasticity) and in the Minnesota headquarters (irregular periphery, distorted street grid, and surrounding stylistic diversity).

The work of Franz Kline provides a visual parallel. The given context at St. Paul could be understood to be like Kline's painting *White Forms* of 1955 (fig. 8). A series of fractured streets within an impacted city grid results in a site of incomplete, but preexisting, gestures in plan, with a large void at its center. Pedersen's characteristic expressionistic gesture results in a filled-up, reparative new order that totally transforms the site. In Kline's painting *Mahoning* of 1956 (fig. 9), a similar resolution occurs in the assertive solid at its center. Kline's work has a parallel approach to problem solving—the dramatic gesture that fills the void and unites apparently disparate fragments.

These expressionist gestures in plan are not always readily apparent in space, but instead are first understood in two dimensions; they are clearly more pictorial than purely sculptural. However, they have one thing in common with Pedersen's use of form: in both instances artistic transformation informs both the site and the new building.

The third characteristic of Pedersen's work is *geometric composition.* All of his buildings exhibit a preference for a geometric structure in plan that juxtaposes the circle and the square, or fragments thereof. (One cannot help but think of Leonardo da Vinci's *Vitruvian Man.*) While the circle occurs in nature, the square is a human construct. One is thought of as being feminine, the other as masculine. The circle encloses but also deflects; the square contains but also defines. One is the pregnant void and the other is the assertive solid. For Pedersen a marriage of the two is highly desirable.

Pedersen's buildings usually occur *in between* these two pure geometric forms. His floor plans are fragments of larger superimposed circles and squares, as seen in the (previously unpublished) analytical diagrams of a selection of Pedersen's most significant buildings and projects of the last sixteen years, organized chronologically (figs. 10–20). Many of these projects are skyscrapers, but this trait is not limited exclusively to tall buildings.

To understand the compositional possibilities of overlapping circles and squares, or those of juxtaposing curving lines with straight lines, the abstractions of Russian constructivists, such as Alexander Rodchenko's *Line Construction* of 1920 (fig. 21), Laszlo Moholy-Nagy's *Yellow Circle* of 1921 (fig. 22), or El Lissitzky's *Proun 19D* of about 1922 (fig. 23), provide interesting parallels to Pedersen's work. The germination of his floor plans can be found in these paintings wherever circles and squares are

7. *Ted Irwin*, Desert Wind *(1986). Courtesy Tropical Studios, Antigua, W.I.*
8. *Franz Kline*, White Forms *(1955). Collection of The Museum of Modern Art, New York.*

9. *Franz Kline*, Mahoning *(1956). Collection of Whitney Museum of American Art, New York.*

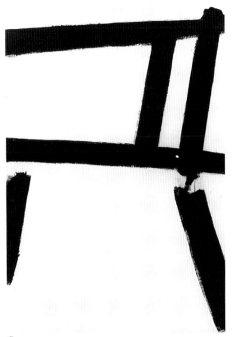

8

7

9

10. *Kohn Pedersen Fox, 333 Wacker Drive (1979–1983), Chicago. Analytical diagram.*
11. *Kohn Pedersen Fox, Houston Office Tower–Block 265 (1981), Houston. Analytical diagram.*
12. *Kohn Pedersen Fox, 125 East 57th Street (1983–1986), New York. Analytical diagram.*
13. *Kohn Pedersen Fox, Washington Mutual Tower (1985–1988), Seattle. Analytical diagram.*

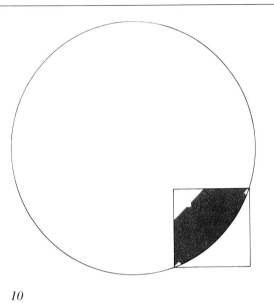

10

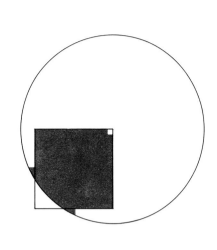

11

14. *Kohn Pedersen Fox, One Fountain Place (1985–1988), Cincinnati. Analytical diagram.*
15. *Kohn Pedersen Fox, Mainzer Landstrasse 58 (1986–1993), Frankfurt. Analytical diagram.*
16. *Kohn Pedersen Fox, Goldman Sachs European Headquarters (1987–1991), London. Analytical diagram.*
17. *Kohn Pedersen Fox, St. Paul Companies Headquarters (1987–1991), St. Paul. Analytical diagram.*

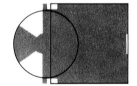

14

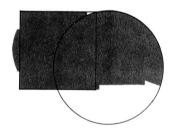

15

18. *Kohn Pedersen Fox, 1250 Boulevard René-Lévesque Ouest (1988–1992), Montreal. Analytical diagram.*
19. *Kohn Pedersen Fox, Three Bellevue Center (1988–1994), Bellevue. Analytical diagram.*
20. *Kohn Pedersen Fox, Concert Tower (1991–1994), Honolulu. Analytical diagram.*

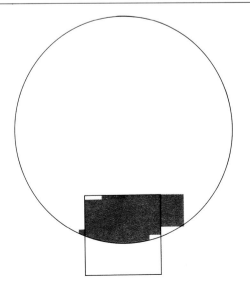

18

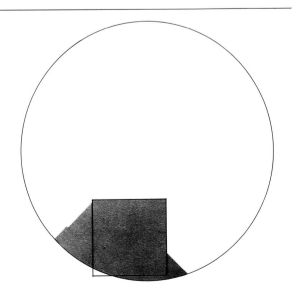

19

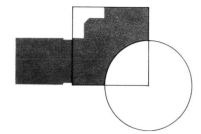

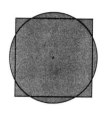

12

13

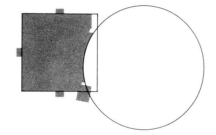

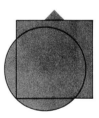

16

17

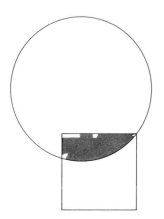

21

superimposed. It is this simple device that is the central theme of Pedersen's work, present even in his earliest buildings. It appears for the first time at the Aid Association for Lutherans Headquarters in Appleton, Wisconsin, and continues in all of his buildings up to the present, including Concert Tower in Honolulu. It can be found at the domestic scale in the Carwill House II and at the large urban scale in the Disney Institute and Town Center.

The combinations in between these perfect forms allow for variation without repetition. It is this core of Pedersen's work that remains constant throughout, regardless of exterior, materials, or stylistic variation. The internal code remains the same.

If one were to make each of the analytical diagrams reproduced here into a single film frame, and then generate a series of intermediate steps smoothly blending the first frame into the second, and then the third, and so on, the resulting film would show that the circle and the square seem to dance together. At the outset (fig. 10) the square overlaps only a small part of the circle. Their proportions are unequal but are in an axial forty-five-degree relationship. As the film progresses, the two forms begin to move, but maintain this relationship. The area in which they overlap, however, grows (fig. 12). These buildings belong to Pedersen's early phase, modern but axially aligned.

As the film continues there is a very brief moment when the circle and the square overlap completely, lying one atop the other in classical proportion (fig. 13). This moment coincides with Pedersen's more sculpturally inert period because the composition in plan does not translate well to three dimensions. The movement between the two forms continues, however, in a set of increasingly dynamic positions, in which the axial relationship disappears and the proportions between the two shapes begin to shift dramatically, as when the circle becomes much larger, swallowing the entire square (fig. 18), or, in a special reversal of roles, when the dominant solid is a square with a circle taking a bite out of it (fig. 16). This shifting movement culminates in perhaps the most dynamic of Pedersen's compositions to date (fig. 20), where an acute angle and a knife-shaped floor plan appear between the two figures. The entire body of Pedersen's work can be viewed as a series of exercises in the compositional possibilities of these two very simple forms.

Two architects have shown the power of metaphor and the power of juxtaposition in architecture. Alvar Aalto explored the possibilities of the juxtaposition of opposites, or duality, in, for example, Villa Mairea (1938–1939), where he sought and emphasized the contrast between water and fire. He heightened this juxtaposition by setting fireplaces in relation to the water in the courtyard's pool. But he also conceived his shallow glass tray to be shaped like a lake shore of his native Finland. This contrast of opposites can be read as the duality between the created and the natural.[12] The other architect who employs metaphor in this unique way is William Pedersen.

In order to find the most rewarding aspect of interpreting, translating, and understanding Pedersen's works and his artistic

22. *Laszlo Moholy-Nagy,*
Yellow Circle *(1921).*
Collection of The Museum of
Modern Art, New York.
23. El Lissitzky, Proun 19D
(1922?). Collection of The
Museum of Modern Art, New
York.

intentions, one can add to Colin Rowe's definition of art, quoted at the beginning of this essay, Samuel Coleridge's definition of architecture—"Now Art, used collectively for painting, sculpture, architecture, and music, is the mediatress between, and the reconciler of, nature and man"[13]—and see how, in the end, the three of them can fit neatly together. Mediating between the circle and the square, Pedersen's architecture—his art—has the capacity to reconcile humans and nature, and to elicit that prolonged suspension of disbelief.

Notes

1. This published quote of Colin Rowe's is rather appropriate but definitely approximate; the source could not be located. Rowe cannot recall the source either, but he was drawing a parallel with Samuel Coleridge, who wrote: "that willing suspension of disbelief for the moment, which constitutes poetic faith." That one appeared in his *Biographia Literaria* (London: J. M. Dent & Sons, 1817), p. 161.
2. Le Corbusier, *Towards a New Architecture* (London: J. Rodker, 1931), p. 153.
3. The classical column of Adolf Loos, the chiaroscuro mountains of Hugh Ferriss, the Mayan monuments of Fernando Mujica, the dramatis personae of Rem Koolhaas, the flying planes of Francisco Rencoret, and others like the lighthouse, the obelisk, and so on, are all cases in point. See, for example, Sigfried Giedion, "Mies van der Rohe: Towards Pure Form," in *Space, Time, and Architecture* (Cambridge: MIT Press, 1967), pp. 381–93; Francisco Rencoret, *New York City: The Edge of Enigma* (New York: Princeton Architectural Press, 1991); and Diana Agrest, "Architectural Anagrams: The Symbolic Performance of Skyscrapers," *Oppositions* 11 (Winter 1977): pp. 26–51.
4. Louis Sullivan, "The Tall Office Building Artistically Considered," *Kindergarten Chats* (New York: Wittenborn, 1947), p. 213.
5. See Christian Norberg-Schulz's introduction to this monograph. See also Rosalind Krauss, "Grids," in *The Originality of the Avant-Garde and Other Modernist Myths* (Cambridge: MIT Press, 1986), pp. 8–22.
6. To understand New York's inevitable icon-obsession, see Rem Koolhaas, *Delirious New York* (New York: Oxford University Press, 1978). As for Chicago's perpetual frame, see Colin Rowe, "Chicago Frame," in *Mathematics of the Ideal Villa* (Cambridge: MIT Press, 1976), pp. 90–117.
7. Arthur Drexler was instrumental in bringing these sets of beliefs to the fore in the last quarter of the century at The Museum of Modern Art in New York, as director of the Department of Architecture and Design. See his *Three New Skyscrapers* (New York: Museum of Modern Art, 1982) and *Transformations in Modern Architecture* (New York: Museum of Modern Art, 1979).
8. See William Pedersen, "Method and Intentions 1976–1989," in *Process: Architecture* (Japan), November 15, 1989, pp. 14–18; "Considerations for Urban Architecture and the Tall Building," in Peter Arnell and Ted Bickford, eds., *Southwest Center: The Houston Competition* (New York: Rizzoli International Publications, 1983), pp. 17–29; and "Architecture and Praxis: A Self-Analysis of the Essential Criteria for the Urban Skyscraper," *The New Art Examiner* 10 (June 1983): pp. 6–10, 30. An interview with Pedersen appears in Barbaralee Diamonstein, ed., *American Architecture Now II* (New York: Rizzoli International Publications, 1985), pp. 177–84.
9. See Ansii Blomstedt, dir., with Christian Laine and Ioannis Karalais, exec. prods., *New Chicago Skyscrapers* (Metropolitan Films and The Chicago Athenaeum, 1990).
10. Sullivan, "Tall Office Building," p. 206.
11. Lao-tzu proposed similar questions of space, time, materials, and their interrelationships. For another reading on space and materials and their juxtaposition, see Robert Hughes, "Christopher Wilmarth," in *Nothing if Not Critical* (New York: Knopf, 1990), pp. 350–52.
12. See Scott Poole, "Elemental Matter in Villa Mairea," in *The New Finnish Architecture* (New York: Rizzoli International Publications, 1992), pp. 18–27. See also Sigfried Giedion, "Alvar Aalto: Irrationality and Standardization," in *Space, Time, and Architecture* (Cambridge: MIT Press, 1967), pp. 618–67.
13. Samuel Coleridge, "On Poesy or Art," *The Complete Works*, vol. 4 (New York: Harper & Brothers, 1853), p. 328.

22

23

Portfolio

Portfolio

333 Wacker Drive

Chicago, Illinois
1979–1983

Procter & Gamble General Offices Complex

Cincinnati, Ohio
1982–1985

Selected Buildings and Projects

With commentaries by the designers

712 Fifth Avenue

New York, New York
1985–1991

This office tower rises above one of Manhattan's best-preserved blockfronts, along Fifth Avenue at 56th Street. A five-story base facing the side street serves as the tower's main entrance and maintains the scale of the neighboring buildings, which are in a special historic-preservation district. The base is connected to a public atrium, where René Lalique architectural glass panels, incorporated into a retail store, are housed in the landmark Rizzoli and Coty buildings. The body of the tower, which is set back fifty feet from Fifth Avenue, frames the nearby Crown Building. The building is clad in Indiana limestone and white Vermont marble, with bronze medallions, polished black granite, and thermal green granite accents. Light and shadow are manipulated with deep recesses on the shaft and crown, providing depth to the walls and liberating the top plaque from the corners.

Plan, typical floor

Plan, ground floor

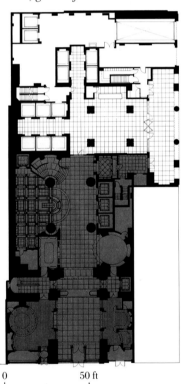

0   50 ft

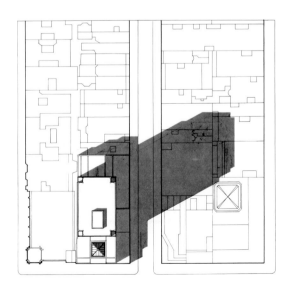

Rising behind a row of newly renovated landmark structures, this building seeks to accentuate the autonomy of their traditional scale. The slender tower emerges, almost like a campanile, independently of its immediate context. However, it seeks to join, by composition, surface, and material, the character of the avenue and the city itself.

William Pedersen

Mellon Bank Center

Philadelphia, Pennsylvania
1984–1990

Set in the heart of Philadelphia's Penn Center area on axis with
the tower of historic City Hall, this fifty-three-story building
initiates a new generation of office buildings that rise above the
traditional 491-foot height established by the William Penn
Statue atop City Hall. A five-story podium, sheathed in granite,
houses interconnected lobbies on JFK Boulevard and Market
Street, as well as retail shops and connections to the city's
underground public transportation and a retail concourse. An
enclosed public winter garden is set between Six Penn Center
and the new tower. The building's base reinforces the local street
walls while the tower's exterior reflects its internal structural
frame. Set back from the street and sheathed in granite,
aluminum, and reflective glass, the office tower, like a slender
obelisk, tapers to projecting cornices beneath an open latticed
pyramidal roof.

Plan, ground floor

Plan, typical floor

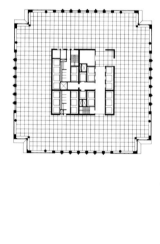

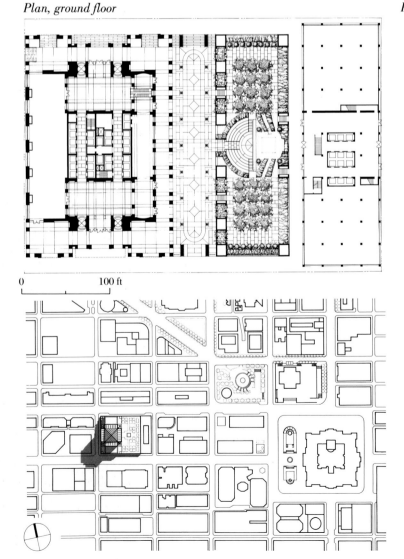

0   100 ft

Its strong biaxial form marks a new center of growth along the Market Street–JFK Boulevard corridor between Logan and Rittenhouse squares. As a new symbolic center, the tower addresses all sides equally.

William Louie

1325 Avenue of the Americas

New York, New York
1987–1990

This thirty-four-story midblock office tower in midtown
Manhattan has entrances on 53rd and 54th streets. The
building's podium contains an exhibition facility that connects
directly to the New York Hilton Hotel. The building steps back
from the podium, rising to face the flanking streets. A city-
mandated through-block connection is provided with a four-story
vaulted glass galleria. The tower, a double slab sheathed in
granite with punched windows, absorbs the thrust of the Hilton
Hotel and relates to the adjoining masonry residential building.
Window frames project from the building face to create a rich
interplay of light and shadow and provide solidity to the walls.
The building's main lobby is centered on the tower's mass but
independent of the galleria. Dual semicircular lobbies lead to the
elevator core through a vaulted hall.

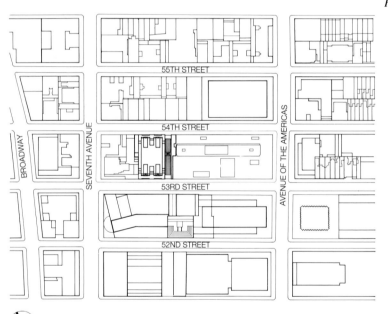

Plan, typical floor

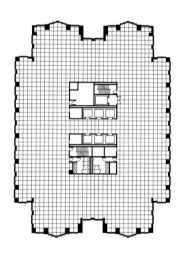

Plan, ground floor

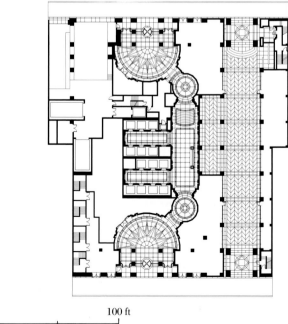

0   100 ft

The layering of windows over granite imparts a solidity to the facade difficult to achieve with modern curtain-wall technology.

William Louie

225 West Wacker Drive

Chicago, Illinois
1985–1989

On a full city block bounded by West Wacker Drive, Franklin Street, Lake Street, and Post Place, this thirty-two-story office building faces the Chicago River and is adjacent to Kohn Pedersen Fox's 333 Wacker Drive of 1983. Occupying the last site before the bend of the river, the building was designed to act as a terminus to a series of masonry buildings from the 1920s and 1930s. The building's main lobby, retail shops, and parking functions are at ground level, while the office space occupies the floors above. The building's massing, facades, and top are part of a unified composition of four slender but solid tower elements, each capped by a cylindrical spire. Vertically organized facades are stretched across these towers, providing a counterpoint to the taut horizontal glass curtain wall of 333 Wacker Drive.

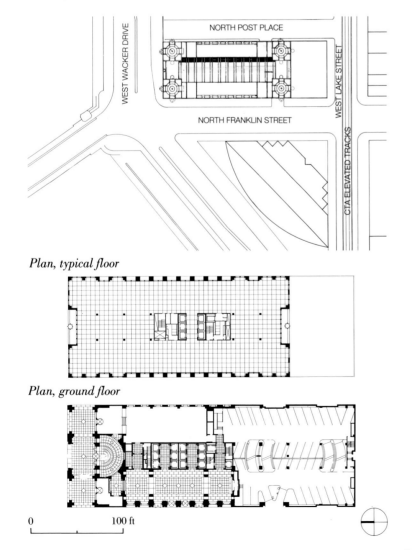

Plan, typical floor

Plan, ground floor

0   100 ft

This building is about continuation, termination, and contrast with its immediate environment of a traditional streetwall of masonry to the east and the simplicity of a dramatic curved form of reflective glass with its base of stone at 333 Wacker Drive as its neighbor to the west.

A. Eugene Kohn

Capital Cities/ABC Headquarters

New York, New York
1986–1989

Occupying an L-shaped site in a predominantly residential
neighborhood on Manhattan's Upper West Side, this twenty-two-
story corporate headquarters is the sixth building for Capital
Cities/ABC designed by KPF. Adjacent to the ABC Phase II
building, completed in 1986, and following the original master
plan of the late 1970s, the design maintains the neighborhood's
street wall and scale with a six-story base with punched windows.
Rising above the base is an office tower, square in plan, of rose
brick with contrasting limestone sills, decorative brick coursing,
and large semicircular bays that project toward the side streets.
Inspired by the neighborhood brownstones, these bay windows
reduce the building's apparent mass and provide executive
offices with large windows and oblique city views. Two-story
windows further reduce the scale of the building's shaft. At the
top, a one-story mechanical penthouse, sheathed in perforated
metal panels, creates a distinctive crown.

Plan, ground floor

Plan, typical floor

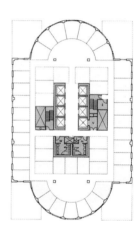

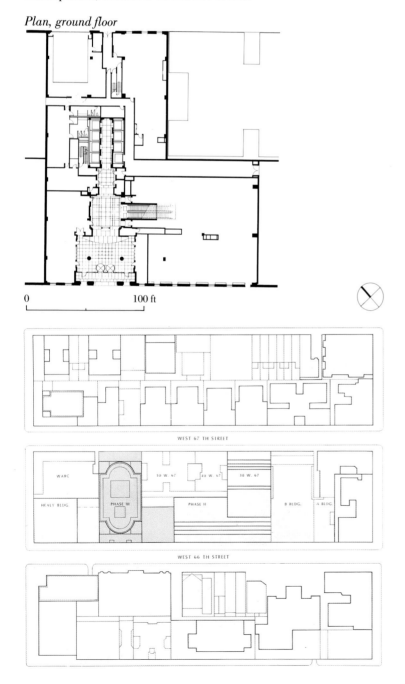

0   100 ft

WEST 67 TH STREET

WEST 66 TH STREET

The soft curve and unique canopy of the tower distinguish this building as the headquarters for ABC, while at the same time, the lower portion blends in with the residential and pedestrian scale and character of this Manhattan neighborhood.

Sheldon Fox

United States Courthouse / Foley Square

New York, New York
1991–1994

This twenty-seven-story U.S. Courthouse is located within lower
Manhattan's civic district on Foley Square, adjacent to Guy
Lowell's hexagonal Municipal Courthouse of 1926 and across
from Cass Gilbert's U.S. Courthouse tower of 1936. A nine-story
base housing two lobbies linked by a gallery, a jury selection
room, and ceremonial courts under a vaulted roof matches the
height of Lowell's courthouse. The tower, which aligns with
Gilbert's courthouse, contains a series of courtrooms and judge's
chambers. These vertically stacked, alternating floors are
expressed on the facade. Sheathed in granite, the courthouse
respects and participates in its honorific context.

Plan, ground floor

Plan, typical floor

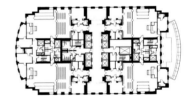

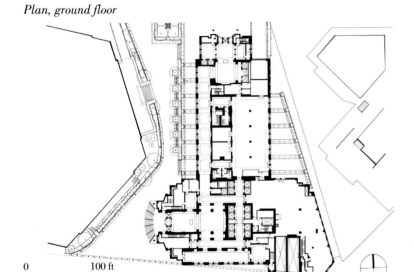

0   100 ft

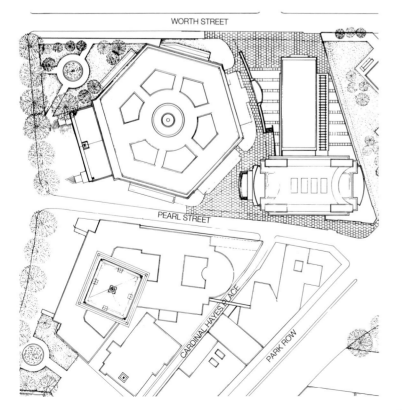

WORTH STREET

PEARL STREET

CARDINAL HAYES PLACE

PARK ROW

90

383 Madison / Scheme III

New York, New York
1987

The site for this office tower is an atypical square block on
Madison Avenue near Grand Central Station. In this scheme,
which responds to zoning requirements for light and air, the tower
stands at forty-eight stories with much the same program as an
earlier scheme designed in 1984. Classical compositional
features are deployed, while detailing at the base is given a
modern character. The building tapers back on all sides to spires
at each corner. These spires are to be lighted at night,
recapturing the slender proportions of early Manhattan
skyscrapers, such as the Empire State and Chrysler buildings.

Plan, 32nd floor

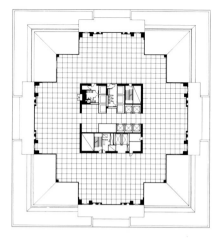

Plan, 22nd floor

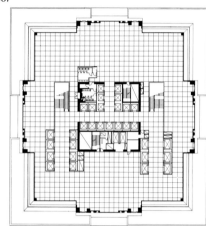

Plan, mezzanine floor

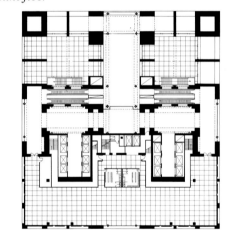

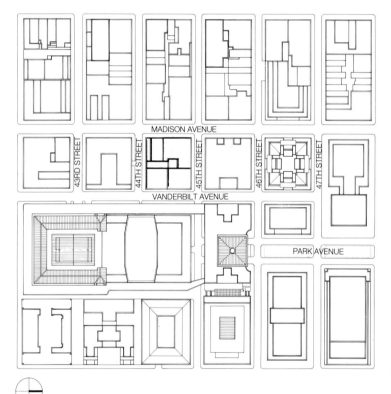

Plan, ground floor

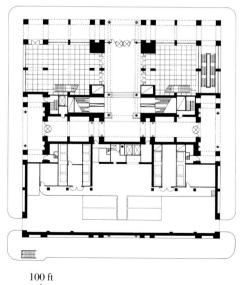

0   100 ft

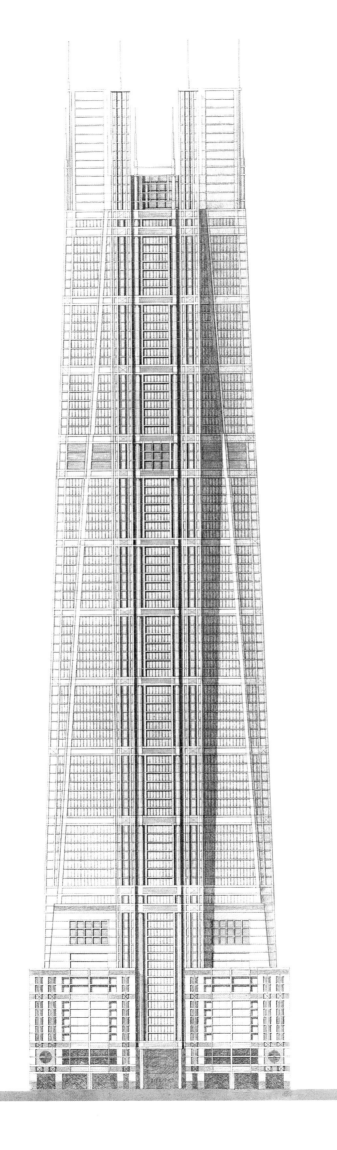

Canary Wharf Tower

London, England
1986–1987

Located on the Thames River east of the City of London, this
complex was designed as the first building group within a master
plan for the large site. The buildings house offices, trading
facilities, a hotel, retail space, and parking. The base of two
fourteen-story buildings forms a street wall on either side of a
fifty-story tower; the three are connected by a continuous
pedestrian arcade. To maximize natural light, office spaces are
arranged in C- or H-shaped wings around a series of shared atria.
A large structural grid, based on fifteen-meter spans, was
required for the open, column-free trading floors. The edges of
the floor slabs are integrated into the building's facades. The
curtain-wall system is a grid of stainless-steel mullions with
tinted glass, ribbed stainless steel, and white marble infill. At the
top of the central tower, a two-wing luxury hotel with rooftop
dining facilities articulates a crown.

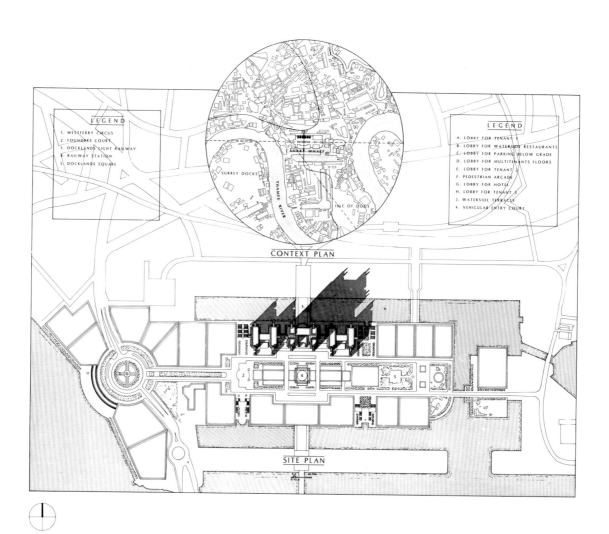

LEGEND
1. WESTFERRY CIRCUS
2. FOUNDERS COURT
3. DOCKLANDS LIGHT RAILWAY
4. RAILWAY STATION
5. DOCKLANDS SQUARE

LEGEND
A. LOBBY FOR TENANT 1
B. LOBBY FOR WATERSIDE RESTAURANTS
C. LOBBY FOR PARKING BELOW GRADE
D. LOBBY FOR MULTITENANTS FLOORS
E. LOBBY FOR TENANT 2
F. PEDESTRIAN ARCADE
G. LOBBY FOR HOTEL
H. LOBBY FOR TENANT 3
J. WATERSIDE TERRACES
K. VEHICULAR ENTRY COURT

CONTEXT PLAN

SITE PLAN

Plan, 43rd–50th floors

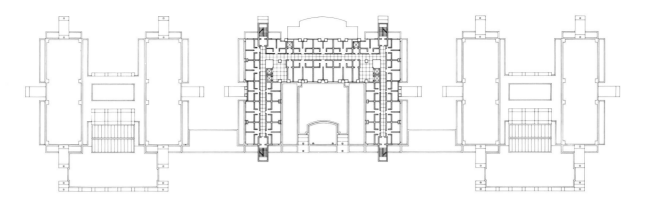

Plan, 17th floor

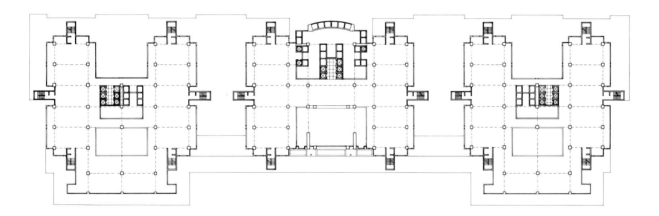

Plan, 3rd–6th floors

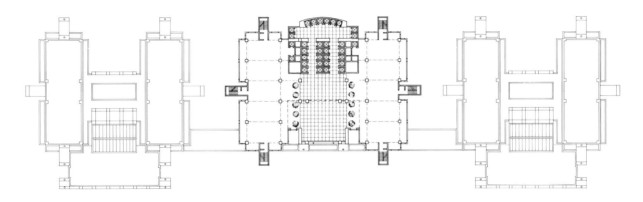

Plan, ground floor

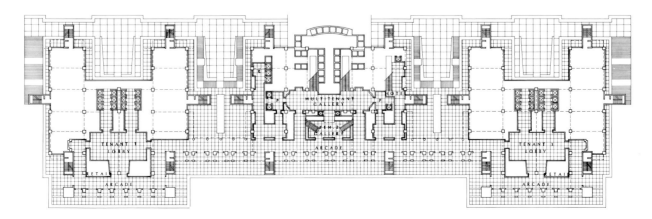

0   50 m

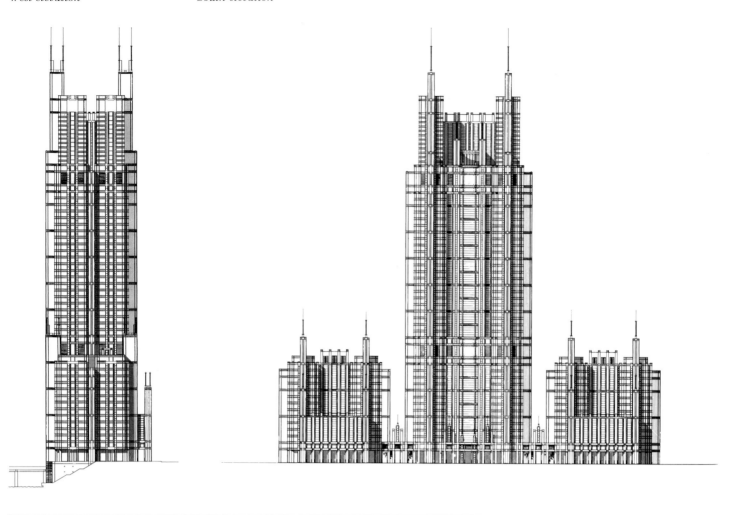

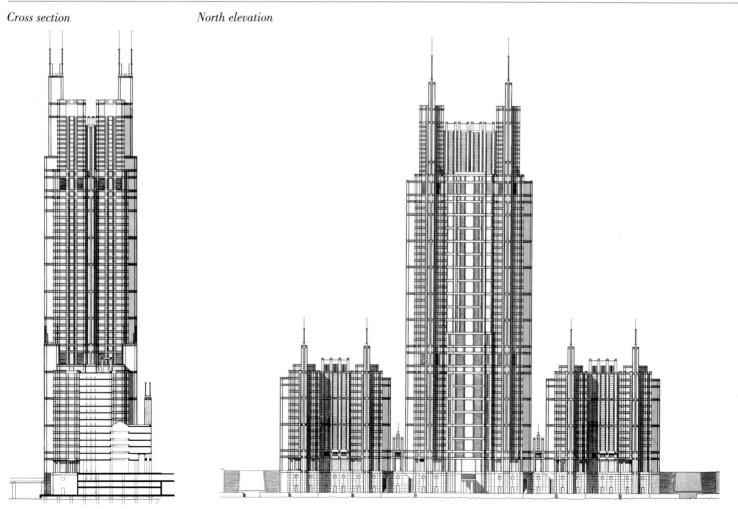

Here the biology of the tall
building, represented by its
structure, its spatial
organization and solar
orientation, and its hierarchy
of surface density, is explored
within the framework of a
classical composition.

William Pedersen

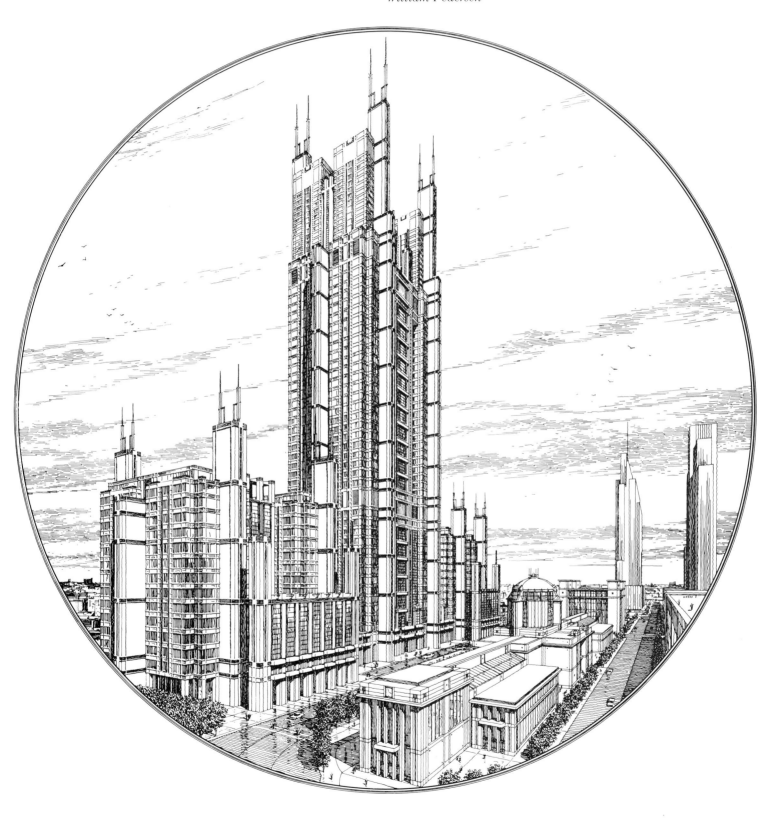

99

311 South Wacker Drive

Chicago, Illinois
1985–1990

This sixty-five-story office building is the first phase of a three-tower complex on South Wacker Drive, adjacent to the Sears Tower. The complex is organized around a winter garden, which serves as entrance and pedestrian hub, and is linked to nearby transportation systems.

The building consists of an octagonal tower embedded into a thick slab along Franklin Street. The tower breaks free of the slab at the fifty-first floor and rises an additional fifteen floors. The two elements are tied together by horizontal strapping at the base and at the thirteenth and forty-sixth floors. At the top, the frame and the tower create a Gothic framework of columns and beams. The large translucent glass cylinder and four surrounding smaller ones are lighted from within. Glowing at night, they are a landmark on the skyline.

Plan, 51st–65th floors

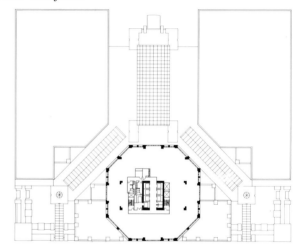

Plan, 47th–50th floors

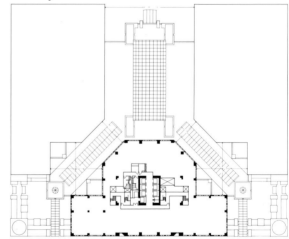

Plan, ground floor

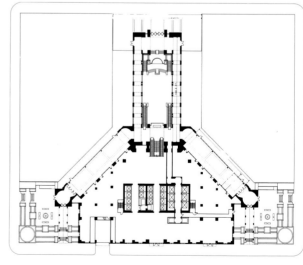

0   200 ft

100

The massing of this skyscraper breaks the building down into a series of elements, giving it legibility and scale as well as allowing it to develop a unique profile on the skyline.

Richard del Monte

Chicago Title and Trust Center

Chicago, Illinois
1986–1992

Located within Chicago's North Loop, where the city's most
important rail and pedestrian networks intersect, this fifty-story,
twin-towered office building, of which one tower is currently
built, completes the triangular plaza formed by the State of
Illinois office building and the City Hall County Building. The
building's base is scaled to these two low-rise structures, while
the twin towers take their height from the Daley Center to the
south. The office towers are composite in form: a masonry-and-
glass liner wraps around a slender metal-and-glass shaft. The two
forms are held together by bundled open glass corners. The
shafts rise above the rest of the structure, each culminating in
three open pylons of metal and glass that are lighted at night.
Below, three canopies swing out from the building to mark the
tower's entrances. At the center of the complex, a curving canopy
identifies a separate approach to a rotunda and a public galleria.

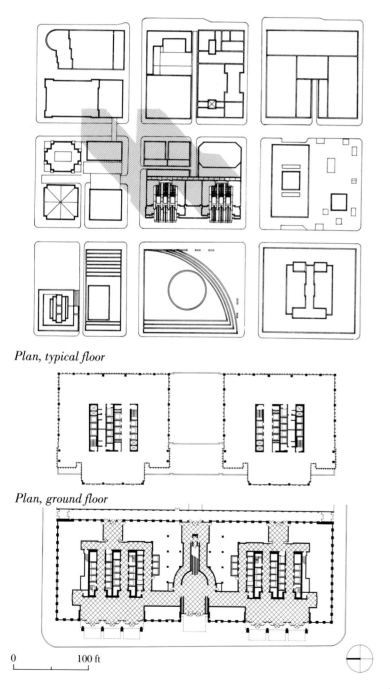

Plan, typical floor

Plan, ground floor

0   100 ft

The facade and its details are inspired by the urban artifacts of Chicago, its bridges, buildings, and railways.

David Leventhal

One Fountain Place

Cincinnati, Ohio
1985–1988

This mixed-use complex, designed to be the tallest structure in Cincinnati, is located on a prominent site in the center of the city. The building houses hotel, retail, and office functions in a five-story podium and a fifty-story tower that culminates in a public observatory. At the base, a large glass-enclosed rotunda acts as an anteroom to a formal five-story retail arcade connecting two city blocks. The tower, set back from Fountain Square, is composed of several stainless-steel-and-glass volumes articulated to reveal their structure. The building was intended by the city planning agency to be an icon for the city.

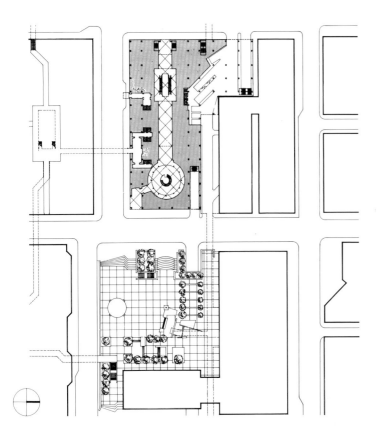

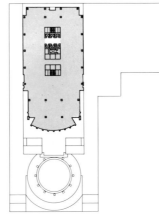

Plan, 20th–35th floors

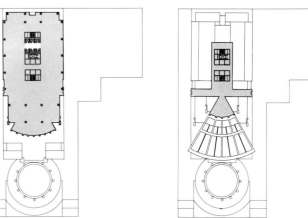

Plan, 50th floor (observatory)

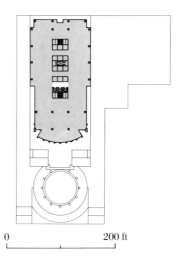

Plan, 16th–19th floors

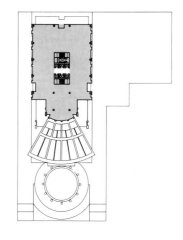

Plan, 46th–49th floors

0   200 ft

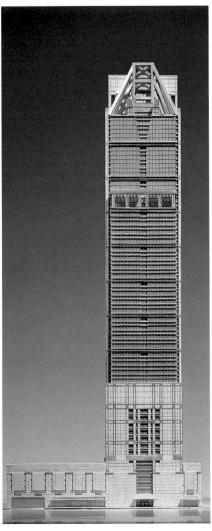

Station Center

White Plains, New York
1986–1988

This building contains the main White Plains commuter railroad station, housing units, office and retail space, a health club, and parking facilities. The project reinforces the edge of the commercial district to the west and, as the city's main railway station, acts as a gateway through its two western portals. The vaulted station intersects the lower block asymmetrically, forming a continuous arcaded entrance on the city side; entrances and service for the private functions are on the park side. Parking and a health club are provided to the north in the lower block, the roof of which forms a new ground plane for the housing to the north and the office block to the south. This podium is laid out with formal gardens that extend the park onto the building. The various terraces and crenellations atop the buildings are individually occupied.

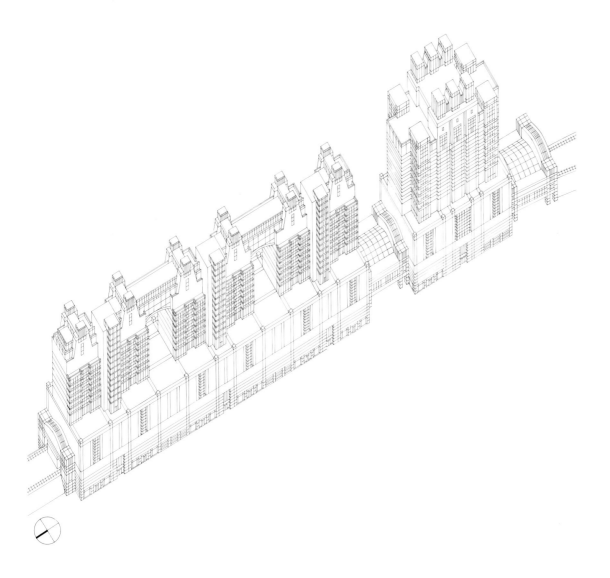

Plan, office/residential floor

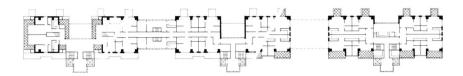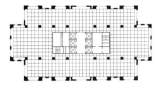

Plan, office/professional office floor

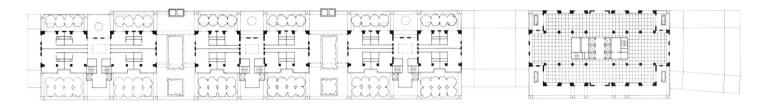

Plan, office/parking floor

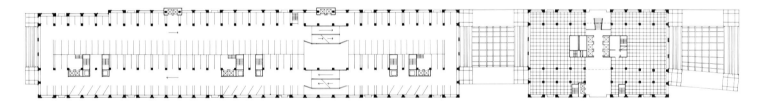

Plan, station floor

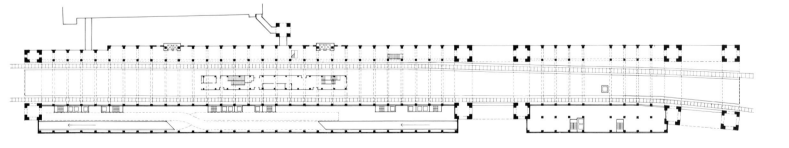

Plan, ground floor

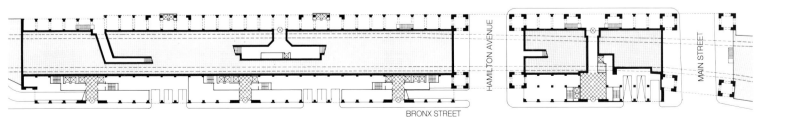

HAMILTON AVENUE

MAIN STREET

BRONX STREET

0   200 ft

113

Goldman, Sachs & Co. European Headquarters

London, England
1987–1991

This ten-story corporate headquarters occupies the former site of the Daily Telegraph Plant, north of Fleet Street in London. The project consists of a new office building, a group of renovated historic buildings, and the re-establishment of Peterborough Court, a component of the site during the nineteenth century.

The building is organized around two axes, one imposed by the site's boundaries to the east, north, and west, and another established by the buildings fronting Fleet Street to the south. Entry is through one of the renovated buildings, establishing the Fleet Street grid as the one that defines public space. The court, entrance gallery, conference rooms, south-facing wall, and rooftop dining rooms respond to this axis. The elevator core, computer areas, loading dock, office space, and fire exits all respond to the axis established by the site's perimeter. Stair towers divide the north, east, and west elevations. On the south, a narrow tower and a shallow convex plane reflect sunlight into the court. At the tenth floor, a vaulted roof housing south-facing dining rooms is combined with smaller rooftop pavilions to create a roofline consistent with the rest of the city. At ground level, the base of the building uses detailing, form, and texture to reflect London's intimate pedestrian scale.

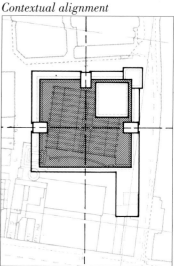

Contextual alignment

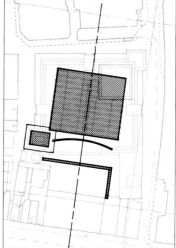

Fleet Street axis

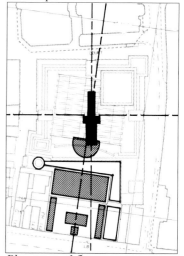

Public spaces

Plan, ground floor

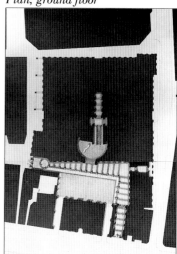

Plan, 7th–9th floors (offices)

Plan, roof

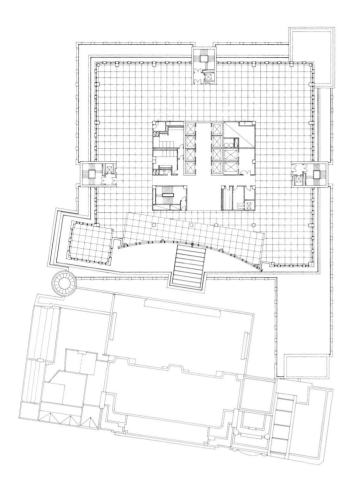

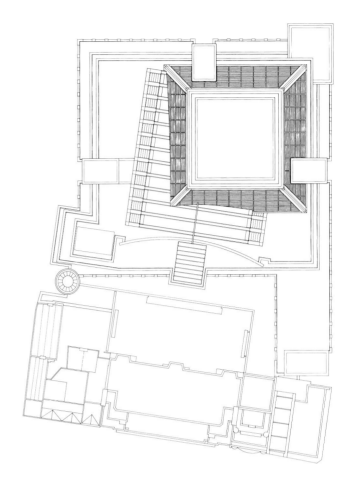

Plan, 2nd floor (trading)

Plan, 10th floor (dining)

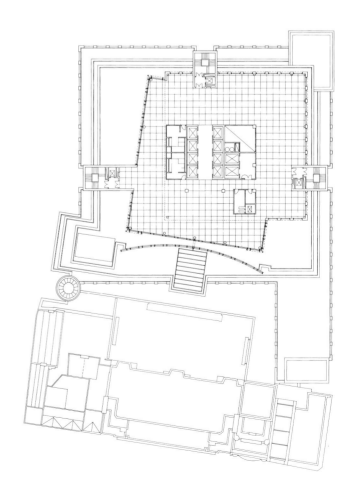

0   20 m

*This building seeks a
contextual equilibrium through
the juxtaposition of several
opposites: the modern and the
classical, the ambiguity of the
whole and the discreteness of
the parts, the tectonic precision
of metal and the volumetric
solidity of stone, the
availability of the public realm
and the withdrawal of the
private realm.*

William Pedersen

*Our building reflects our
client's corporate and civic
responsibility. By designing
highly detailed public spaces
and by breaking down the
overall massing of these headquarters we sought to represent
the company's vision for itself
and its desire to be a good
neighbor to the nearby St.
Paul's Cathedral.*

Lee Polisano

The ensemble of lobby, courtyard, and gallery at Peterborough Court alludes to the building's larger formal attitudes, even as it acknowledges the impacted quality of London's more localized street condition with its network of figural and interstitial spaces.

Craig Nealy

St. Paul Companies Headquarters

St. Paul, Minnesota
1987–1991

The triangular site, at a shift in the St. Paul city grid, is flanked
by two notable structures: the Hamm Building, clad in terra
cotta, and the Landmark Center, a romanesque courthouse.
The St. Paul Companies Headquarters, a complex for a large
insurance company, presented the opportunity to complete
the site.

A low rectangular block defines the edge of St. Peter's Street, not
only serving as a visual base for the building but also referring to
the Hamm Building across the street. The cylindrical glass tower
is the fulcrum on which the entire composition pivots; it acts, in
conjunction with Hamm Plaza (also designed by KPF), as the
visual terminus for the pedestrian street approaching from the
east. The basilica-like form is the entry to the complex, uniting
old and new and, with its smaller scale, opening a dialogue
between both. The circular cafeteria is aligned with the steeples
of the church across the street and is the focal point of the upper
garden. The main tower, with its pyramidal metal roof, relates to
the variety of roof forms in the area, including the more distant
State Capitol and the St. Paul Cathedral.

The facades, consisting of stone grids with punched window
openings, provide visual weight and serve as the ground against
which the more figural elements develop. The use of local stone
ties the new building to its surroundings while clearly
articulating the planar and non-load-bearing function of stone in
modern construction.

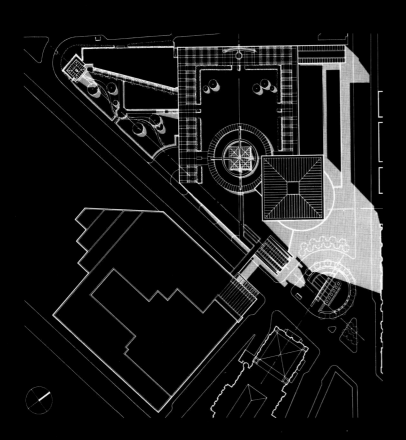

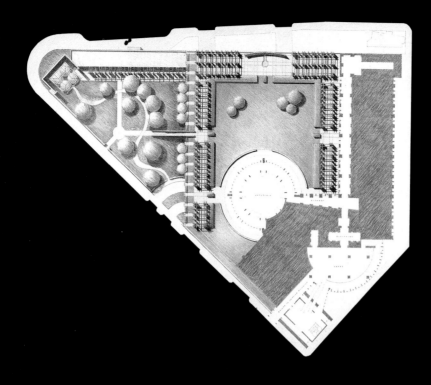

Plan, ground floor

Plan, 3rd–9th floors

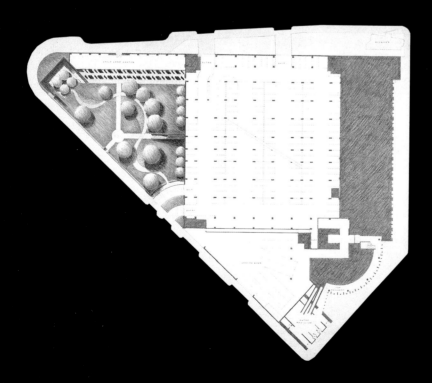

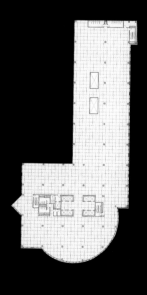

0   100 ft

The strategy, somewhat different within the body of our work, of disposing almost discrete pieces, each with a specific urban role, enables a large corporation to reveal its diverse programmatic constituency.

William Pedersen

The grouping of forms does not attempt to mimic its surroundings, but instead tries to give concrete form to the forces at work on this site. It challenges the viewer to understand these forces through an understanding of the building. Each of the elements has a distinct role to play in the process.

Richard del Monte

*The St. Paul Companies
charge to us was to embody
both their corporate spirit and
their civic pride. It is a rare
opportunity for a building both
to serve so dramatically to
reinforce the fabric of its city
and also to respond so clearly
to the environment and its
purpose by the expression of
its functional and aesthetic
elements.*

Robert Cioppa

Canary Wharf

London, England
1987–1991

These ten-story office buildings are part of Canary Wharf, the
new financial district east of central London. Forming a long
urban wall along the Thames River, the two buildings border
Cabot Square, a new public space within the complex.

Each facade was generated by Canary Wharf itself. One side is
broken down into separate elements, including turrets and
colonnaded screens. These elements respond to specific site
conditions, such as the large public square, the retail galleria,
and the nearby high-rise office buildings. The other side
responds to the Thames River with a broad, sweeping curtain
wall above and intricately detailed retail facades below. Both
buildings are clad in heavily veined, aqueous-gray Vermont
marble, white-painted metal, and clear glass. Two enclosed
skylighted atria with facades of stucco and glass punctuate each
building, bringing light and air into the large floorplates below.

The two buildings form a long urban wall, much like the great mercantile structures that once lined the wharfs of the Thames River.

David Leventhal

Mainzer Landstrasse 58

Frankfurt am Main, Germany
1986–1993

This building in the new Mainzer Landstrasse commercial strip in Frankfurt, just south of the Westend residential community, includes an office block and tower for the headquarters of DG Bank, residential apartments, and a central winter garden. The base of the complex incorporates the residential and office components and also serves as a step to the higher office tower. The multiple superimposed facades and volumes reinforce the building's strong symmetry. The winter garden, located between the tower and the residential and office blocks, is placed on a north-south axis for maximum exposure to sunlight. It is designed as an enlarged civic version of the great European palm courts, or crystal palaces, and creates a new central focus for the Westend community.

The central spine of the office tower anchors the building on the Frankfurt skyline while the building's divisions and breaks correspond to neighboring office towers along Mainzer Landstrasse. The tower rises in a curved shaft to 208 meters, using lighter materials such as reflective glass and white-painted steel. It terminates in a three-story loggia beneath a great cantilevered crown that beckons toward the old center of Frankfurt.

Plan, 2nd–4th floors

Plan, 40th–47th floors

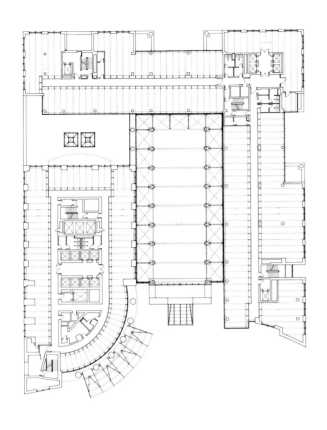

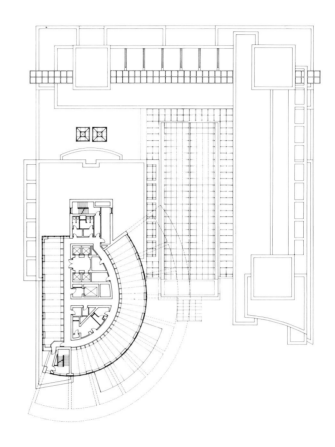

Plan, ground floor

Plan, 9th floor

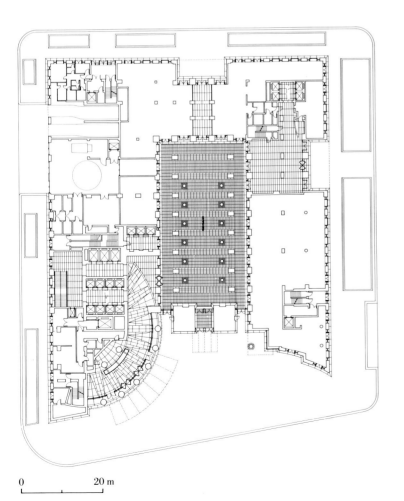

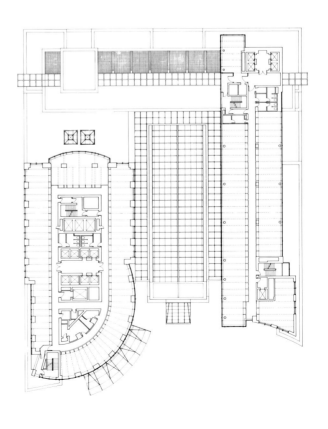

0   20 m

151

For us, this building represented a significant breakthrough in the composition of the tall building. In joining together three parts, two of which act in an oppositional dialogue to a third component that stabilizes their relationship, we were more capable of addressing issues relating to formality and informality, figure and abstraction, opacity and reflectivity, symbol and function.

William Pedersen

The different facade systems are used to emphasize discrete volumes while referring to the dichotomies of modern versus traditional architecture and collective, free-plan layout versus the individual office.

Paul King

1250 Boulevard René-Lévesque Ouest

Montreal, Canada
1988–1992

This forty-seven-story office building is located in the western part of the central business district of the island city of Montreal, Quebec. The building, now housing the Montreal offices of IBM Canada, occupies a prominent position on the boulevard, a major east-west commercial axis since the completion of Place Ville Marie in the late 1970s. The building reflects Montreal's desire to spur growth in the business district. The tower is adjacent to the landmark Windsor Station and is one block from Dorchester Square, the district's main public space.

The nearly rectangular site is formed by a street grid defined by Mount Royal to the north and the St. Lawrence River to the south; the parti was developed around these dominant features. The massing of slender, interlocking stone slabs addresses Mount Royal—rising almost to the height of the mountain's peak—and acts as a support armature for the curved glass-and-aluminum wall, which is centered on the copper dome of the cathedral in Dorchester Square. The faceted, rectilinear elements look east and south over the park, the city, and the St. Lawrence River, while the curved element extends from the lobby at the base to the building's top, where it is capped by a horizontal wing.

The massing of the L-shaped lower base extends the street walls and reduces the scale of the tower at pedestrian level. A landscaped public plaza sheltered by the building's form relieves the northeast corner of the site, which might otherwise be crowded by pedestrian traffic from three neighboring towers. Immediately next to the plaza is a six-story public winter garden that serves as the building's entrance from the boulevard. The winter garden also connects to a street-level retail arcade, the metro system, and, via tunnels, to two adjacent buildings.

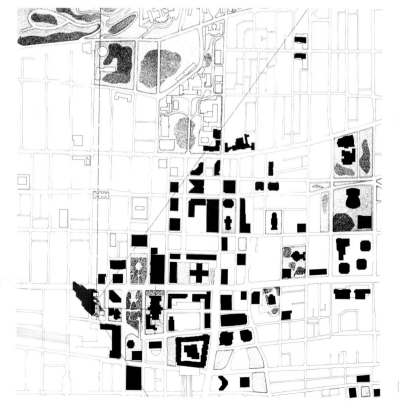

160

Plan, 5th–9th floors

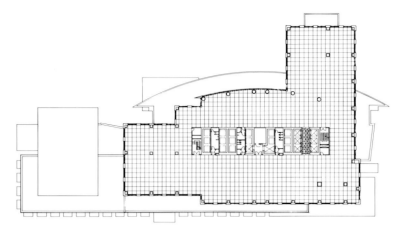

Plan, mezzanine floor

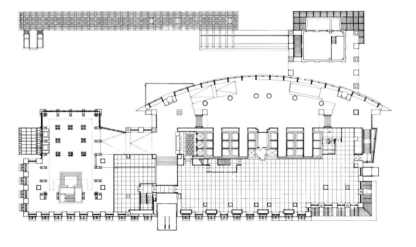

Plan, restaurant floor

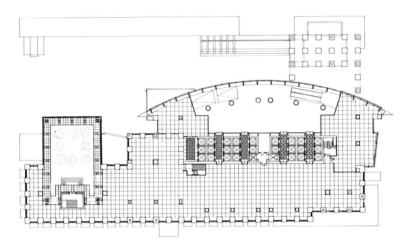

Plan, ground floor

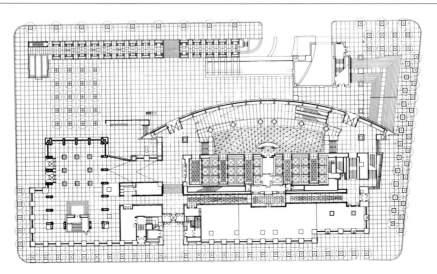

0   30 m

Plan, 29th–33rd floors

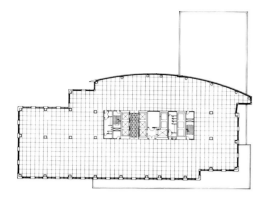

Plan, 48th floor

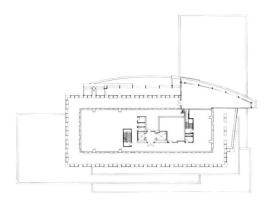

Plan, 20th–25th floors

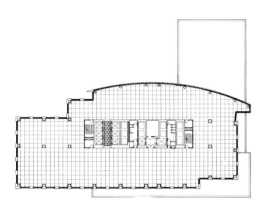

Plan, 47th floor

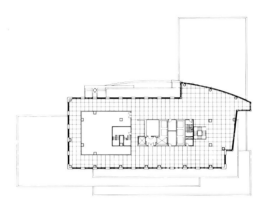

Plan, 16th floor

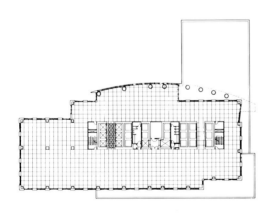

Plan, 43rd–45th floors

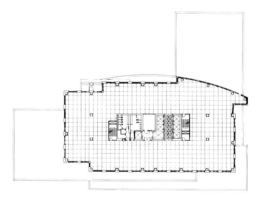

Plan, 11th–15th floors

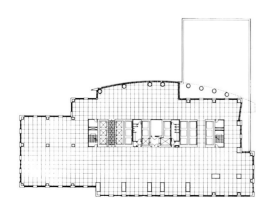

Plan, 37th–41st floors

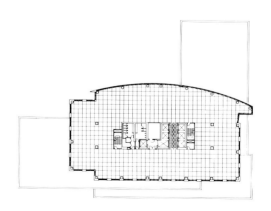

This building evolved from the almost generic compositional discoveries of our Frankfurt tower. Here, however, we sought a more integrated relationship between the two salient parts. Vertically striated stone surfaces enable a curving glass wall, horizontally composed, to emerge rather than collide. The result is a structure emanating a presence which is simultaneously formal and informal.

William Pedersen

Here we had the opportunity to develop an abstract and integrated tectonic vocabulary which is at once explicitly urban in its relationship to Montreal and highly self-reflexive of its object: nature.

Richard Clarke

Varying scale, strong identity, careful detailing, and new expression coexist to create a fresh new image for the skyscraper.

John Koga

Rockefeller Plaza West

New York, New York
1987–1991

Facing Seventh Avenue at Rockefeller Center's western edge, between 49th and 50th streets adjacent to the Exxon Building and plaza, this fifty-five-story office building responds to strict zoning requirements for both New York City and the Times Square Theater District. The 1.6-million-square-foot building also houses performing arts rehearsal studios and is linked to the underground concourse network of the center.

The contrasting models of corporate and public modernism—Rockefeller Center and Times Square—set the stage for the project and inform its design. A central vertical core pins the building to the site and defines it on the skyline, joining the axis of the GE and Exxon buildings. Variously sized elements are rotated around this core to terminate the east-west axis of the complex and create a new relationship to Times Square to the south. The changing scale and irregular forms of these elements allow the building to anchor itself in the midtown Manhattan cityscape. The building is clad in limestone and clear glass, with stainless-steel ornamentation placed on the surface of the stone to articulate building setbacks and shimmer in the sunlight.

A two-tiered podium, slid toward the west, adds to Seventh Avenue's street wall. Its surface is covered by electronic signage, and a building entrance is indicated by a tower of light. An irregular configuration created at the Exxon plaza provides the main entrance to the building. A portion of the building facing Times Square is disengaged and transformed into a metal-and-glass sign. Lighted at night, it brings the building into the bright ambience of Times Square.

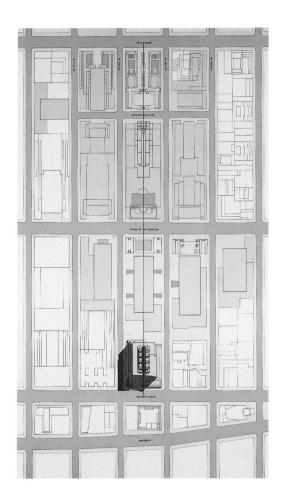

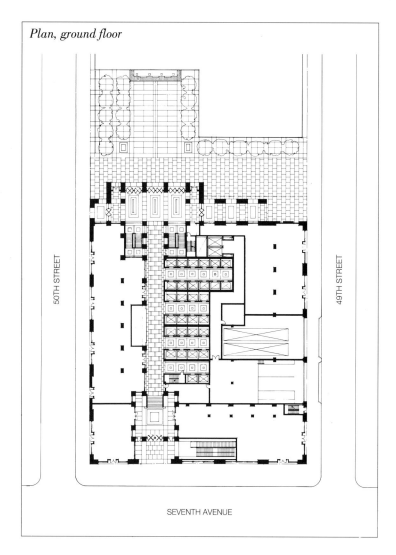

Plan, ground floor

50TH STREET

49TH STREET

SEVENTH AVENUE

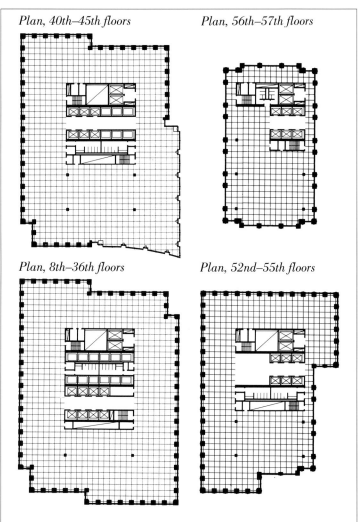

Plan, 40th–45th floors

Plan, 56th–57th floors

Plan, 8th–36th floors

Plan, 52nd–55th floors

0   100 ft

Here we seek the Janus-like ability to address, meaningfully, the demands of two contrasting urban models: the nobility of Rockefeller Center and the visual cacophony of Times Square. The resulting composition can be read, in its totality, as almost de Stijl. However, within its parts it is rooted in classicism. This compositional synthesis negotiates the resolution of early and late intentions within our work.

William Pedersen

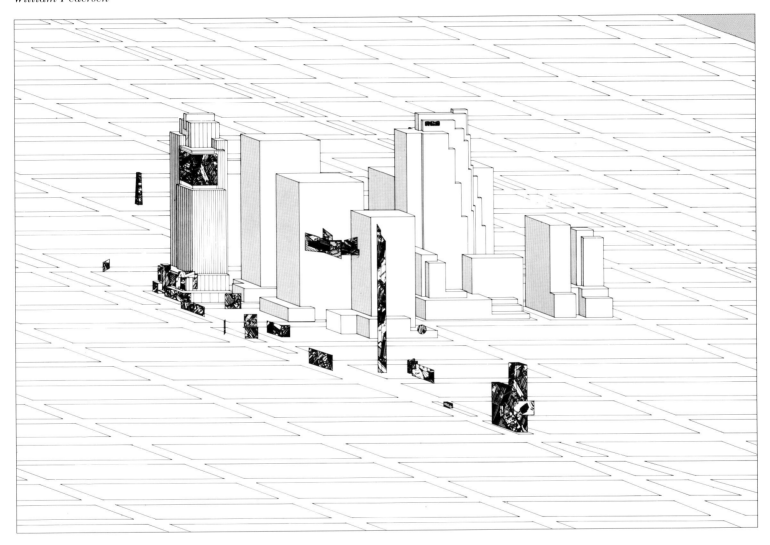

Our primary responsibilities for this project were to meet the demands of its diverse site conditions in concert with the mandated zoning requirements and the owner's goal to create the western gateway to the Rockefeller Center Complex. The design attempts to respond to these influences, yet still create a singular architectural statement with its own integrity.

Gregory Clement

Three Bellevue Center

Bellevue, Washington
1988–1994

Three Bellevue Center is a proposed office building for Bellevue, a new city facing Seattle directly across Lake Washington. The building was conceived as the intersection of three distinct abstract volumes atop a figural base. A rectangular horizontal volume fronts 108th Avenue N.E. and defines a new pedestrian corridor. A curving vertical volume—inspired by the locale's nautical overtones—defers to the adjacent building and plaza. A central core emerging at the top skewers the curved and rectangular volumes, locking them into place.

A curtain-wall system identifies each of the different volumetric aspects of the building. The vertically organized walls on the south and east facades are contrasted with the more horizontal wall that stretches across the curved facade to form a metaphorical sail facing Lake Washington. The systems are interwoven to provide continuity and scale to the entire building.

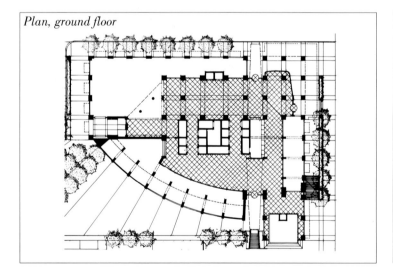

Plan, ground floor

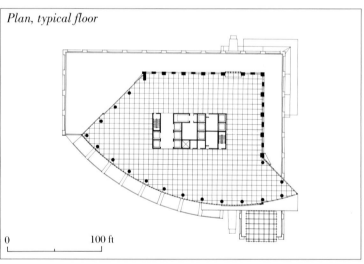

Plan, typical floor

0   100 ft

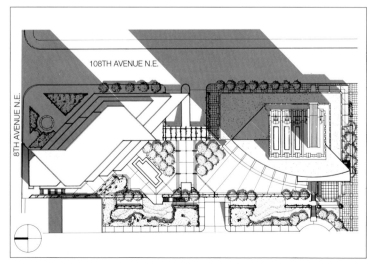

108TH AVENUE N.E.

8TH AVENUE N.E.

Facing Lake Washington, this building evokes an imagery of sail and mast. The abstractness of the tower's form is countered by the classically centered composition of its lower base. This juxtaposition is intended to heighten the intensity of human interaction with the building as it meets the ground.

William Pedersen

We attempted to synthesize the different geometric forms by the interweaving of two distinct curtain walls. What emerges is a vocabulary that explains and celebrates movement.

Peter Schubert

Chifley Tower

Sydney, Australia
1987–1992

This forty-two-story office tower is located at the edge of downtown Sydney, on an irregularly shaped site next to Chifley Square. The site opens onto the expansive public green of the Royal Botanical Gardens and the Domain to the east. Beyond the green and to the north lie the city's famous harbor and Opera House. Most notable of the varied buildings surrounding the site are some old Victorian sandstone structures and art deco buildings.

At ground level, an interior room opens onto the redesigned Chifley Square. This room and a through-block arcade provide access to three levels of shops and restaurants. The office spaces, with separate entrances on Chifley Square and Bent Street, are housed in two double-height trading floors and conference facilities that adjoin a garden set atop a five-story podium that brings coherence to the street wall. The office-tower mass, a composition of shifted rectilinear volumes with varying heights that correspond to those of neighboring buildings, rises at the north end of the site to minimize the shadow cast on the square. The resulting facades respond to different site conditions. A broad curving wall of lightly reflective glass looks toward the harbor and the Domain, while the city facade is patterned with punched windows and other curtain-wall elements.

The overall composition has a dynamic profile on the skyline, provided by its crown, a radio mast and microwave dish enclosure, to the north. The strong central rectilinear mass locks into the city's north-south street grid while sponsoring distinct but simultaneous responses to the harbor, the city, and the pedestrian.

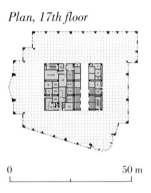

Plan, 31st–38th floors

Plan, 17th floor

0   50 m

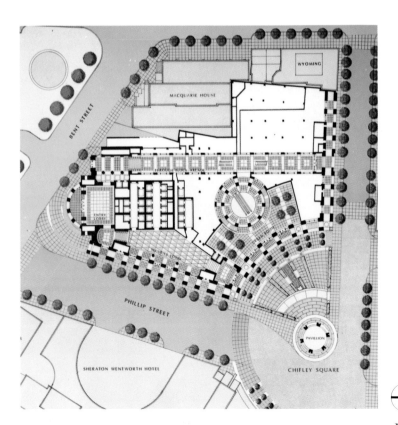

Recognizing the long love affair of Sydney with its harbor and views, an expansive curved glass form is oriented in that direction. The tall mast placed atop the building in combination with the billowing glass form is intended to symbolize the harbor's activity.

The design is an energetic one which attempts to recognize and rectify the many conditions of the site. The active geometry is unified by the common language of punched and vertically grouped windows and a granite palette reminiscent of some of the more notable Victorian buildings of Sydney.

William Louie

Bank Niaga Headquarters

Jakarta, Indonesia
1989–1993

Located on Jalan Sudirman, one of Jakarta's principal arteries, this headquarters complex for a large commercial bank accommodates a diverse program on a site organized into quadrants. Facing the boulevard is a twenty-seven-story office tower, expressed as two interlocking volumes of granite and glass, occupying one full quadrant. The tower is further articulated by a series of brise-soleils and is capped by a helipad. Also facing the boulevard, a four-story banking hall with a butterfly-wing roof occupies another quadrant. A mosque with a steeply pitched pyramidal roof and a podium with gardens and fountains, accommodating parking below, occupy the remaining two quadrants to the rear.

Plan, 3rd floor

Plan, typical floor

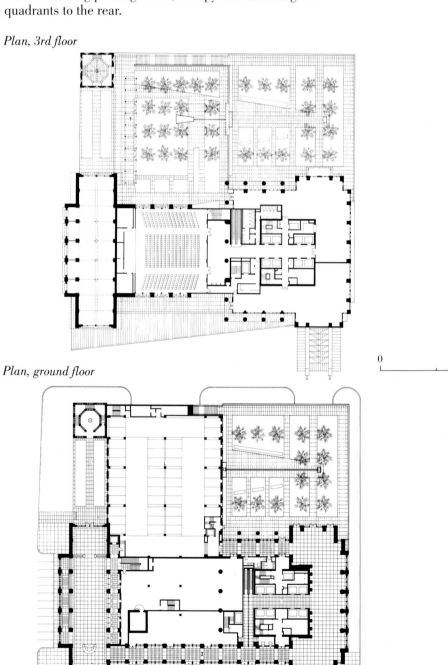

0   30 m

Plan, ground floor

550 South Hope Street

Los Angeles, California
1988–1992

The twenty-seven-story office building sits on the eastern side of South Hope Street, in downtown Los Angeles. This new building was designed to relate to its immediate neighbor, Bertram Goodhue's Los Angeles Public Library of 1926, and to George W. Kelham's California Club building of 1929 across the street.

The building is organized around a central slab of the same width as the California Club yet perpendicular to it, allowing the two buildings to be read as a pair and thus framing, in perspective, the tower of the Public Library as the terminus of Hope Street. The tower also has a vertically striated back datum plane and a horizontally ordered glass curtain wall punctured by a vertical mast. Flamed and polished Swedish granite is woven into the verticals and horizontals throughout to create a unified reading, which is reinforced by a figural base. This base defines the street wall and generates a relationship to the adjacent smaller building through scale. The context is further reflected in the use of beige and red-orange granites similar in tone to the ensemble of honorific buildings. Retail functions as well as the two-story entrance lobby are located at the Hope Street level, while a court garden at the mezzanine level and adjacent to the library accommodates outdoor dining functions.

Plan, roof

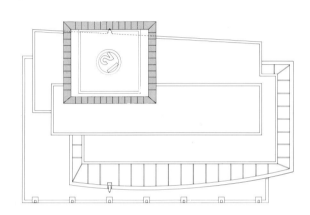

Plan, typical floor

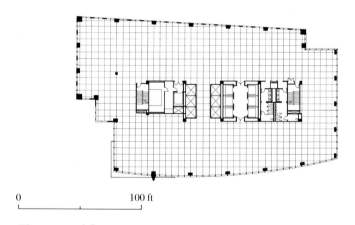

0   100 ft

Plan, ground floor

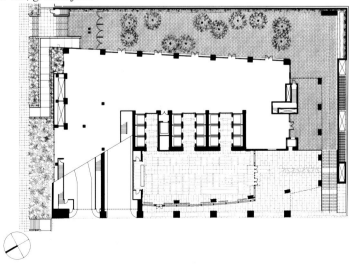

THE BANK OF CALIFORNIA
SINCE 1864

Key to the design of this building is its relationship to the California Club and the Los Angeles Public Library achieved by its massing and color. This uniquely Californian skyscraper speaks of its important location in the downtown area while accomplishing a handsome, efficient, and economical office building.

A. Eugene Kohn

Tobishima Headquarters

Tokyo, Japan
1990

Situated in Tokyo Teleport, a new city being built in Tokyo Bay, this headquarters complex consists of a twenty-four-story office tower, a banking hall, art gallery, public hall, shops, and gardens. The tower, composed of three volumes of granite and glass, anchors the edge of the site. An undulating horizontal curtain wall faces the bay, while above it a meeting hall surfaced in mirrored glass reflects the distant city of Tokyo. An arrangement of smaller-scaled objects housing the other functions is installed at the building's base, presenting a landscape of pavilions and gardens analogous to traditional Japanese garden design.

Plan, 23rd floor

Plan, 7th–21st (odd) floors

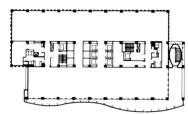

Plan, 6th–20th (even) floors

Plan, 4th and 5th floors

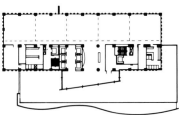

Plan, ground floor

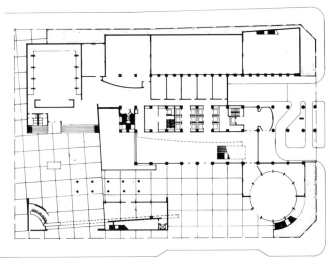

Plan, 3rd floor

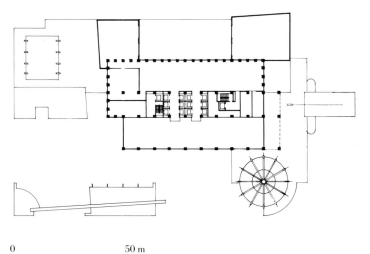

0   50 m

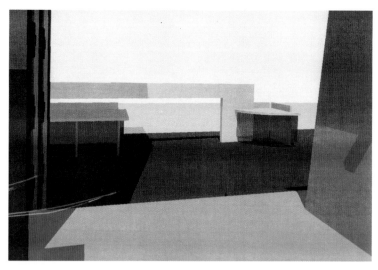
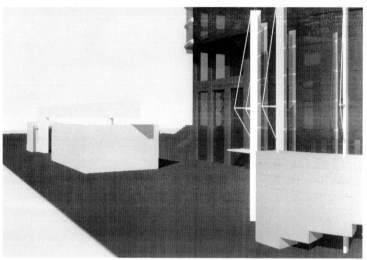

Morrison Tower

Portland, Oregon
1989–1994

Morrison Tower provides office space and retail facilities at S.W. Morrison and 3rd Avenue near Pioneer Square, in Portland's pedestrian-oriented arts district. A three-story stone base houses public spaces, art galleries, and restaurants to encourage community use. A twenty-eight-story office tower rises above the podium in three interlocking volumes. Two curved curtain walls of metal and glass with stone spandrels acknowledge both Mount Hood and Mount St. Helens in the distance and together form a prow facing the Willamette River. A vertical element—a narrow rectangular form extending from base to top—locks the building into the city grid while acting as backbone to the mass of the tower. The building's summit is composed of the intersection of the three forms.

Plan, 31st and 32nd floors

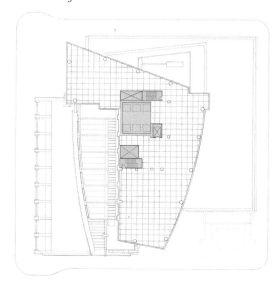

Plan, typical floor

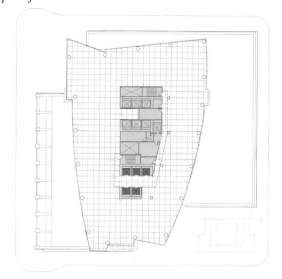

Plan, ground floor

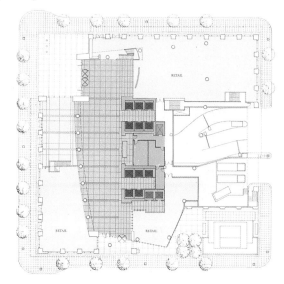

0   100 ft

The abstractness of the tower's larger composition seeks a dialogue with the city, the river, and the mountains, while the vertically centered repetition of the base reflects the scale and texture of adjacent traditional structures.

William Pedersen

The spiraling form emerged from a need to address the distant views of Mount St. Helens and Mount Hood. The resulting silhouette joins the drama of the surrounding landscape.

Peter Schubert

Ameritrust Center

Cleveland, Ohio
1988–1995

This sixty-story bank headquarters and hotel complex faces
Public Square, the historic center of Cleveland. The site is also
adjacent to the landmark Terminal Tower, an early twentieth-
century skyscraper that was once the tallest building outside of
New York City.

As the office tower rises above the hotel base, its mass and visual
center of gravity shift to the north, away from the slender profile
of Terminal Tower. A curved reflective-glass curtain wall
terminates Euclid Avenue, which enters the square at a diagonal.
The tower is capped by a metal-and-glass crown symbolizing
both the city's industrial past and its high-technology future. The
granite-and-glass base maintains the harmony and scale of the
historic buildings surrounding the square, while a skylighted
atrium on the second floor, housing public spaces, provides a
window overlooking Public Square.

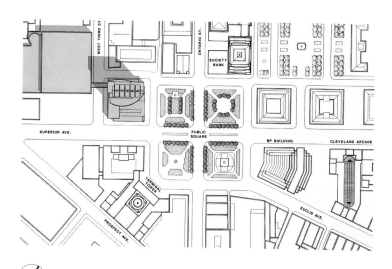

Plan, typical high-rise floor

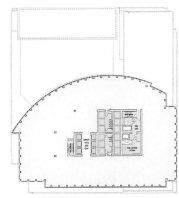

Plan, typical low-rise floor

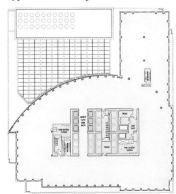

Plan, typical hotel floor

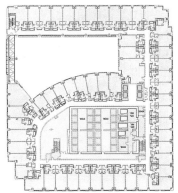

Plan, ground floor

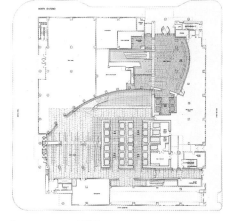

0   100 ft

This skyscraper of multiple uses responds to the many urban forces that come together at this extremely prominent site on Public Square in this quintessential mid-western American city. The expression of the building's top reflects the industrial past of Cleveland and its hi-tech future.

A. Eugene Kohn

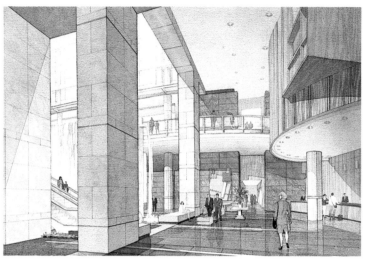

World Bank Headquarters

Washington, D.C.
1989–1996

The design for the World Bank Headquarters complex was the winning entry in an international competition. For a site on Pennsylvania Avenue in an area dominated by buildings from the 1960s and 1970s, the scheme incorporates buildings by Gordon Bunshaft and Vincent Kling into a unified entity.

The building consists of a thirteen-story superblock surrounding a large covered courtyard. The existing structures comprise two of the three masonry wings that frame the project's glazed north wing. The courtyard identifies the bank as a community, connecting and integrating the separate buildings and their diverse functions within one institution. The canted glass wall facing Pennsylvania Avenue lifts off from the ground to reveal the large open-plan lobby, its adjacent public spaces, and the covered courtyard and sculpture terrace beyond. The strong urban presence of these elements is symbolic of the institution's desire for openness and accessibility for its constituents and the public at large.

Although Washington is a city of classical architecture, the design distances itself from this vocabulary because of its allusions to colonialism abroad. Instead, the project is inspired by its context, specifically Vincent Kling's modern structure; it modifies and enhances the scale of the Kling building.

The individual architectural elements of precast concrete and white-painted aluminum have been detailed to a high level of abstraction; their recombination and juxtaposition provides depth and variety of expression. Within the central court, references to world cultures occur in linear watercourses, monumental flights of steps, and pyramidal glazed pieces. On the roof, conference room canopies, masts, and the bowed courtyard skylight give form to the building's programmatic elements and provide a distinctive profile on the Washington skyline.

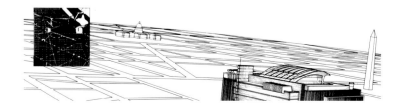

Plan, typical floor

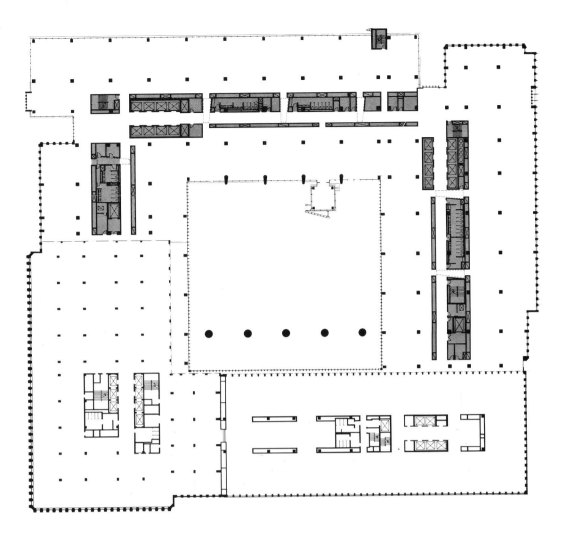

Plan, ground floor

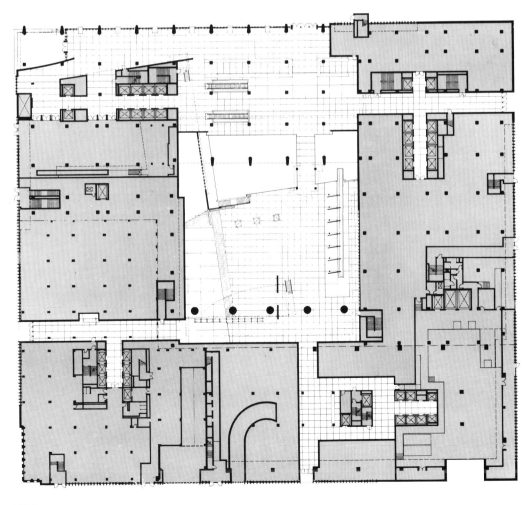

0   100 ft

Acknowledging that representation by a classical, hence colonial, language would be anathema to some of the members of the bank, we chose to work within a modern language that emerges from the desire to express community, openness, and contextual linkage. This language, sponsored by existing structures, is transformed into an intense dialogue between vertical and horizontal surfaces.

William Pedersen

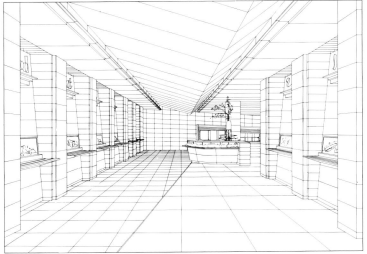

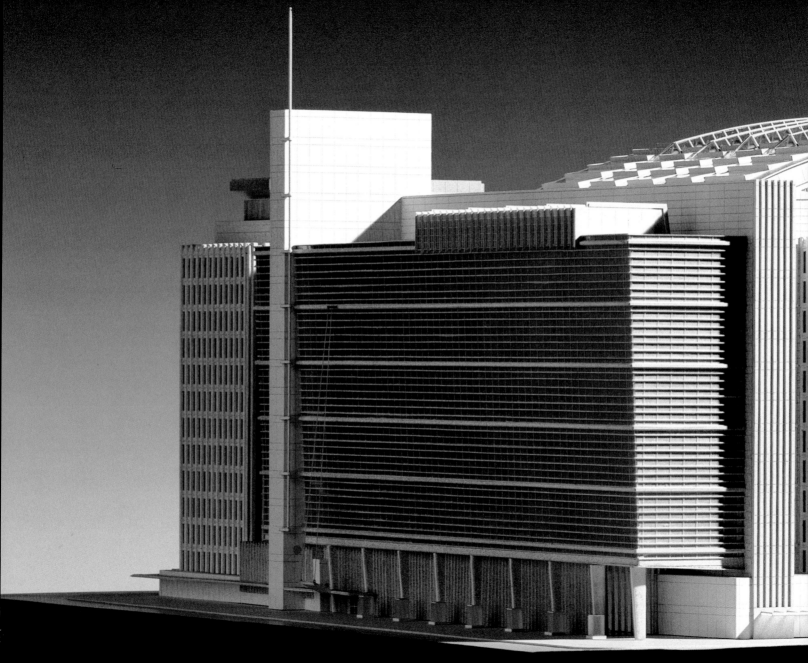

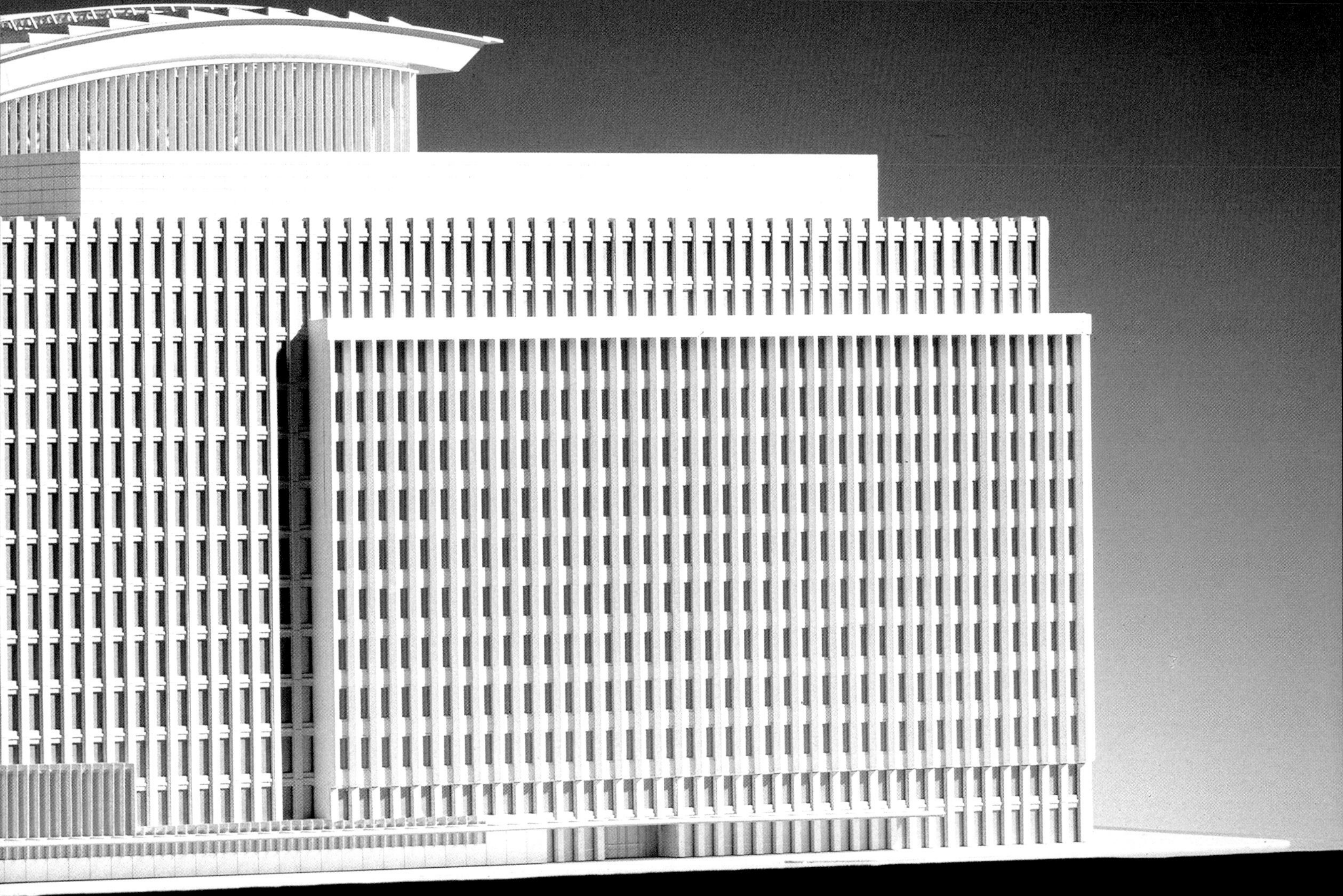

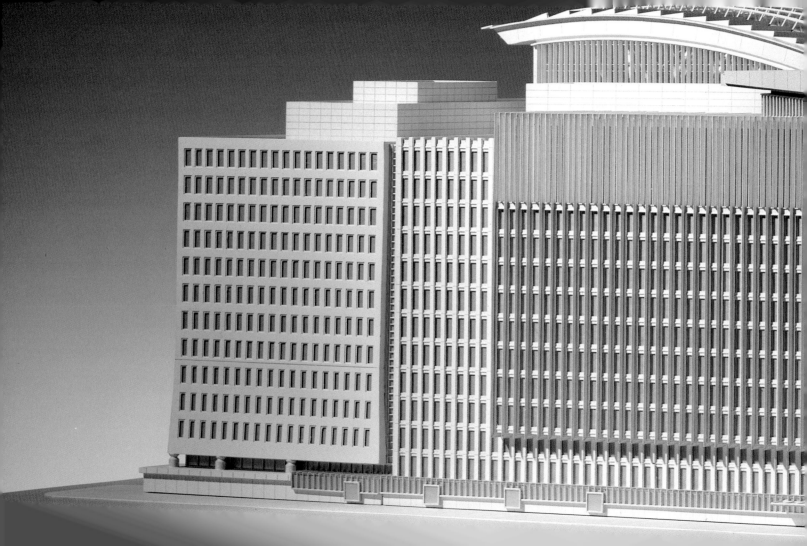

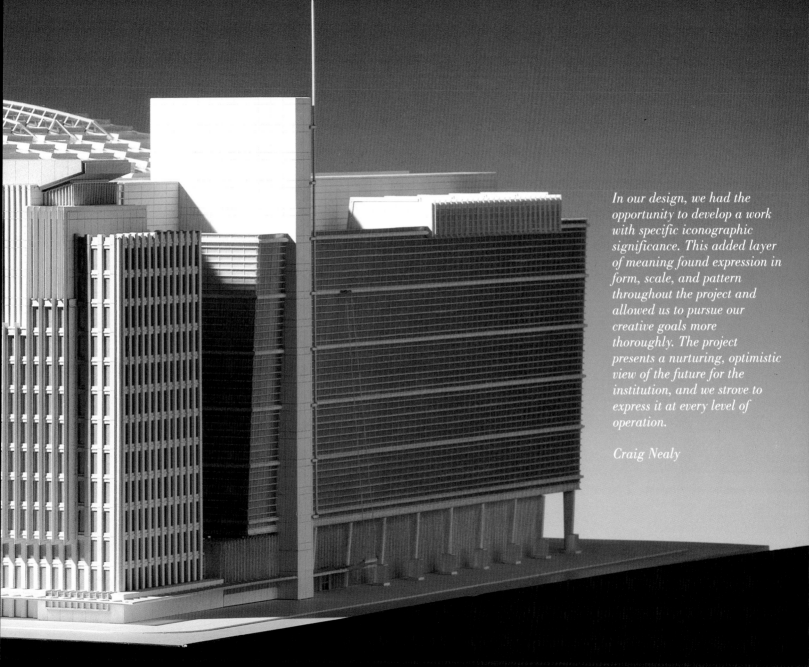

In our design, we had the opportunity to develop a work with specific iconographic significance. This added layer of meaning found expression in form, scale, and pattern throughout the project and allowed us to pursue our creative goals more thoroughly. The project presents a nurturing, optimistic view of the future for the institution, and we strove to express it at every level of operation.

Craig Nealy

Federal Reserve Bank of Dallas

Dallas, Texas
1989–1992

The site, on a shallow rise at the northern edge of downtown Dallas, looks over the sunken Woodall Rodgers Freeway to the low buildings of the arts district and offers views of the city to the south and the surrounding residential district. Banking functions dictated a design providing a secure operations facility with a large, flexible plan. The program also called for a building offering efficient and direct delivery of operational goods, a complex inter- and intradepartmental network, and employee amenities. The site plan anticipates a fifty-year expansion program.

These goals generated an extensive ground floor accommodating the securities, check, and general delivery services as well as the vaults and related departments. Public access is through a main entrance, opening into a double-height lobby, which includes the securities department, teller windows, and a guard station. Parking is below grade, allowing freer circulation above ground. An elevated garden level on the roof of the first floor still leaves room on the site for future expansion.

The main employee entrance is on the second floor, which is organized around a central courtyard that provides natural light to the interior spaces. It contains facilities such as the cafeteria, lounge, auditorium, exercise and day care areas, central training/conference center, and a currency museum. Elevator cores at either end of the courtyard anticipate and encourage the flow of employees to and from these amenities.

The tower housing executive offices is canted to address Pearl Street, the approach from the city. Building materials include a warm cross-cut Indiana limestone accented by a gray Stanstead granite base. Energy-efficient, lightly reflective glass serves for spandrel panels, which are held in place by a crisp white aluminum mullion system.

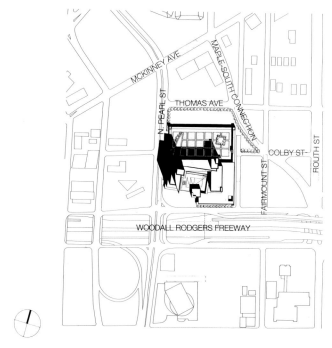

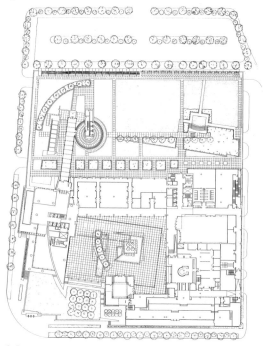

Plan, garden floor

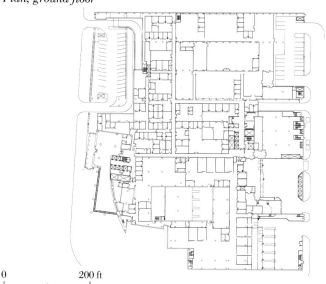

Plan, ground floor

0   200 ft

Plan, typical high-rise floor

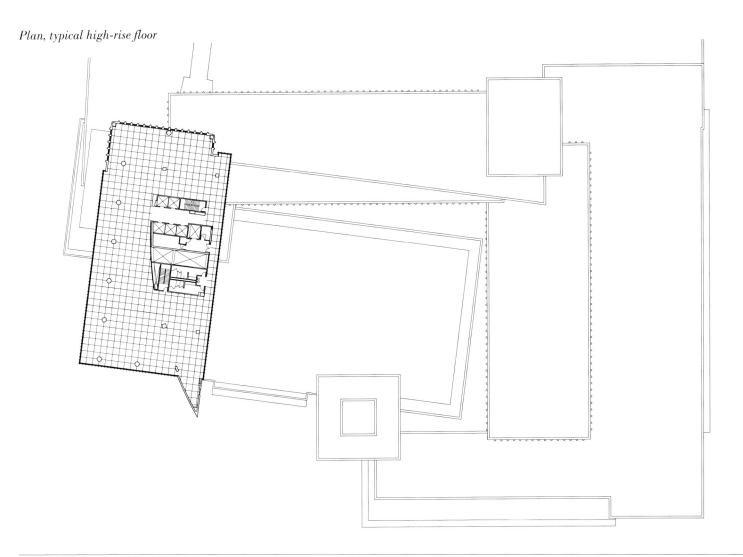

Plan, typical low-rise floor

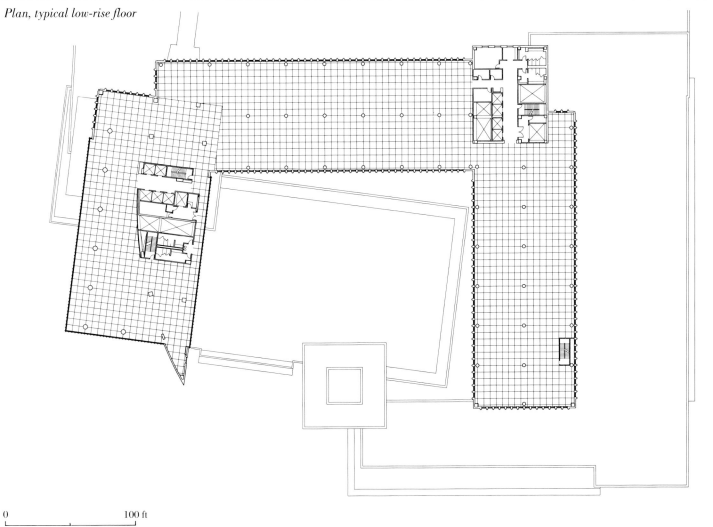

0   100 ft

The spiraling ascension of volumes focuses on a collective void, while a fine-grained striation of stone and glass allows form to dominate surface. Monumentality, representative of a Federal presence, is purposefully tempered by informality, to seek a more human balance.

William Pedersen

Our design is rooted in the concept of community that is the heart of the bank's collective identity and is inspired, in part, by the seemingly limitless, sweeping landscape that characterizes Dallas's prairie condition. The square courtyard typology was adapted to create a dominant horizontal field populated by proportionally interrelated vertical elements employed to articulate object perimeters and to scale and delimit the organizing internal forces.

Richard Clarke

Meydenbauer Convention Center

Bellevue, Washington
1989–1993

As part of a new Civic Center for Bellevue, this convention
center is a pivotal piece in the city's master plan. The rectangular
low-rise building is composed of separate yet interlocking
volumes that attempt to redefine this institutional building type.
The typical convention center is here given a more human scale,
with a program that includes an exhibition hall, meeting rooms, a
theater, and retail spaces as well as a circulation tower and a
vaulted pre-function space. Components such as the shallow
curved roof and smaller roof forms give the building a distinctive
presence. The center is clad in a combination of indigenous
and contemporary materials, including precast, stucco, metal,
wood, and glass. Scale and texture are skillfully used to define
mass and volume and will influence future construction in the
Civic Center.

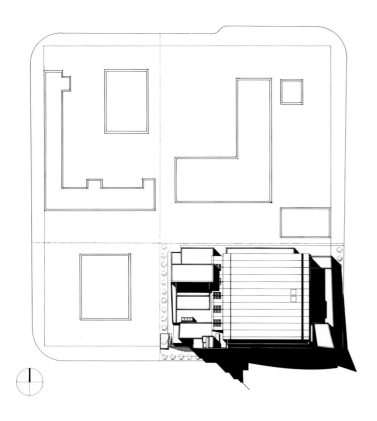

Longitudinal section

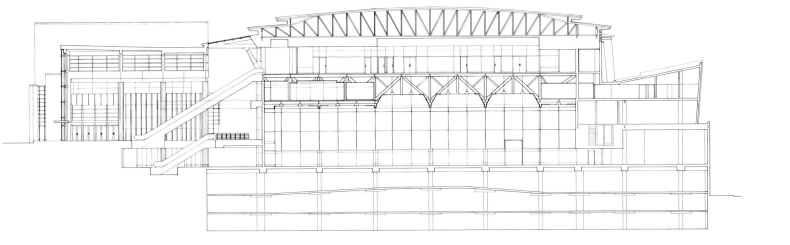

Plan, ground floor

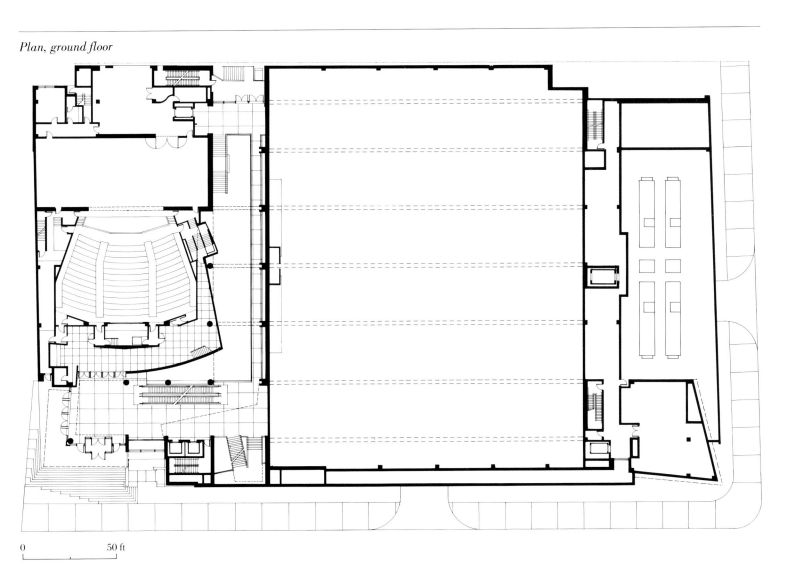

0   50 ft

The landscape of the structure's roof is intended to explain its function while simultaneously exploiting the sharpness and reflectivity of metal. Conceived as a sculptural joining of distinct parts, this building intends to introduce a humanity to a building type normally bereft of it.

William Pedersen

The arrangement and identity of forms in this project create a whole new repertoire of volumes for a building of this type.

John Koga

147 Columbus Avenue

New York, New York
1990–1992

Offices and studio support facilities for the ABC television network are housed in this ten-story office building at the corner of Columbus Avenue and West 66th Street in Manhattan. The design consists of two rectangular volumes. Punched windows and cast-stone detailing articulate the side-street elevation. The Columbus Avenue elevation uses an expansive curtain wall to take advantage of views toward Lincoln Center. The two volumes intersect with a faceted curtain wall at the corner, providing oblique views to Central Park and the ABC complex. A mast ties the composition together and signals the presence of ABC within the community.

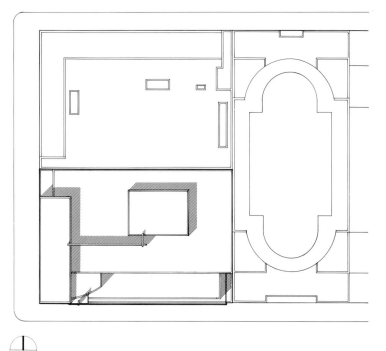

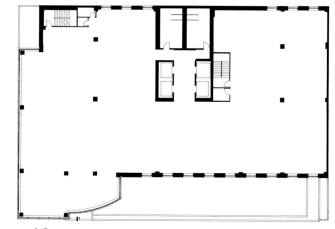

Plan, typical floor

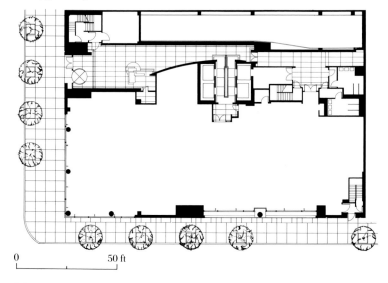

Plan, ground floor

0   50 ft

269

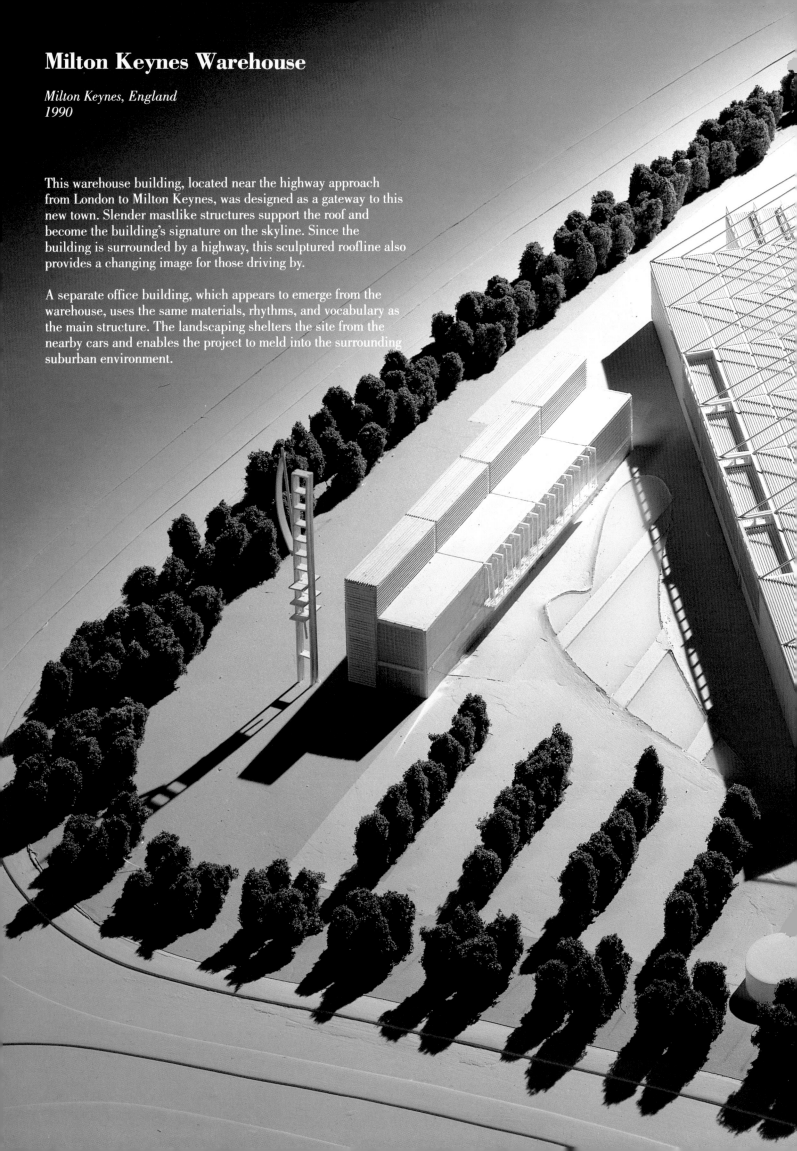

Milton Keynes Warehouse

Milton Keynes, England
1990

This warehouse building, located near the highway approach from London to Milton Keynes, was designed as a gateway to this new town. Slender mastlike structures support the roof and become the building's signature on the skyline. Since the building is surrounded by a highway, this sculptured roofline also provides a changing image for those driving by.

A separate office building, which appears to emerge from the warehouse, uses the same materials, rhythms, and vocabulary as the main structure. The landscaping shelters the site from the nearby cars and enables the project to meld into the surrounding suburban environment.

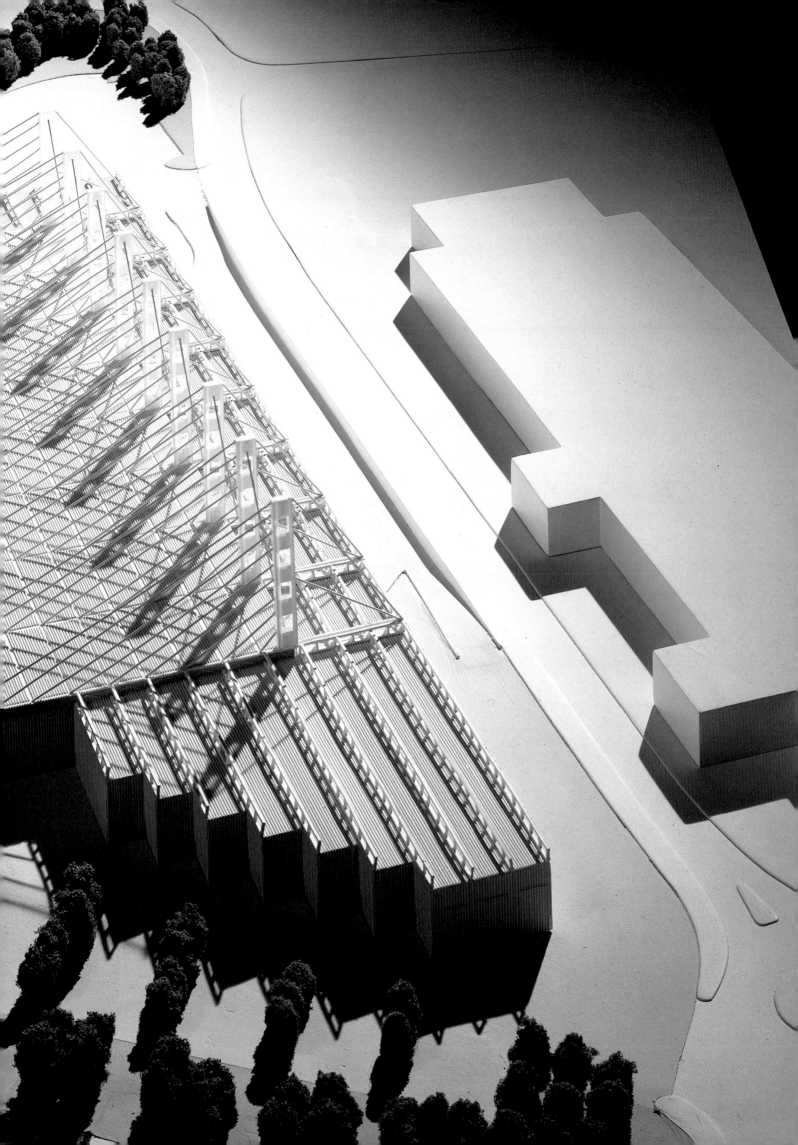

State House / 58–71 High Holborn

London, England
1989–1994

This nine-story office building, located in London's legal district between High Holborn, Sandland, and Red Lion streets, replaces a structure from the 1960s. The new building, a pinwheel in plan, accommodates retail shops on the ground floor and offices above, around a central atrium. A north-south walkway through the building connects two city blocks and historic inns. The building's facades maintain the street lines of the adjacent low-rise structures. A small towerlike element at one corner, where High Holborn bends, identifies the building in the immediate area and on the skyline.

Plan, 7th floor

Plan, 4th floor

Plan, ground floor

0   30 m

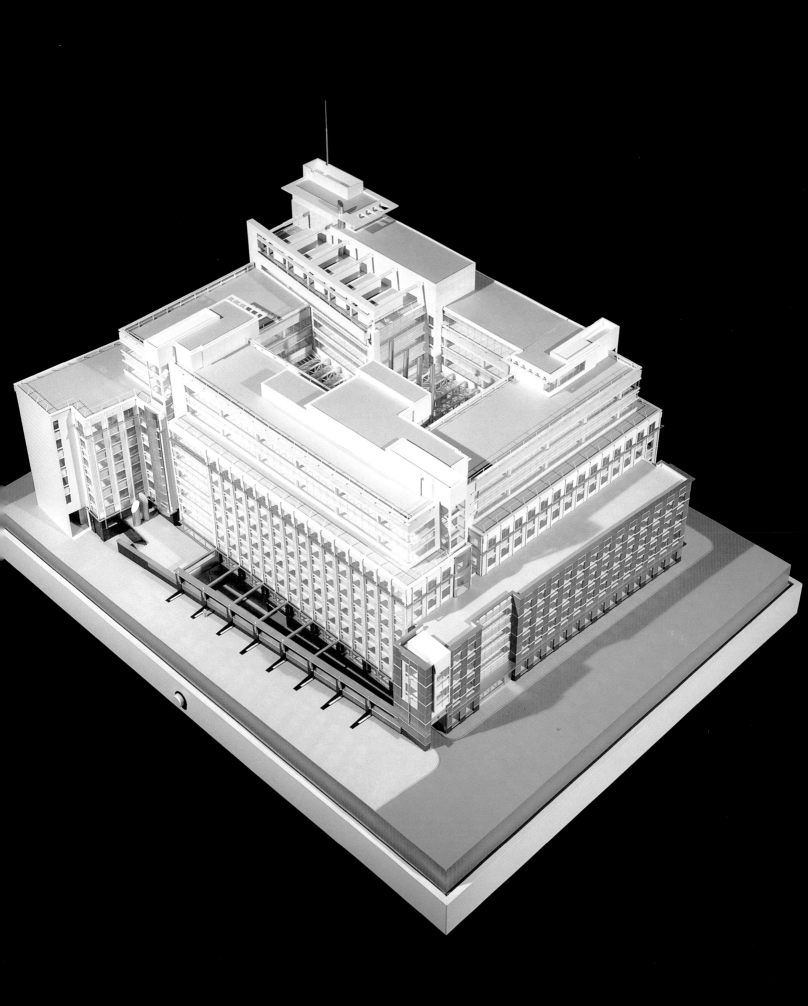

St. Paul Companies South Building

St. Paul, Minnesota
1990–1992

Located at the edge of St. Paul, adjacent to the Landmark Center, this amalgamation of five buildings dating from the 1920s to the 1980s was to be entirely reclad in order to relate to the new headquarters, also by KPF, across the street. A vertically ordered curtain wall, of precast limestone piers and lightly reflective glass infill panels, sits above a horizontal granite base around the entire perimeter. At the main corner, a glass-and-metal curtain wall rises and turns the corner, establishing a dialogue with the new main entrance. A bridge links the two structures, framing the view of the cathedral beyond.

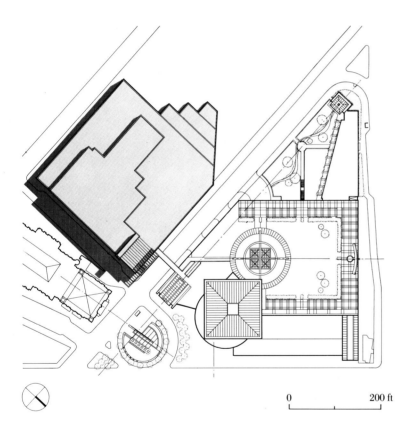

0   200 ft

276

Carwill House I

Stratton Mountain, Vermont
1988–1989

Sited on a high rocky slope facing Stratton Mountain, this house
was designed as a community of pavilions, each with specific
solar and view orientations. Three Platonic pieces, which anchor
the house and its composition, are transformed from a pure
square at the entry pavilion, to a more directional study pavilion,
and, finally, to a skeletal exercise pavilion. The pavilions are
united by a series of linear spaces. This progression
demonstrates the structural and material assemblage of the
house. Materials include stone, wide cedar planks, a wood
skeleton, and lead-coated copper.

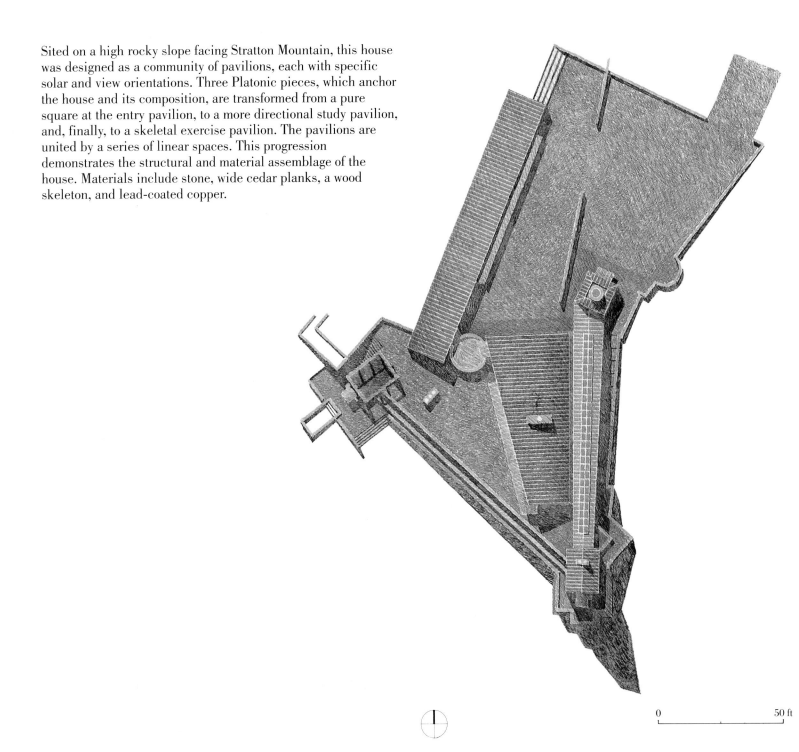

0   50 ft

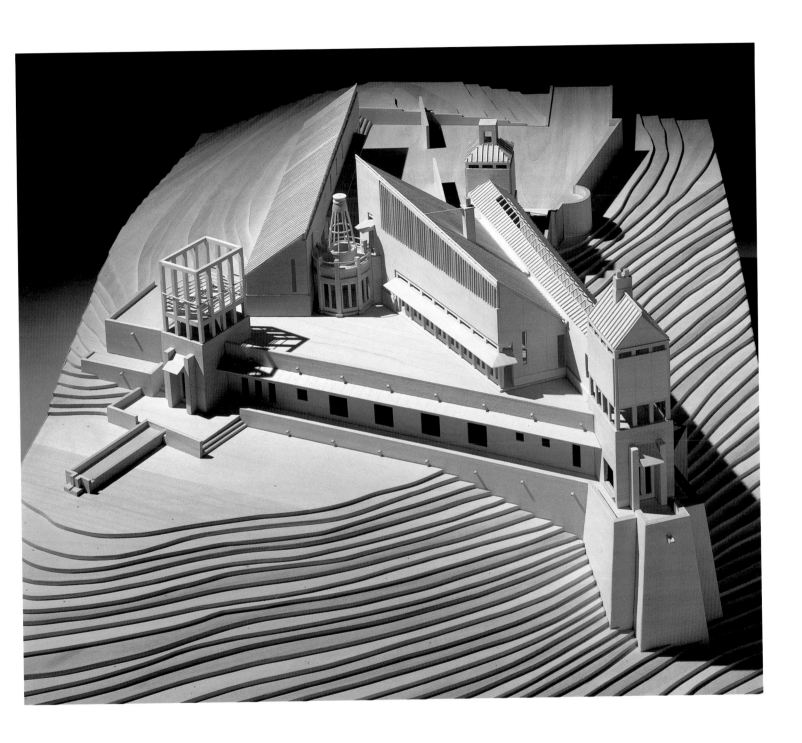

Carwill House II

Stratton Mountain, Vermont
1989–1991

The site for this house is at the highest point of a residential development. From this point the terrain slopes steeply to the south toward Stratton Mountain, a ski resort. The landscape is densely wooded and bedrock lies immediately below the surface; large outcroppings are evident throughout the site.

A slice across the crown of the site created a sheer wall of cut rock. The house is shifted away from this face to form an entry court and frame the panoramic view of Stratton Mountain. The design of the house is based on interlocking geometrical forms, creating a tension that exploits the site's strong geography and views while adhering to the community's strict design regulations and the client's programmatic requirements.

A cylindrical tower, scaled down by a canopy, marks the entrance to the house. The living and dining wing is to the south of the cylinder, oriented toward the mountain and surmounted by a high shed roof with a curving ridge. The bedroom and service wing is an attenuated trapezoidal form that projects northward and benefits from eastern exposures. Three vertical pieces—entrance rotunda, main stair, and chimney—act as anchors. Key volumes and roofs are clad in lead-coated copper; the walls enclosing the other forms, in large planks of rough-hewn cedar; and the base of the house, as it meets grade, in Vermont slate.

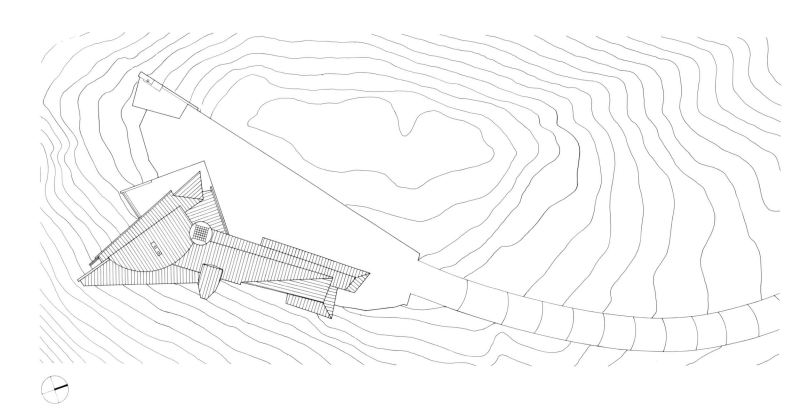

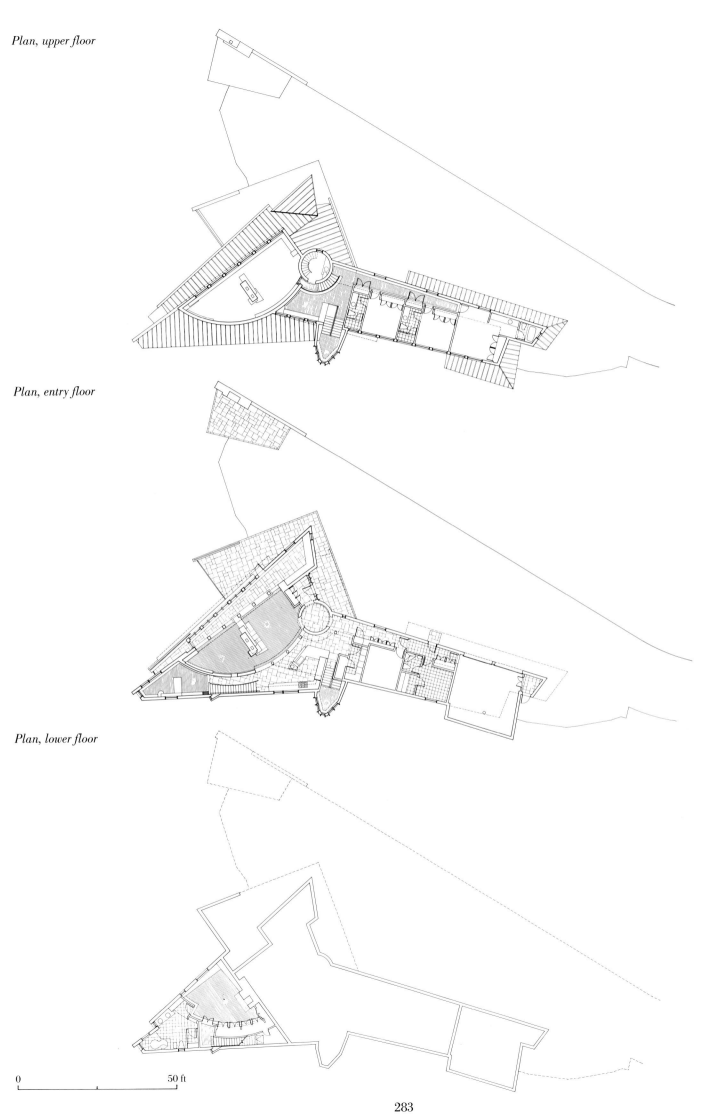

Plan, upper floor

Plan, entry floor

Plan, lower floor

0   50 ft

This is a highly personal and sculptural essay on the character of a mountain house. A tension between the curvilinear and the linear is accentuated to create an interior of constantly fluctuating juxtapositions.

William Pedersen

The synthesis of the vernacular and the modern is one of the house's central themes. The cladding system expresses the synthesis by using a traditional siding material, cedar, and organizing it in a grid of large panels with exposed fasteners.

Joshua Chaiken

Mills House

Shelter Island, New York
1990–1992

Set at the water's edge on Shelter Island, this house was designed
to serve as both residence and small museum for a contemporary
craft-furniture collection. The house is a series of geometric
forms that respond to orientation and context. The open-plan
ground floor features a conical form supported on columns that
provides focus to the living area. Private spaces, including two
bedrooms and a library, are on the second floor. A small pavilion
houses a breakfast area below and a reading nook above, while a
larger pavilion, containing the master bedroom, has an exterior
staircase leading to a rooftop belvedere. A V-shaped roof defines
the porch, which wraps around the first-floor living area.
Materials include bluestone for the base and chimney, cladding
of cedar panels attached to a wood frame with stainless-steel
bolts, and lead-coated copper roofs.

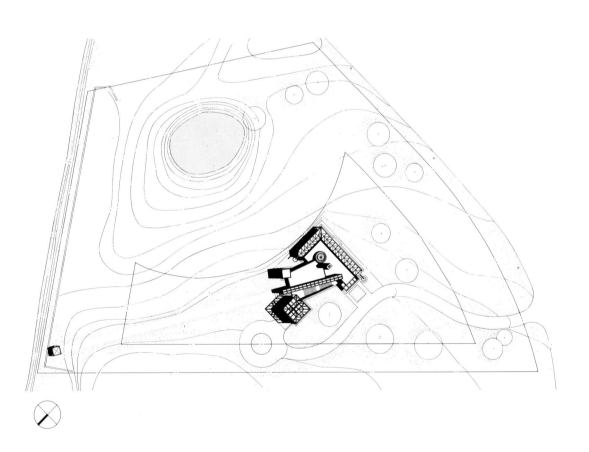

Plan, upper floor

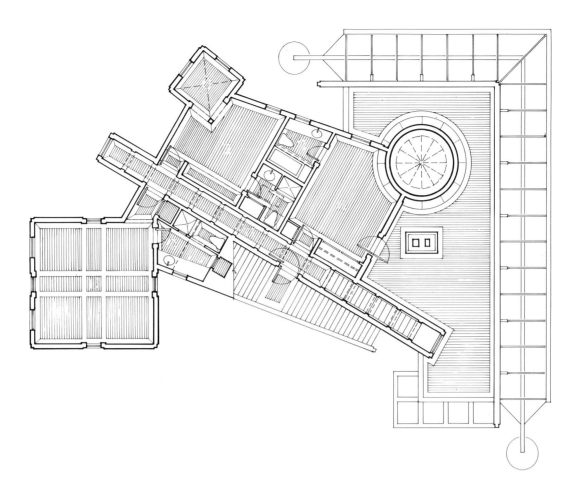

Plan, ground floor

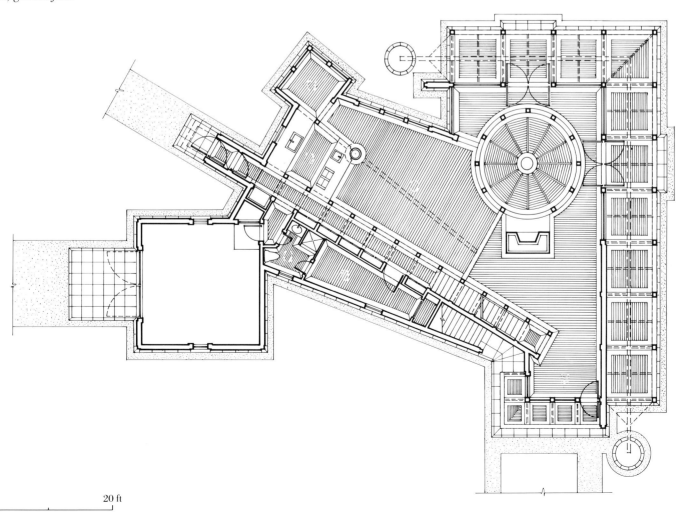

0   20 ft

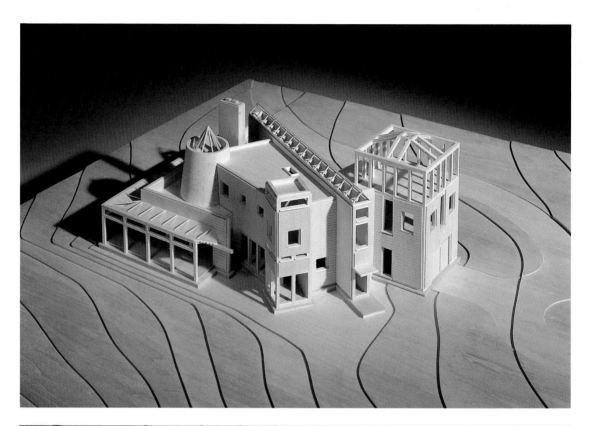

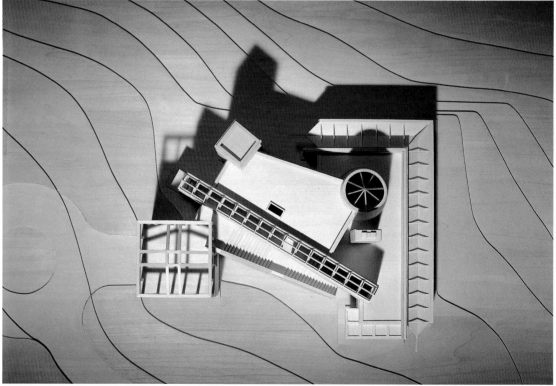

294

The rigorous tectonics of this island house structure a composition of symbolically conceived forms brought together in a "conversational" relationship.

William Pedersen

Hanseatic Trade Center

Hamburg, Germany
1990–1993

This mixed-use complex is located within the harbor district on a
site at the end of Kehrwieder/Sandtorhoft, two islands that are
part of Hamburg's Speicherstadt, or storage city. Three linear
buildings, containing offices, a hotel, and retail space, are
designed to relate to and extend the district in scale, texture, and
materials, while their endpieces serve as termini for the islands.
A public plaza, encompassing both land and water, includes new
landscaping, public paths, and a floating theater adjacent to the
ferry docks. A small museum dedicated to the history of the port
is proposed as well. A circulation network of public walks,
bridges, and a new pedestrian corridor links the complex to the
old city. A fifteen-story cylindrical office tower serves as a focal
point for the bridges that span the river and will allow
connections to future development sites.

Plan, typical floor

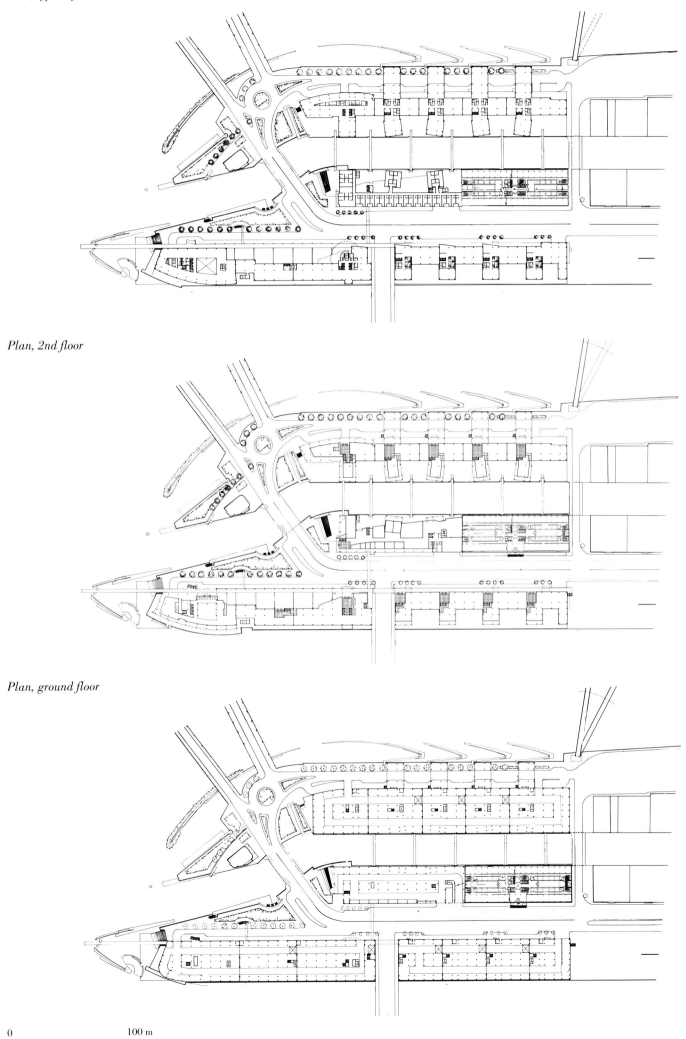

Plan, 2nd floor

Plan, ground floor

0   100 m

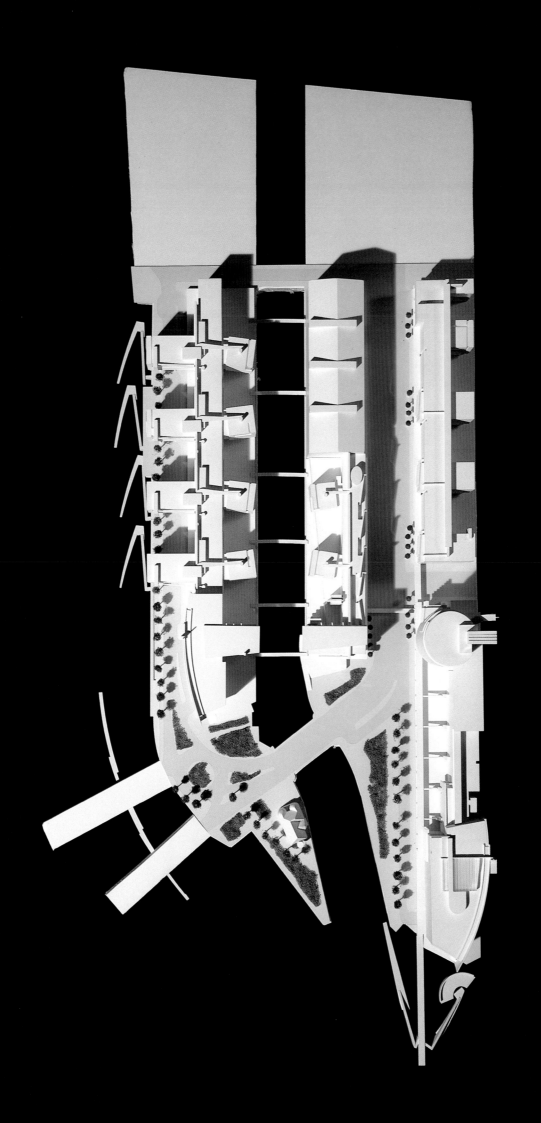

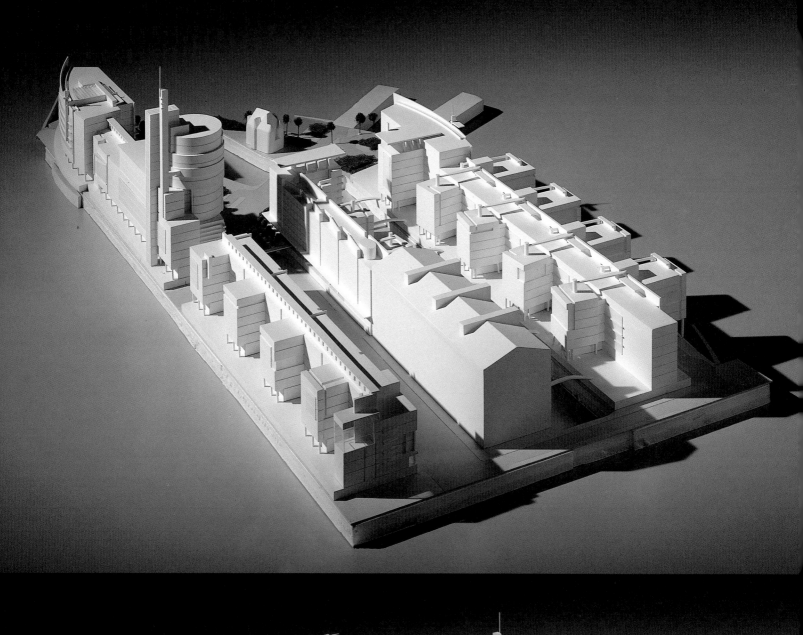

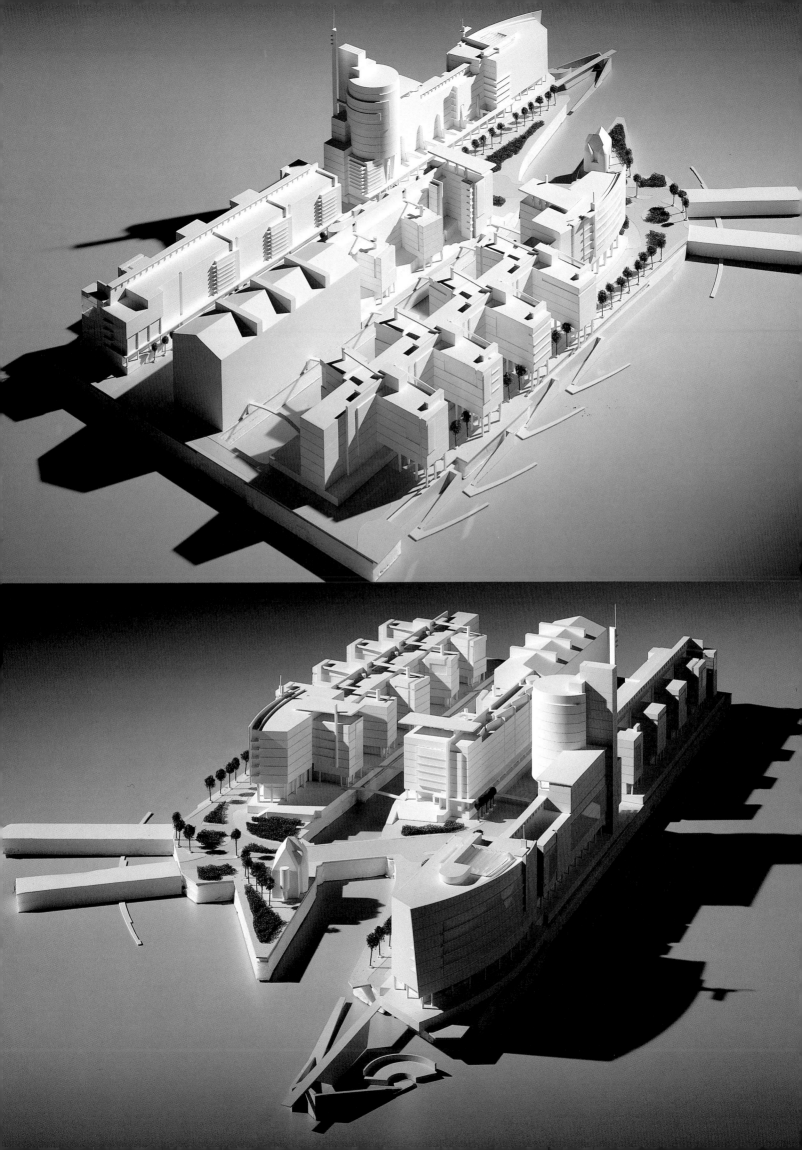

Platz der Akademie / Block 30

Berlin, Germany
1991–1992

This mixed-use building, located at the southeast corner of
Berlin's Platz der Akademie, occupies an important block and
takes its formal and textural cues from the surrounding historic
district. The seventeenth-century protective ramparts that once
extended onto the site serve as a metaphor that forces the east
wall to bow out, while the north wall peels back to reveal the
inner public court and link it to the Platz. The shape of the
eastern wall is derived from the circles of the nearby Deutsche
Dom, Schauspielhaus, and Altesmuseum. The facades were
developed from the example of the Schauspielhaus, with
extended horizontals and closely spaced verticals.

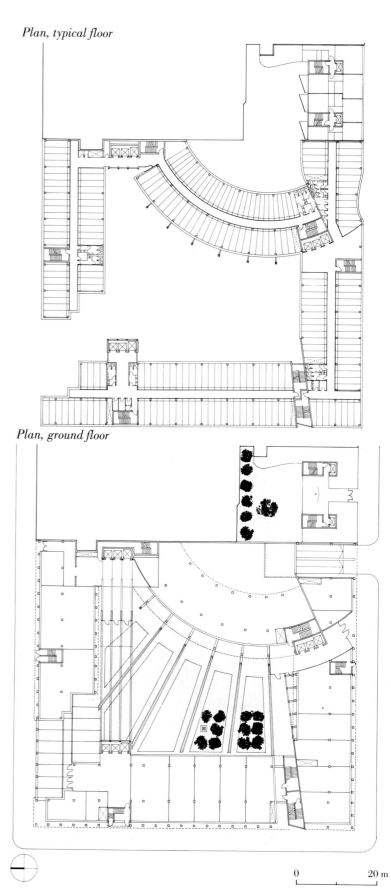

Plan, typical floor

Plan, ground floor

0   20 m

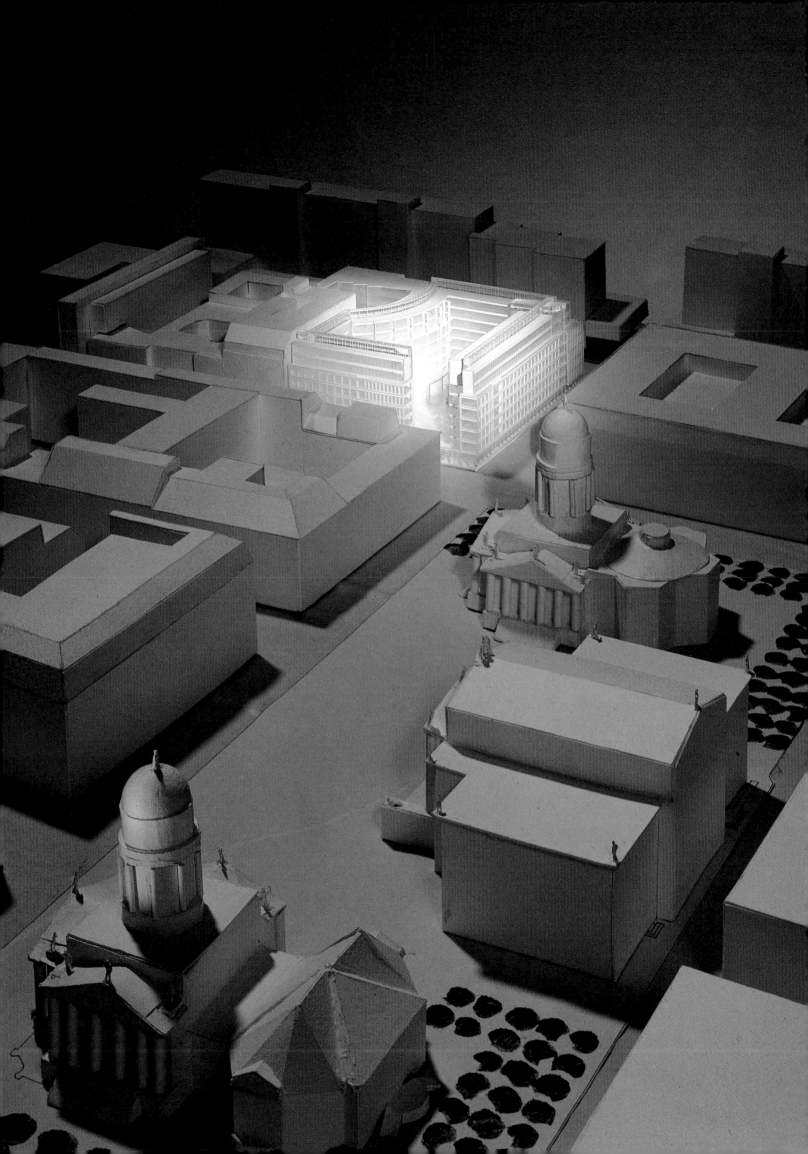

University of Pennsylvania / Revlon Campus Center

Philadelphia, Pennsylvania
1990–1995

This new, multi-use student center at the northern edge of the university's campus contains spaces for the performing arts, a black-box theater, auditorium, bookstore, student activities offices, food service facilities, student lounges, and retail space. The design is part of KPF's master plan for this area of the campus. The massing responds to the diversity of both the program and the site conditions. The building forms are organized around a garden court, which brings outdoor activities into the site while allowing pedestrian circulation diagonally through it. A large skylighted rotunda creates an inviting open entry atrium and organizes the discrete program components. The highly articulated exterior wall is composed of brick with stone accents and trim, recalling the texture and character of much of the campus.

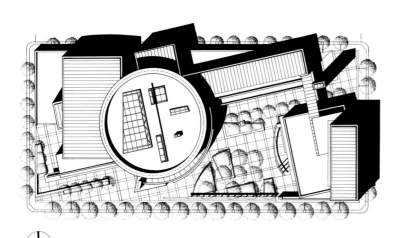

Plan, 4th floor

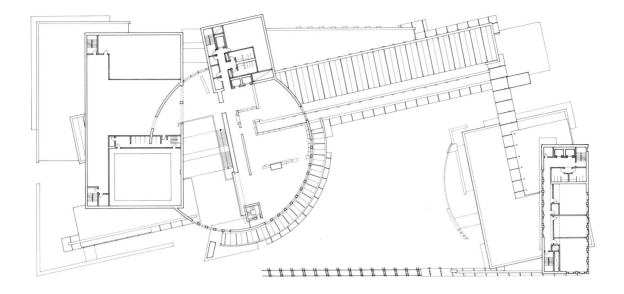

Plan, 2nd floor

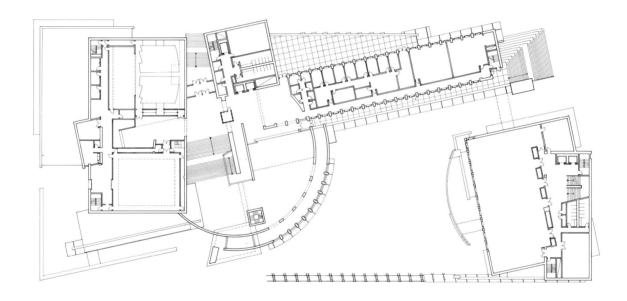

Plan, ground floor

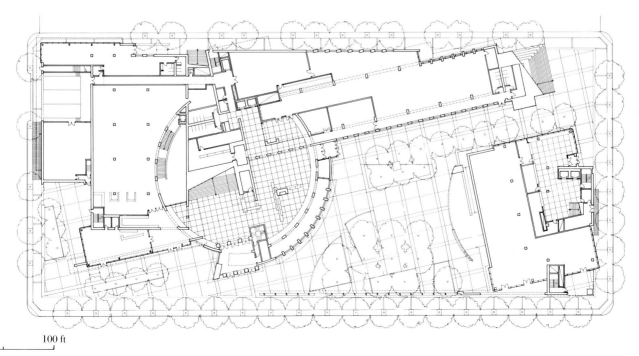

0   100 ft

*Most of the significant
functions of this complex
program establish an
interaction with the central
rotunda which, in itself, is a
symbol of the gathering
together of Penn's diverse
constituency.*

William Pedersen

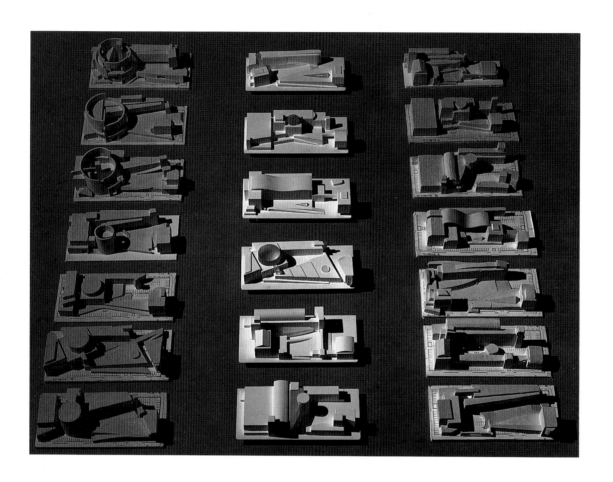

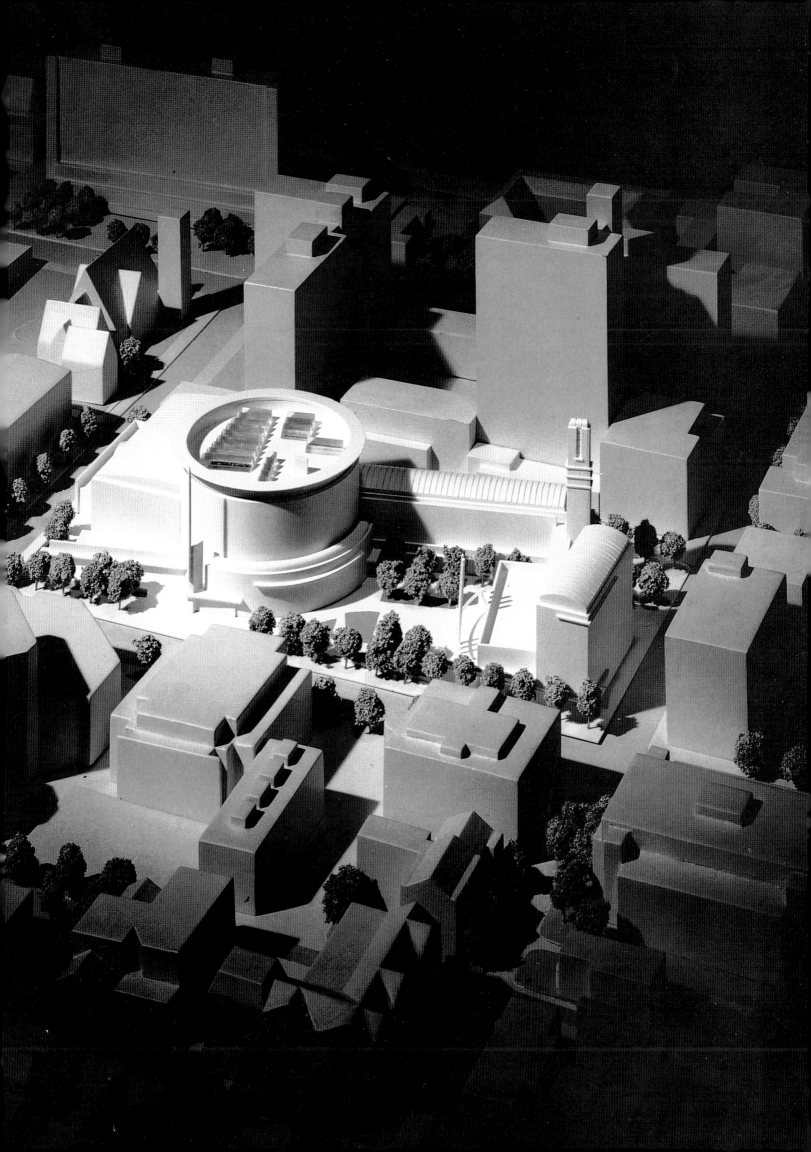

Newport Harbor Art Museum

Newport Beach, California
1990–1991

This contemporary art museum, located to the south of Los
Angeles, takes advantage of its low-lying suburban scale,
California climate and light, and ocean views. The museum
complex houses temporary and permanent art and sculpture
galleries within a series of interior and exterior spaces, as well as
retail, educational, and administrative facilities. Each function is
expressed with a distinct building element, all assembled amid
gardens and contained within a low perimeter wall that insulates
the visitor from street noise while still optimizing light and views.
A gently curved spine forms a major circulation axis and offers a
constantly changing perspective of the indoor galleries and
outdoor sculpture courts. The museum is entirely composed of
planar stucco walls, recalling indigenous building materials and
emphasizing qualities of light, color, and the surrounding
landscape. The galleries are illuminated by skylights.

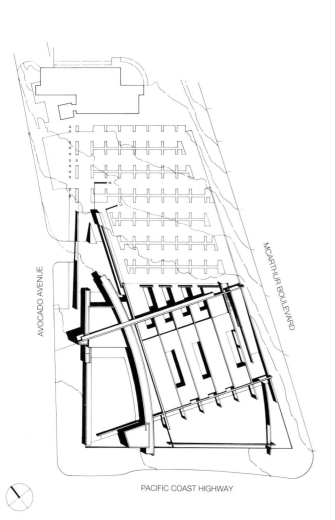

312

Plan, gallery level

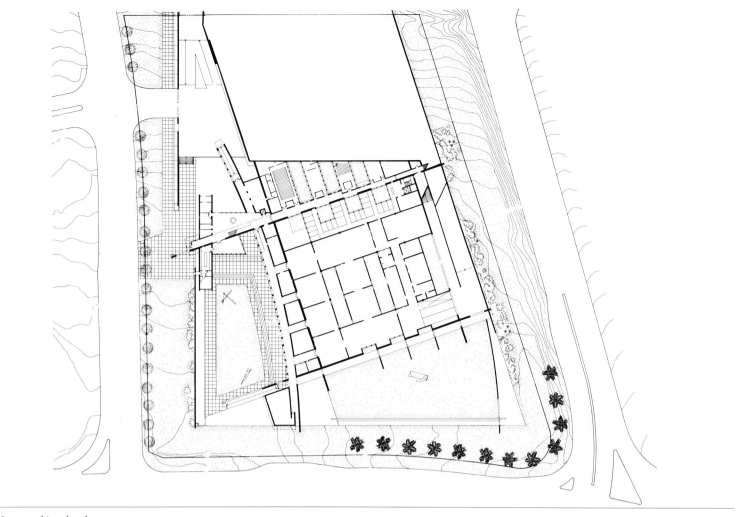

Plan, parking level

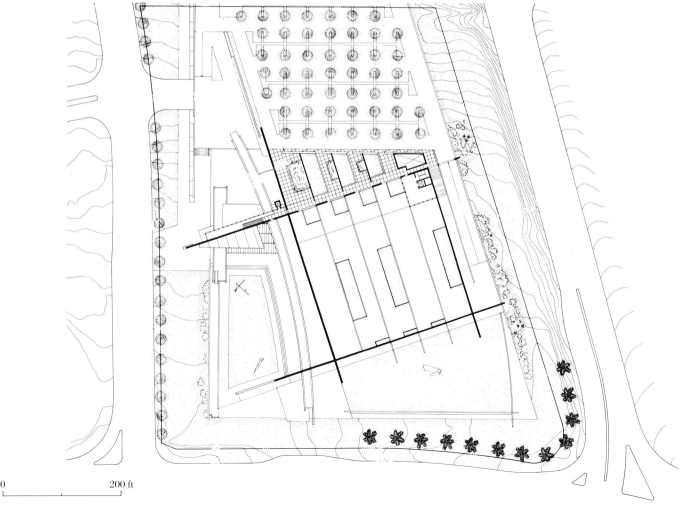

0 200 ft

*Limited by zoning to a single
level, this horizontal structure
seeks to create a hierarchical
fabric of exterior courtyards
and internal rooms, within
which a dialogue among
nature, architecture, and art
will be made possible.*

William Pedersen

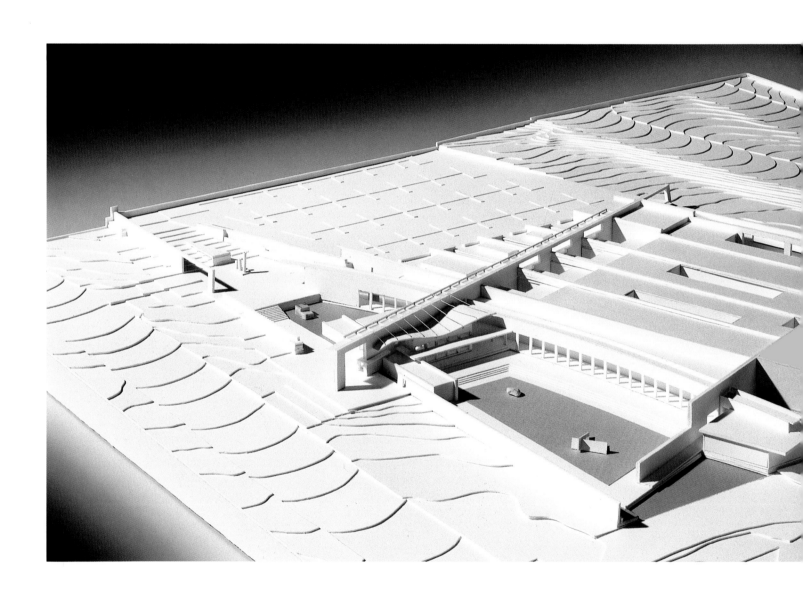

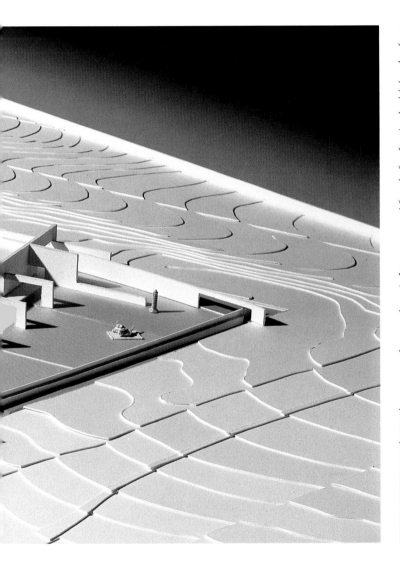

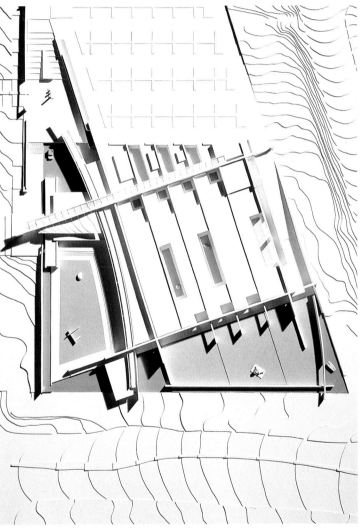

Disney Institute and Town Center

Osceola, Florida
1991

Outside Orlando, Florida, and within the district of Walt Disney World, this flat, two-hundred-acre site includes open and heavily forested wetlands. The site would be connected to the Florida Turnpike by a new proposed roadway and interchange. The project comprises a new Disney-sponsored academic institute and resort town for approximately twenty thousand people.

The program for the institute consists of a series of small theaters and auditoriums, conference and classroom facilities, and a large performing-arts hall. The program for the town calls for two hotels, a health club, retail and professional spaces, a golf clubhouse and course, and both permanent and time-share residential areas.

Inspired by the American university campus, Renaissance ideal cities, and Spanish town planning in the New World, the design for the new community is organized along two major intersecting axes, University Boulevard and Main Street. The resort town occupies two quadrants and the academic institute another two. These four quadrants create distinct neighborhood districts and are surrounded by a boulevard of royal palms that ties them together while giving an identity to the town within. Both the institute and the town are pedestrian-oriented and focused on a large central lake. An appropriate architectural language for the community was developed from regional influences and traditional building materials.

Here we bring together, by collage, a number of significant urban planning strategies based on a framework of two perpendicular roads, which are in themselves a version of the Roman decumanus and corda. The resulting composition strives for an equilibrium between the whole and its diverse parts, the city and nature, collective memory and personal fantasy.

William Pedersen

The concepts of American town planning were embraced in pursuit of the ideal balance between imposition, intervention, and deference.

Peter Schubert

Hamm Plaza

St. Paul, Minnesota
1989–1992

Located in front of the Hamm Building and the new St. Paul
Companies Headquarters building, and adjacent to the historic
Landmark Building, this urban plaza was designed in
collaboration with the sculptor Jackie Ferrara. It was conceived
as the unifying element in what was once a triangular vehicular
island and as the terminus for a series of streets and building
axes. Hamm Plaza is an artistic response to the significant
buildings that border the triangular space, combining sculpture
and architecture and providing a pedestrian oasis with sitting
areas, fountains, and landscaping in the heart of St. Paul.

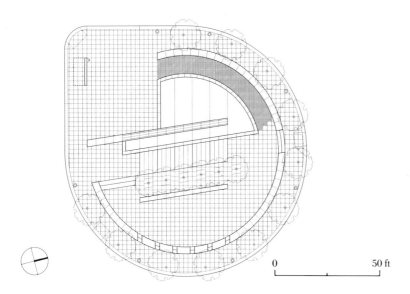

0   50 ft

Niagara Toll Station

Niagara Falls, New York
1990

On the approach to Rainbow Bridge, where the city meets the landscape, this toll station was designed with various symbolic elements within a rectangular precinct aligned with the city grid. A sweeping arc of flags, one for each state, organizes the scheme, connecting entry and exit points and serving as a monumental gateway for vehicles and pedestrians. The entry/inspection and exit/toll facilities are sited in counterpoint to the arc and to traffic movement. A metal tower with a series of cables supports a glass-and-metal canopy, lighted at night, over the inspection lanes.

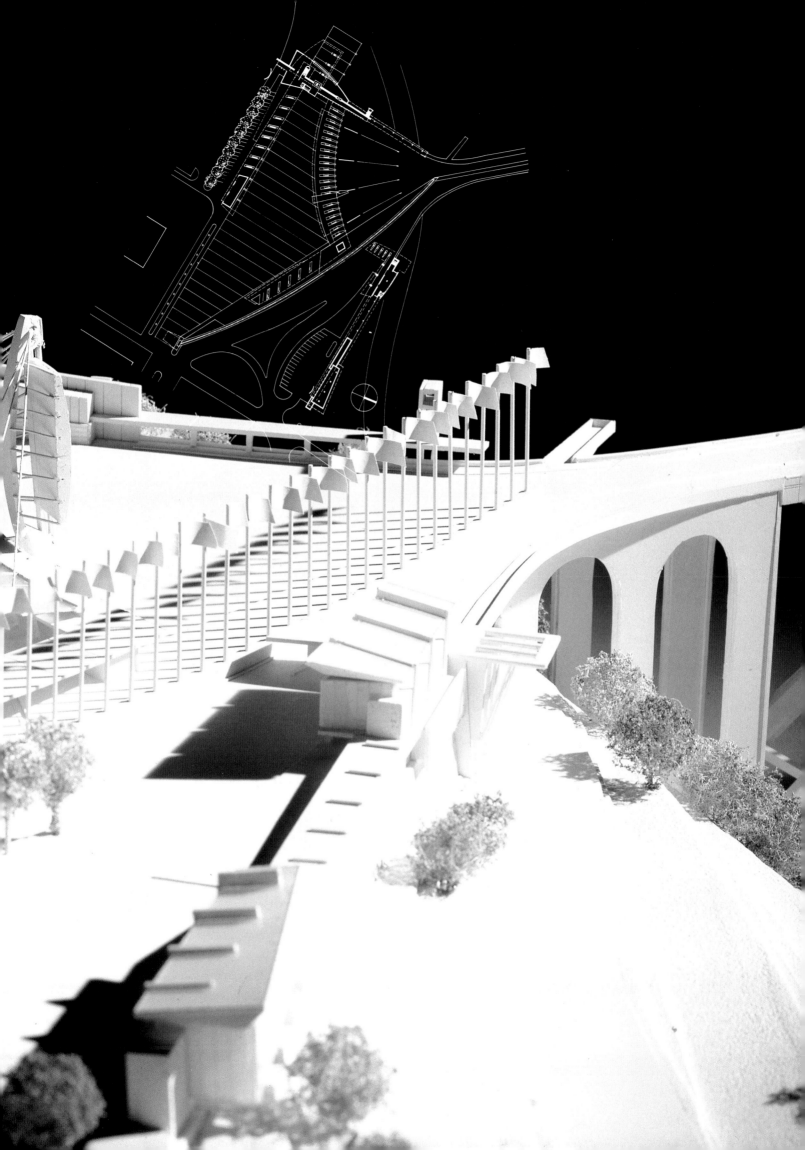

Tokyo Marriott

Tokyo, Japan
1990

This mixed-use project is part of a new large-scale urban
development in Tokyo Bay. The site is bounded by a highway, an
elevated pedestrian walkway, and a commuter railway. The
complex consists of two towers enclosing a public courtyard. The
taller hotel tower responds to three contextual forces: the center
of Tokyo across the bay, the center of the new city, and Mt. Fuji
in the distance. The smaller residential tower, placed at an angle
to the hotel, forms with it an entrance to this urban complex.
Low-rise buildings at the base house office, retail, conference,
and ballroom facilities.

Nagoya Station Building

Nagoya, Japan
1990–1999

This mixed-use station building is situated in the western part of Nagoya, Japan's third-largest city. Nagoya, midway between Tokyo and Osaka, is connected to the rest of Japan by high-speed bullet trains. The complex, which contains cultural, retail, hotel, office, and station facilities, is adjacent to the rail tracks and functions as the main regional transportation hub, linking rail, subway, and bus lines.

The project is composed of two towers rising from an eighteen-story base. The contrast between horizontal base and vertical towers creates a dynamic sculptural composition, which, combined with the siting of the complex, forms a gateway into the city. The base houses a twelve-story department store as well as a museum, health club, multipurpose hall, restaurants, and other retail functions. A two-story glass-enclosed "sky-street" near the top of the base connects public functions below to the towers above. A third tower with exterior shuttle elevators connects the ground level to the sky-street. The circular fifty-three-story hotel tower provides a variety of room types and views; the fifty-one-story office tower is formed by the juxtaposition of rectilinear and cylindrical forms. The hotel tower has a restaurant and banquet rooms on the top floors; the office tower, an observatory. Both towers are capped by rooftop helipads.

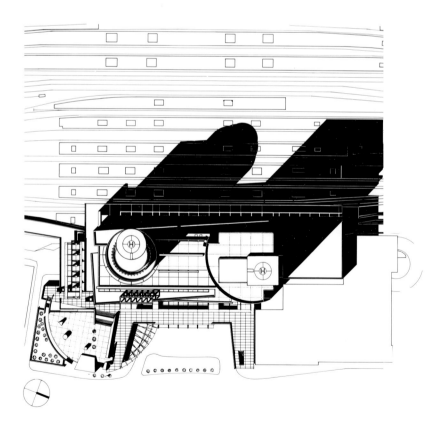

Plans, typical high-rise floor

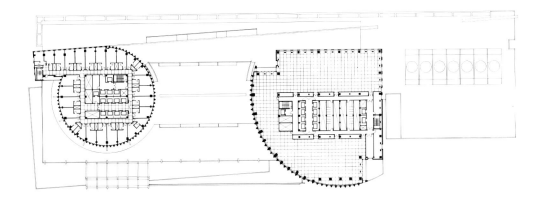

Plan, sky-street floor

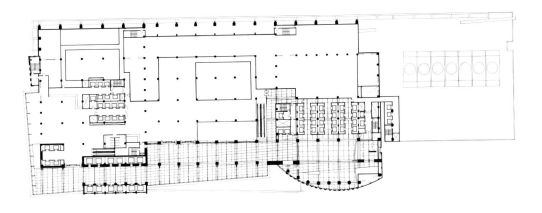

Plan, ground floor

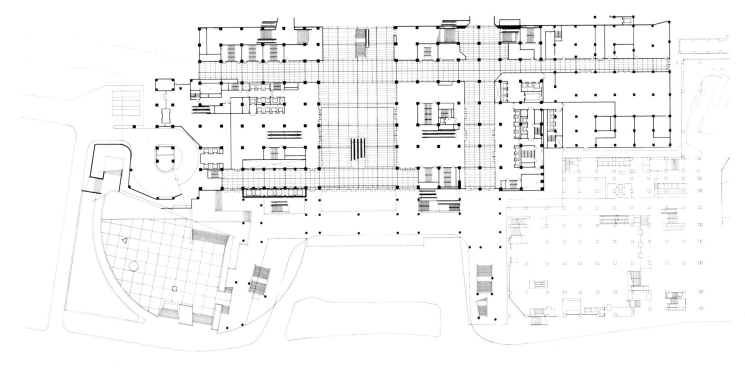

0   50 m

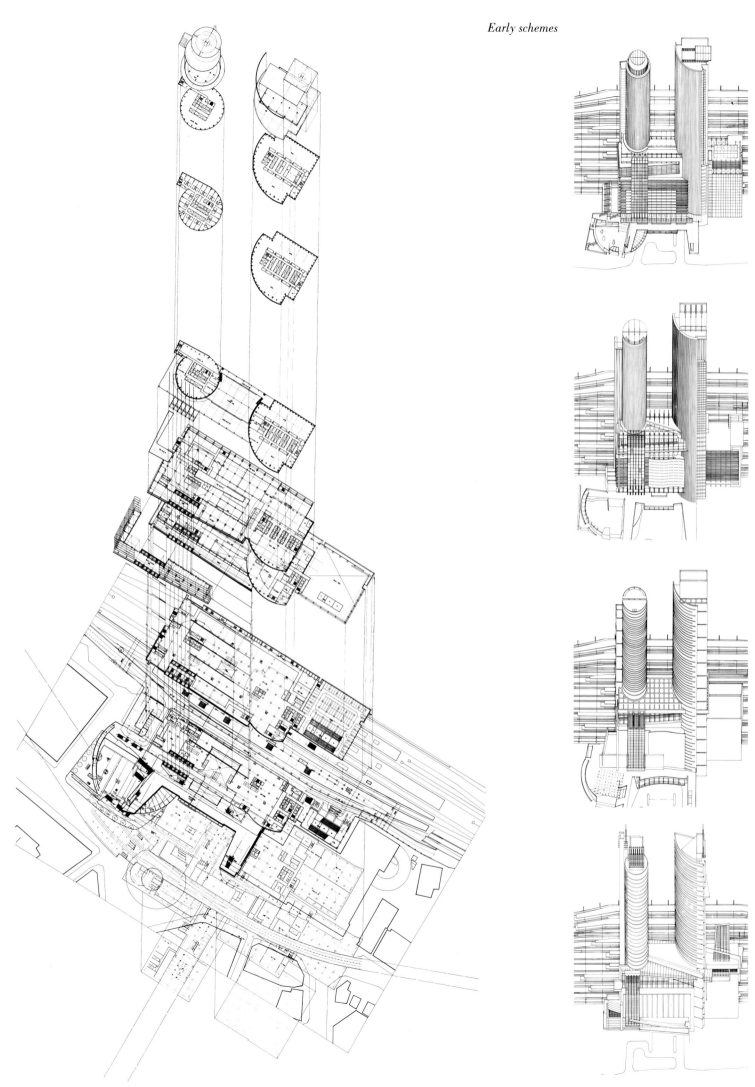

East elevation

North elevation

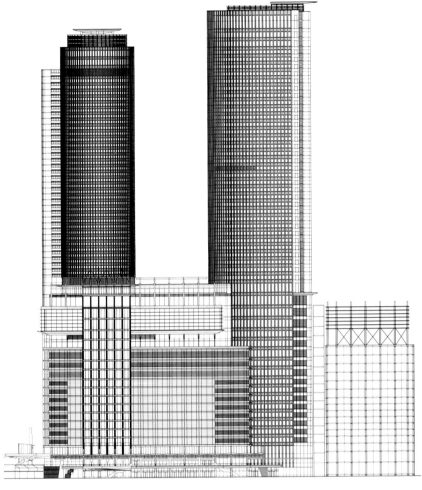

West elevation

South elevation

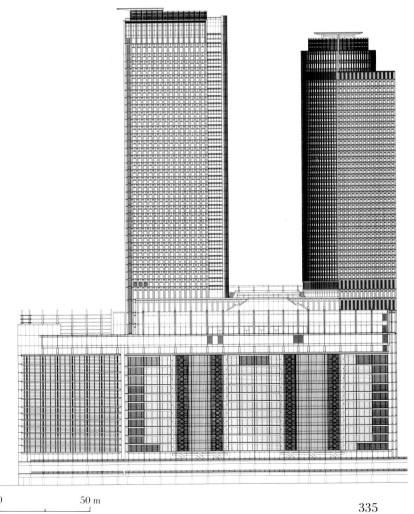

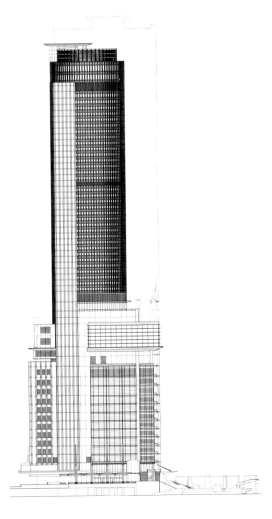

0   50 m

High-speed bullet trains travel
north-south across this country,
their tracks creating a
metaphorical artery. This
concept of movement finds its
way into the making of the
building and its dramatic
architectural expression.

Paul Katz

The unique qualities of this project derive from the marriage of clarity of concept and idea with complexity of program and content. This relationship, which exists at various scales within the project, generates a consistent architectural vocabulary and an ordering device that make this building a statement for Nagoya's future.

John Koga

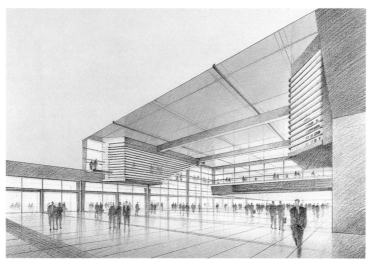

JFK Terminal One

Queens, New York
1992

This terminal, at the entrance to John F. Kennedy International Airport, was designed to serve five international airlines; it also acts as a gateway to the rest of the airport. On the approach to the terminal, an inclined aluminum drum serves as a sign for the airlines and also identifies the building itself. Inside are individual first-class lounges with views of the Manhattan skyline. On the upper level is a grand hall wrapped by continuous glazed walls and canted aluminum piers that support a scalloped metal-clad roof. The main concourse hovers above the tarmac and is enclosed by horizontal bands of floor-to-ceiling glass; departure and arrival gates are organized along a central circulation spine. The terminal's overall form is intended to evoke a sense of movement and flight reminiscent of aircraft design.

In our terminal design, we used architecture to articulate the process of flight and to give voice to the emotions surrounding international travel.

Craig Nealy

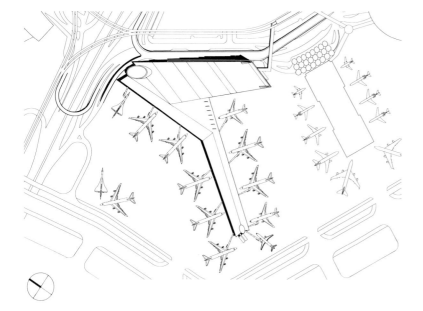

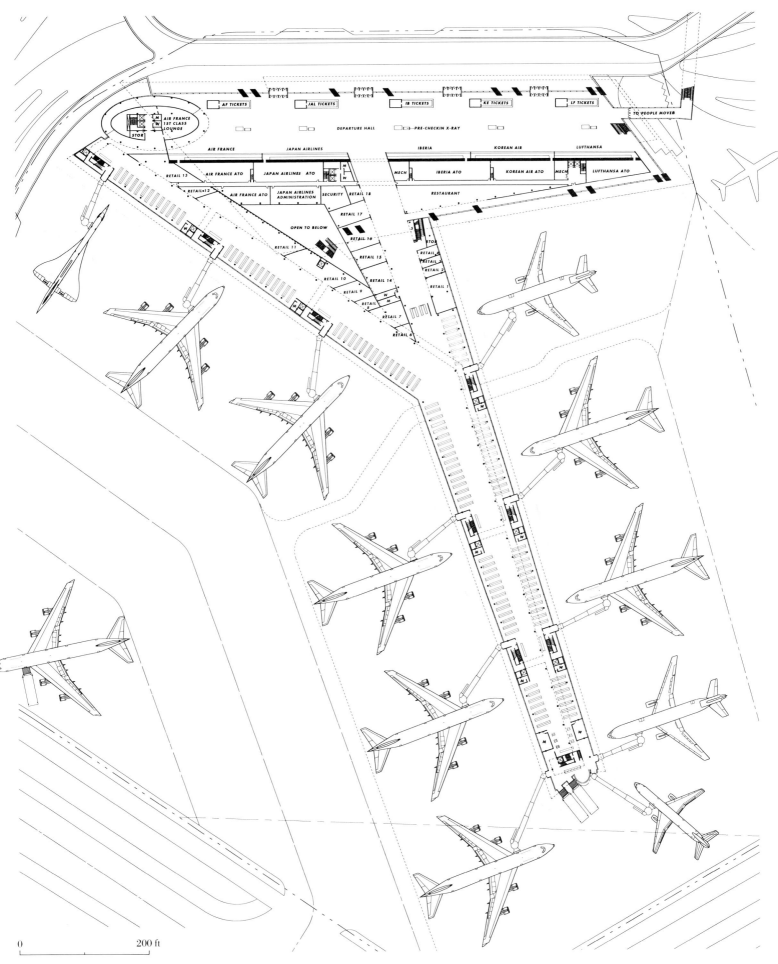

AF TICKETS | JAL TICKETS | IB TICKETS | KE TICKETS | LF TICKETS

AIR FRANCE 1ST CLASS LOUNGE

STOR

TO PEOPLE MOVER

DEPARTURE HALL · PRE-CHECKIN X-RAY

AIR FRANCE · JAPAN AIRLINES · IBERIA · KOREAN AIR · LUFTHANSA

RETAIL 13 · AIR FRANCE ATO · JAPAN AIRLINES ATO · MECH · IBERIA ATO · KOREAN AIR ATO · MECH · LUFTHANSA ATO

RETAIL 12 · AIR FRANCE ATO · JAPAN AIRLINES ADMINISTRATION · SECURITY · RETAIL 18

RESTAURANT

RETAIL 17

OPEN TO BELOW

RETAIL 16

RETAIL 11

RETAIL 15

RETAIL 10

RETAIL 14

RETAIL 9

RETAIL 1

RETAIL 8

RETAIL 7

RETAIL 6

0 — 200 ft

Longitudinal section

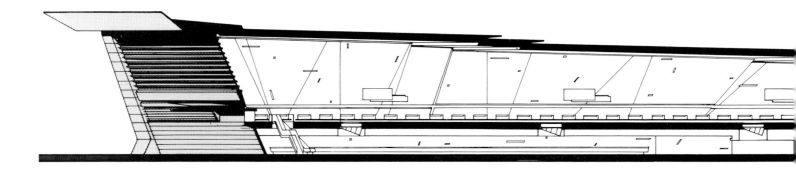

North elevation

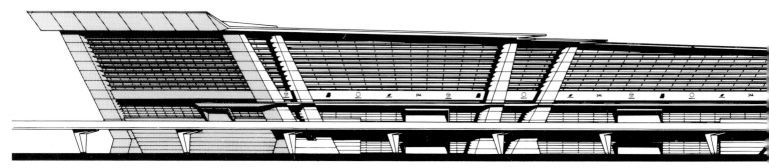

0   50 ft

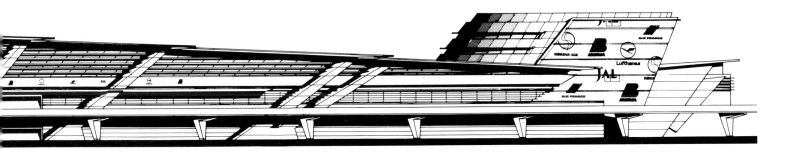

M. Project

Machida, Japan
1991–1992

This large-scale mixed-use complex creates a new town center
for Machida, a suburb of Tokyo located near the Yokohama
harbor. The program includes a two-hundred-room hotel with
wedding facilities, banquet rooms, restaurants, office space, a
shopping center with a movie theater, a museum, ten triplex
apartments, a bus depot, and parking. The office, hotel, and
function rooms are grouped in a horizontal slab building capped
by a series of rooftop pavilions. This structure is lifted off the
four-story plinth by pilotis. The building's plinth reflects
disparate conditions around the site and accommodates the
remaining programmatic functions.

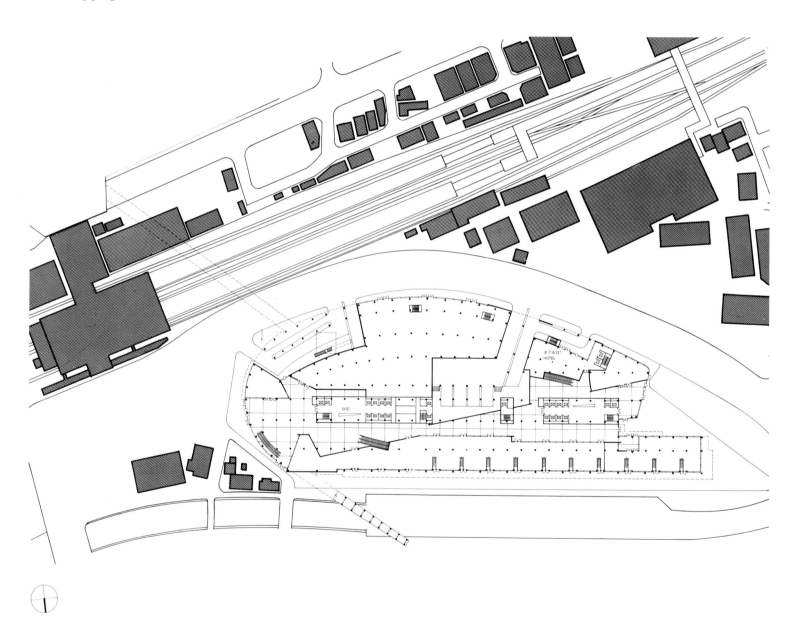

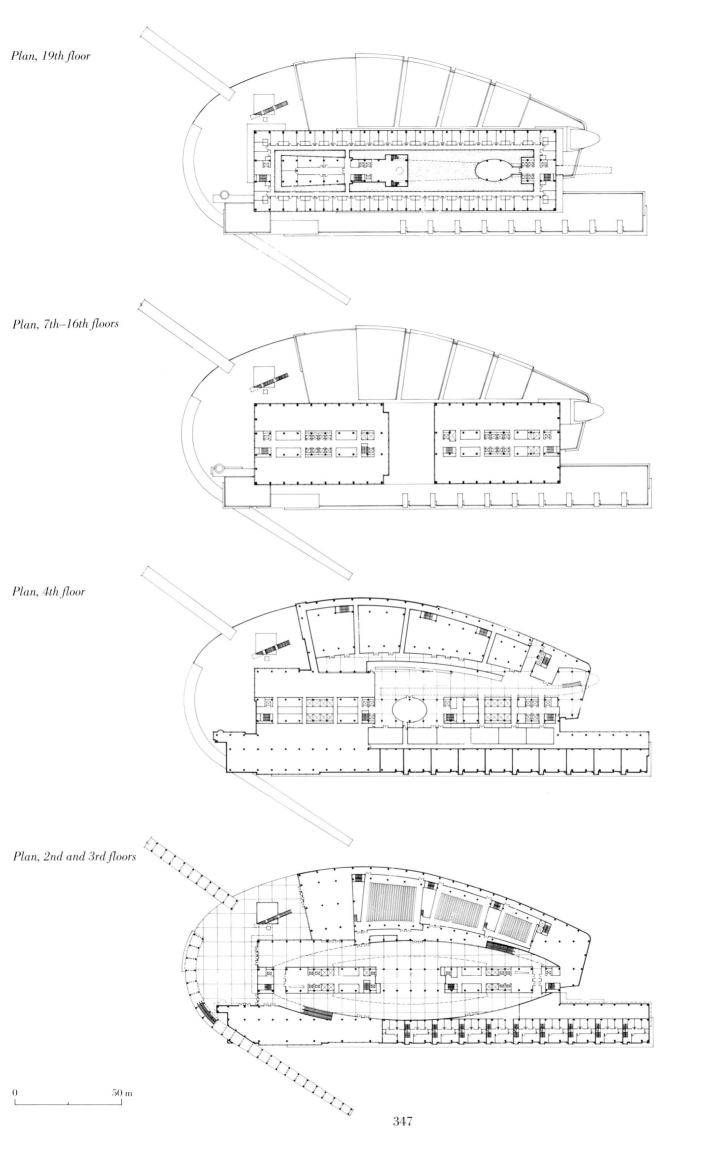

Plan, 19th floor

Plan, 7th–16th floors

Plan, 4th floor

Plan, 2nd and 3rd floors

0   50 m

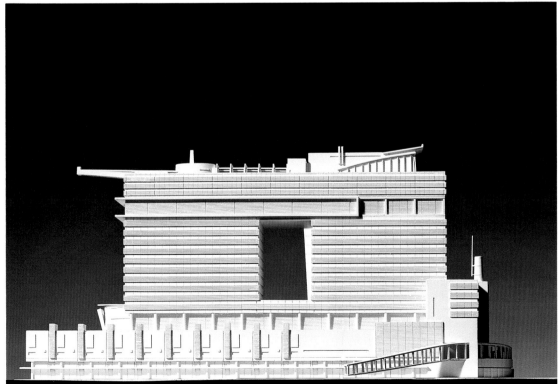

Concert Tower

Honolulu, Hawaii
1991–1994

At the intersection of Kapiolani Boulevard and Ward Avenue within Honolulu's Mauka district, the Concert Tower site is near Blaisdell Center, the city's principal cultural center. The new thirty-story office building acts as a gateway to this district, which includes an art museum, concert hall, and performance arena. A four-story base accommodates the building's main entrance lobby, rehearsal studio spaces for union musicians, and a cafe facing a garden plaza and monumental water feature. Above this podium, the tower rises with a curving curtain wall oriented toward the park and a rectilinear curtain wall that locks into the city's grid. These two forms, expressed in metal, stone, and tinted glass with a system of vertical and horizontal brise-soleils, respond to the site and to solar orientation and dominant views. The elevator core is expressed on the outside as an organizing element in the fenestration.

Plan, typical floor

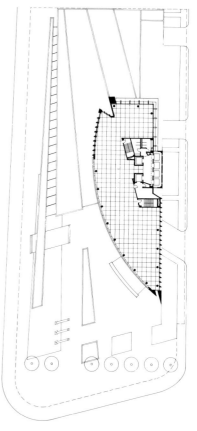

Plan, ground floor

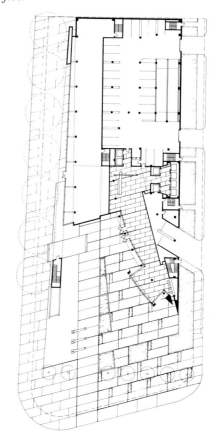

0   100 ft

Honolulu is a city dominated by the dialogue between the mountains and the sea. This small office tower seeks to represent that reality by a two-part composition that orients itself in a distant relationship with the symbolic focus of the city—Aloha Tower.

William Pedersen

The drama of a single narrow blade emerges from the rift between landscape and seascape to slice the trade winds of the Pacific.

Peter Schubert

Warsaw Bank Center

Warsaw, Poland
1991–1995

At a prominent intersection in Warsaw's central district across from the Palace of Culture and a large public park, this twenty-seven-story building will accommodate the corporate headquarters for the National Bank of Poland, additional office space, a health club, shops, and a restaurant. The building consists of three principal elements: a horizontally articulated base housing the main lobby, shops, and six levels of parking; a vertically organized office tower which is set back from the base; and a penthouse level, containing public functions, with a horizontal setback. At the top, the building's geometry is revealed and expressed.

Plan, 32nd floor

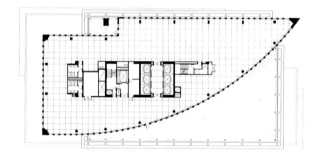

Plan, 8th–18th floors

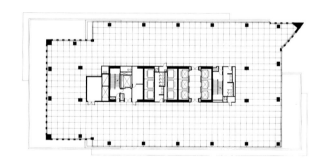

Plan, ground floor

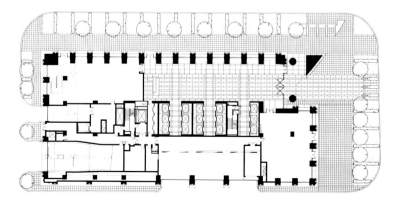

0   20 m

355

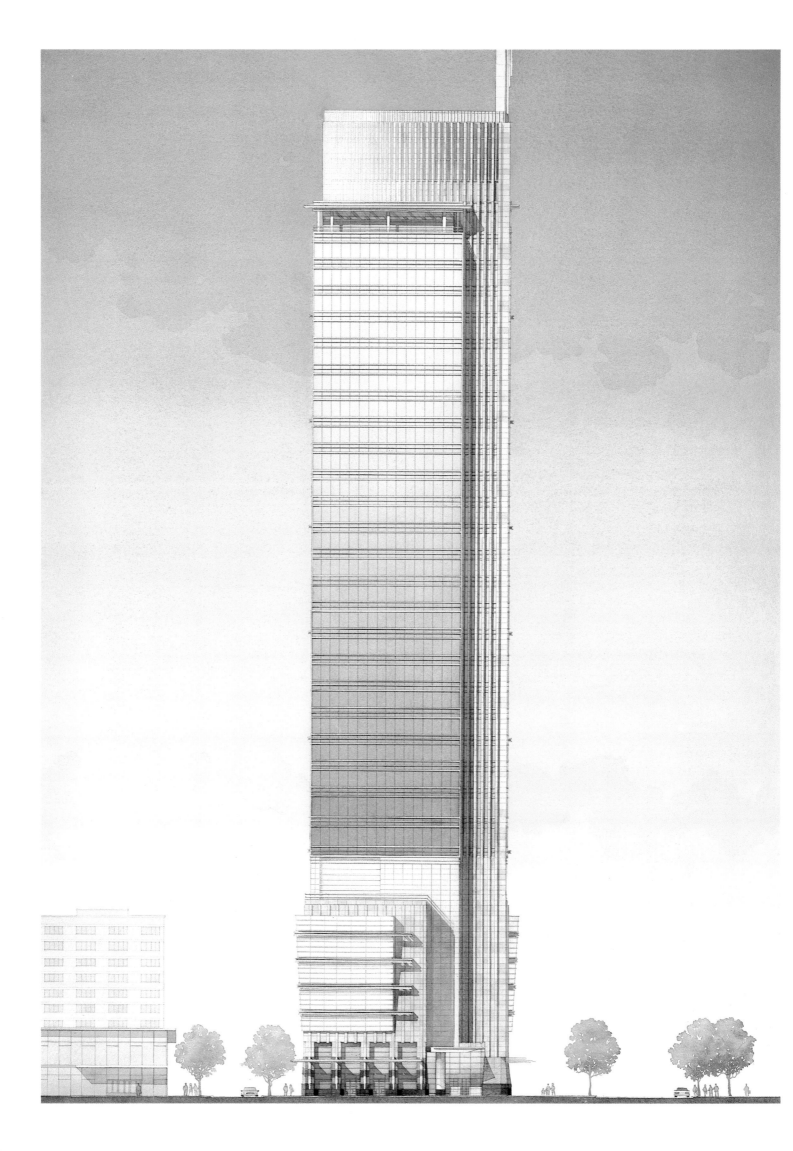

The dual design goals here were to provide a culturally influenced and dynamic figural counterpoint to the static urban domination of the Palace of Culture and to give the city its most finely scaled and modern free-plan office tower.

Richard Clarke

Coraceros Complex

Viña del Mar, Chile
1992

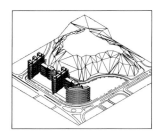

This mixed-use complex, which is on a large site facing the Pacific Ocean at the northern edge of this resort city, was conceived as an extension of the garden city. A curved hotel at the intersection of Avenida Jorge Montt and Avenida del Norte faces the city to the south and the ocean to the west. Three residential high-rises take advantage of solar orientation and views; they sit above a horizontal deck with pools, sunning and viewing areas, gardens, and a children's play area. Retail space is organized around a large covered court with promenades on two levels. The dramatic slope behind the complex has been left open for passive recreation and nature trails. Above, a serpentine residential building follows the contours of the hill and encloses sports facilities and gardens. A large portal frames the view and houses a funicular for residents.

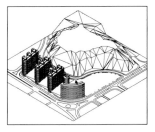

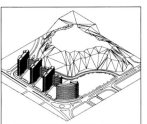

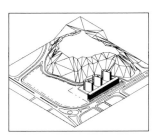

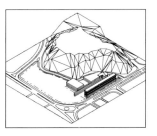

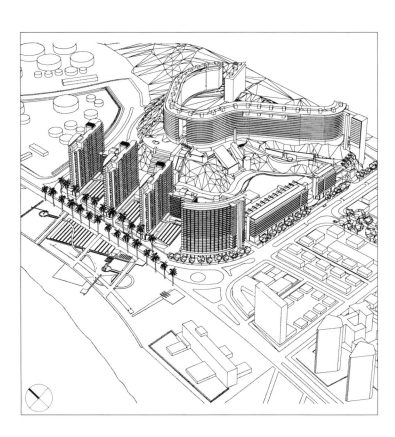

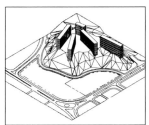

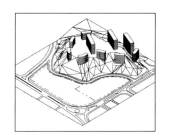

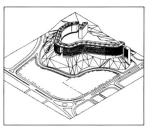

First Hawaiian Center

Honolulu, Hawaii
1991–1995

This thirty-story bank headquarters and office building is on a full-block site in Honolulu at the intersection of Bishop and King streets next to Bishop Park, in the heart of the city's financial district. The building sets back from King Street, a major pedestrian artery, allowing for a public arcade and a zoning-mandated plaza at ground level. A parallelogram-shaped podium, housing a three-story banking hall and the main entrance lobby, refers to the lower scale of nearby buildings and the angle of Merchant Street. The office tower, composed of two nestled triangles that share an exposed elevator core, responds to the landscape, solar orientation, views, and nearby high-rises. The facades are articulated with a limestone-and-glass curtain wall with vertical sun-shading to the east and west and with a metal-and-glass curtain wall with horizontal sun-shading to the south.

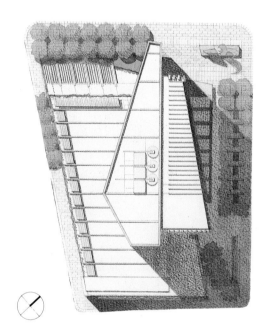

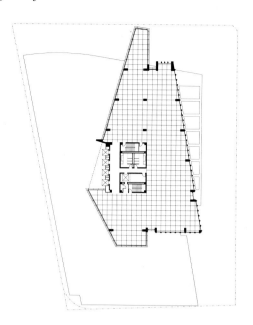

Plan, typical high-rise floor

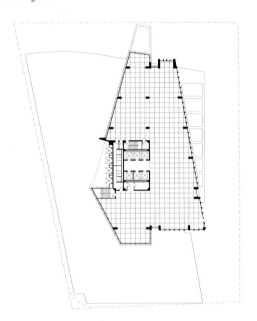

Plan, typical low-rise floor

Plan, ground floor

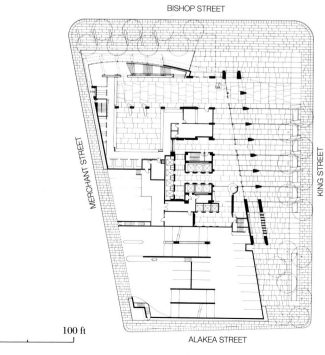

0   100 ft

Again we sought to represent the dialogue between the mountains and the sea with the two-part composition of the tower. The somewhat prismatic geometry is intended to heighten the juxtaposition while surface texture recedes to accentuate the dominance of form. Nature, through landscape, negotiates the interaction of the public and private realms.

William Pedersen

Two nestled, vertical, and inflected forms rise and cant to make a composition full of juxtapositions and to begin a meaningful dialogue between the city and the landscape.

Peter Schubert

Singapore Arts Center

Singapore
1992

The Singapore Arts Center, at the edge of the bay on one of
Singapore's most visible sites, represents this tropical city's
cultural aspirations. The narrow, water's-edge site allows for
spectacular city views. The arts center program includes a
concert hall and lyric, medium, adaptable, and developmental
theaters. Adjoining retail and office space will support the
complex financially.

The main entrance, immediately off Raffles Avenue, leads to the
concert hall to the east and the four theaters to the west. Thus,
the concert hall stands alone between the grouped theaters and
the mixed-use commercial spaces to the east. A small "floating"
theater for special events projects over the bay and over an open
public promenade along the water.

Inside the complex, a large boat-shaped concourse facing the bay
acts as a veranda overlooking the promenade below. From this
veranda, each hall is entered separately from a grand stair rising
from a lower-level garden to a lobby which extends into the
volume of the concourse. This main space is continually
animated: before performances, during intermission, and from
the exterior promenade.

Plan, roof

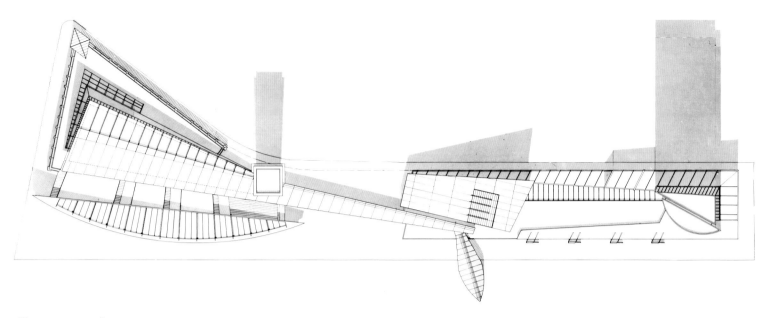

Plan, concourse floor

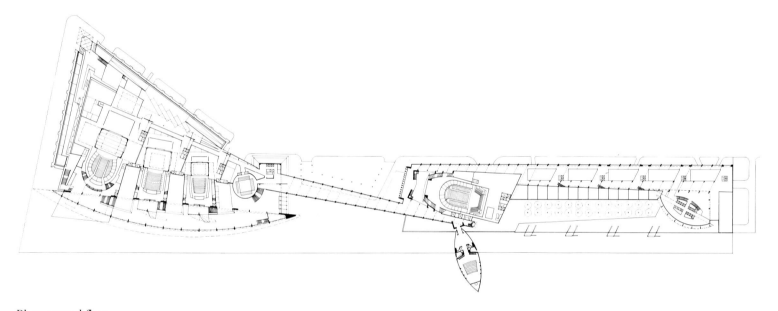

Plan, ground floor

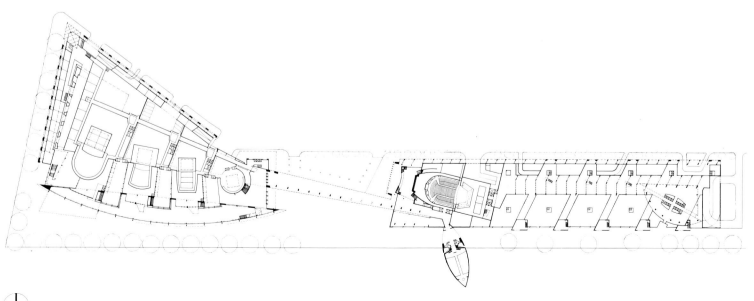

0   100 m

369

Section through lyric theater

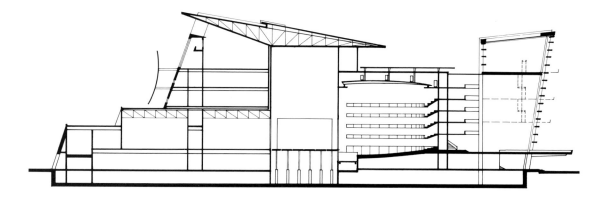

Section through medium theater

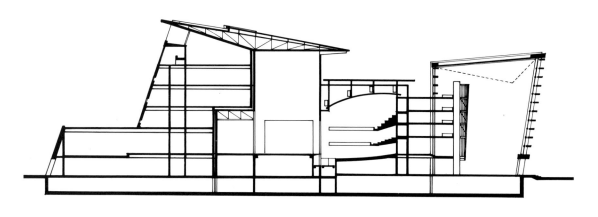

Section through adaptable theater

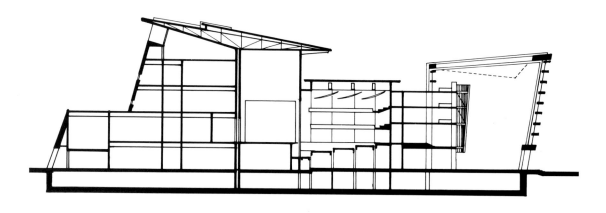

Section through developmental theater

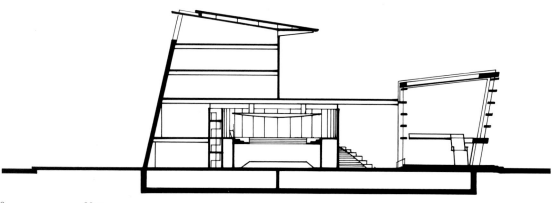

0   20 m

South elevation

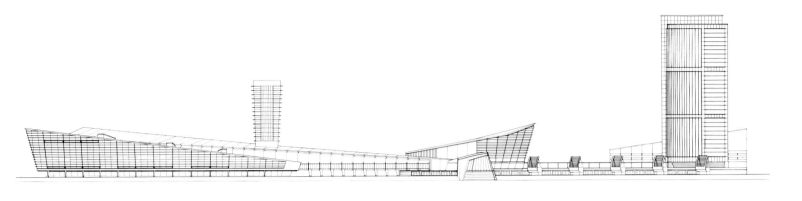

Longitudinal section looking north (through theaters)

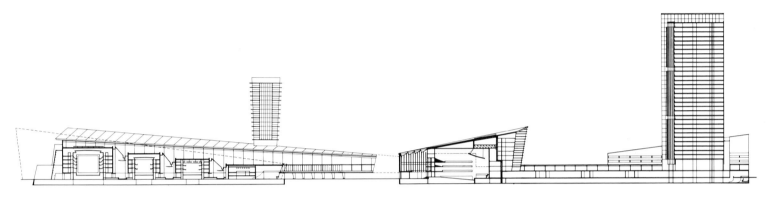

Longitudinal section looking north (through back of house)

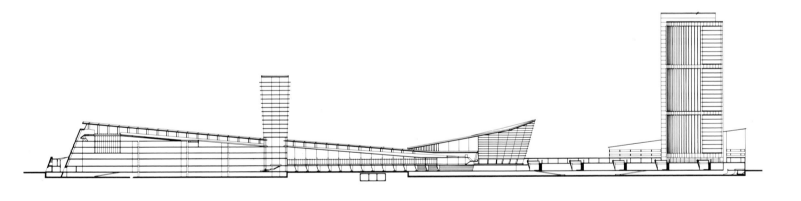

North elevation

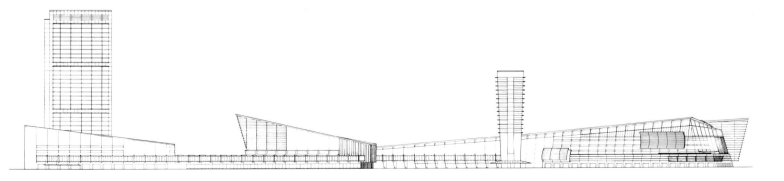

0   100 m

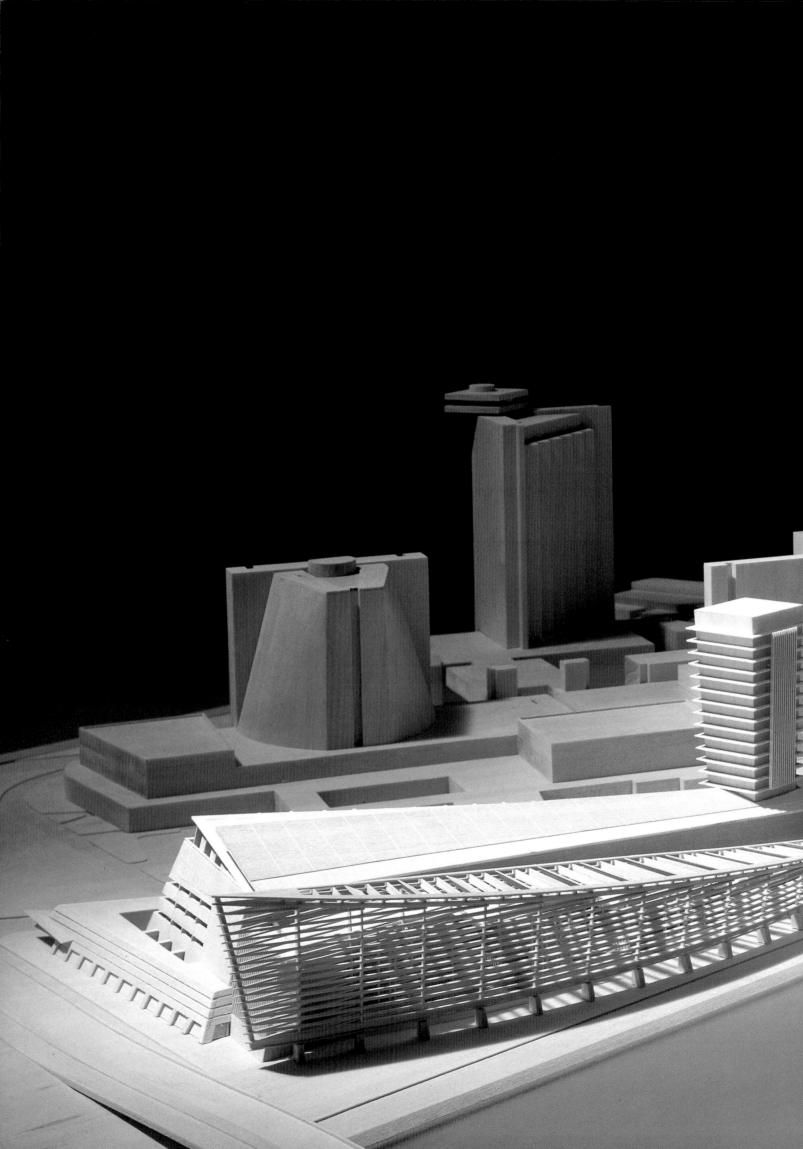

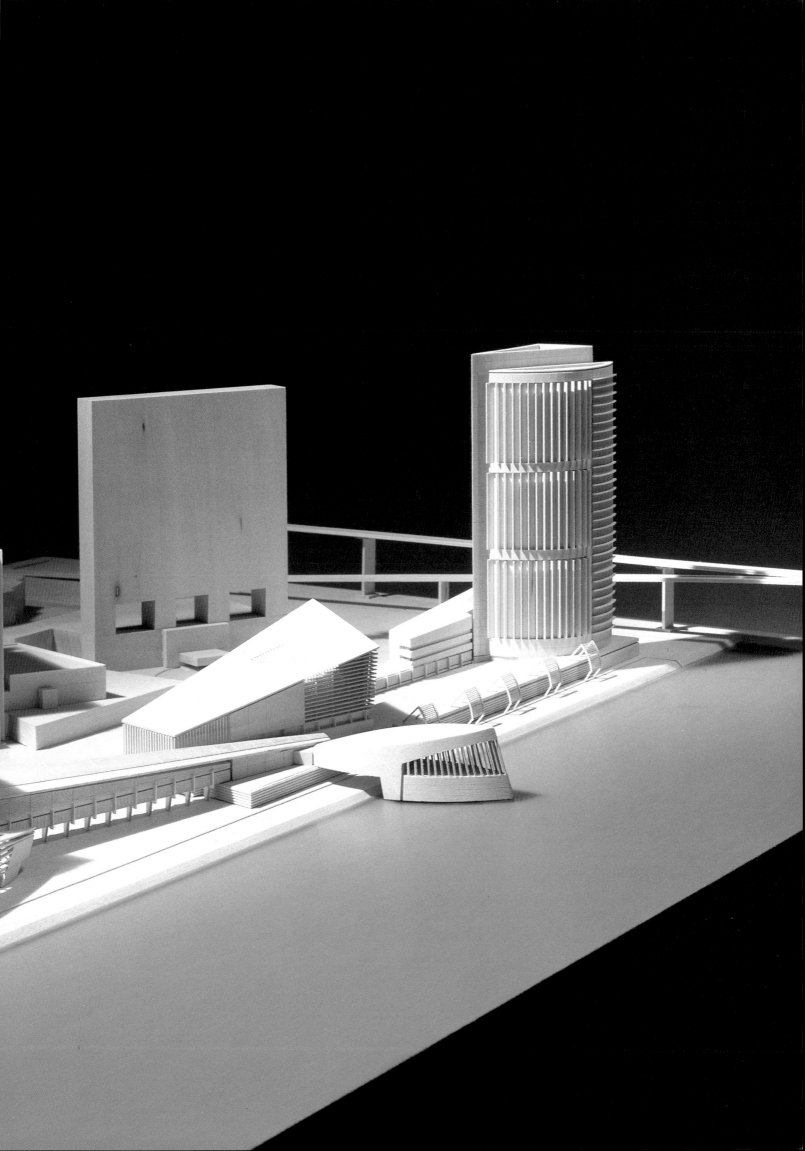

A civilization is often judged by the quality of its artistic legacy. The arts are a measure not only of a society's greatness but also of its optimism for the future. Correspondingly, civic buildings have always been intended as bold gestures toward the public realm of the culture they celebrate.

William Pedersen

As a result of its superb location within the city, the Singapore Arts Center must operate poetically as the new icon of this tropical city. The boat-shaped veranda that connects the theaters will launch a dramatic exhibition within Singapore. It is intended to become a stage set for players both inside and out to observe, exchange, and participate in the theatrics of art and modern life.

Peter Schubert

Postscript

Architecture is the subject of my photography. My work celebrates the ambiguous in architecture. Often, foreground becomes background and background becomes foreground; positive and negative rotate. Curved forms are flattened, scale is distorted, and perspective is exaggerated.

Since 1984, I have photographed fifteen KPF buildings in the United States and London. They have always provided me with fine subject matter for my investigation into architecture.

In KPF buildings, the outside wall surface often seems to be three-dimensional. This encourages a variety of readings. Photographing the walls as fragments generates a transformation of the subject matter: architecture. This allows me to re-create and reinterpret its meaning. I find the play of light off these three-dimensional surfaces especially interesting. When photographed from a close position, window patterns seem to vibrate. Once again, this architecture is further transformed— by light.

KPF has been innovative in its use of materials. These materials often absorb, reflect, or transmit light, which affects their reading as forms. I find in the interior of their buildings rich and complex combinations of materials, which are easily transformed to accommodate ambiguous interpretations of form.

I have been inspired by the architecture I have photographed. My aim was to capture the monumental presence, poetry, and essence that these particular buildings convey.

Judith Turner
New York, 1992

Partners

A. Eugene Kohn

A. Eugene Kohn was born in Philadelphia, Pennsylvania, in 1930. He received a Bachelor of Architecture degree in 1953 and a Master of Architecture degree in 1957, both from the University of Pennsylvania, where he was a Theopolis Parsons Chandler Graduate Fellow. Mr. Kohn is a former lieutenant commander of the United States Navy.

Prior to founding Kohn Pedersen Fox Associates in 1976, Mr. Kohn was President and Partner of John Carl Warnecke and Associates (1967–76); Design Director of Welton Becket Associates New York (1965–67); and Senior Designer at Vincent G. Kling Associates in Philadelphia, Pennsylvania (1960–65), where his designs received two American Institute of Architects National Honor Awards. Mr. Kohn is Partner-in-Charge for many of KPF's projects and is responsible for the firm's new commissions.

Mr. Kohn has been practicing architecture for over thirty years and is registered in twenty-five states. He is a Fellow of the American Institute of Architects and a member of its Octagon Society. During 1988, Mr. Kohn held the position of President of the New York City Chapter of the A.I.A. He is also a member of the Royal Institute of British Architects, the New York Building Congress, the Philadelphia Chamber of Commerce, the Municipal Art Society of New York, and the Urban Land Institute. He has served on the board of directors of the Architectural League, the Chicago City Ballet, and the Sheltering Arms Children Service as well as on the Advisory Board for the Master of Science degree in Real Estate Development at Columbia University's Graduate School of Architecture, Planning, and Preservation, and on the Yale University Committee on the Art Gallery and British Arts Center. Mr. Kohn is a trustee of the University of Pennsylvania and serves on the Board of Overseers at the University of Pennsylvania's Graduate School of Fine Arts and the Wharton Real Estate Center Advisory Board, in addition to the Board of the National Realty Committee.

Mr. Kohn has lectured extensively on the subject of contemporary architecture, and has been invited to participate in conferences throughout the world. He has delivered keynote speeches to professional associations, civic and educational organizations, and industry and trade groups in Los Angeles, Chicago, Washington, D.C., New York, London, Hong Kong, Tokyo, and Kuala Lumpur, as well as in Sydney, Brisbane, Melbourne, and Perth in Australia, and in Wellington, New Zealand. Mr. Kohn spoke in several cities in the former Soviet Union on behalf of the United States Information Agency. He has also served on numerous design and award juries. As a visiting critic and guest lecturer, Mr. Kohn has appeared at Bucknell, Harvard, UCLA, University of Pennsylvania, Penn State, University of Kentucky, University of Tennessee, Clemson University, and the University of Wisconsin. Many of Mr. Kohn's articles on architectural issues have been published in the United States and abroad.

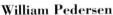

William Pedersen

William Pedersen was born in St. Paul, Minnesota, in 1938. He received a Bachelor of Architecture degree from the University of Minnesota in 1961 and was a recipient of the school's Gargoyle Club Prize. In 1963 he received a Master of Architecture degree from the Massachusetts Institute of Technology, where in 1963 he was a Whitney Fellow. In 1965, he won the Rome Prize in Architecture and studied for two years at the American Academy in Rome. In addition, Mr. Pedersen was honored with the 1985 Arnold W. Brunner Memorial Prize in Architecture, awarded by the American Academy and the Institute of Arts and Letters, the 1990 University of Minnesota Alumni Achievement Award, and an Award of Recognition from the St. Paul Chapter of the A.I.A. For his work at Kohn Pedersen Fox, Mr. Pedersen has received consecutive *Progressive Architecture* Design Awards from 1987 through 1990. He won the A.I.A. National Honor Award in 1984 for 333 Wacker Drive in Chicago, Illinois, and again in 1987 for the Procter & Gamble Corporate Headquarters in Cincinnati, Ohio.

Prior to joining in the founding of Kohn Pedersen Fox in 1976, Mr. Pedersen was Vice-President of John Carl Warnecke and Associates (1971–76), an Associate with I.M. Pei and Partners (1967–71), and a Designer with Eduardo Catalano (1964–65) and Pietro Belluschi (1963). He is the firm's principal Design Partner.

In 1982, *Newsweek* magazine ("The New American High Rise," November 8) recognized Mr. Pedersen as a major influence in the evolution of the tall office building in America today. He has had several essays published, including "Considerations for Urban Architecture and the Tall Building" in *Southwest Center: The Houston Competition* (Rizzoli, 1983), "Architecture and Praxis: A Self-Analysis of the Essential Criteria for the Urban Skyscraper" in *The New Art Examiner* (June 1983), and "Method & Intentions 1976–1989" in *Process: Architecture* (November 1989). He has also been interviewed for *American Architecture Now II* (Rizzoli, 1985) and "Skyscrapers" in *National Geographic* (February 1989). In addition, he has been profiled in *New York Magazine* (September 11, 1989) and *Business Week* (January 28, 1991).

Mr. Pedersen frequently lectures throughout the world and serves on academic and professional juries and symposia. He has been a visiting critic at the Rhode Island School of Design (1982), Columbia University (1983), and Harvard University (1984), and he has held the Eero Saarinen Chair at Yale University (1986). Mr. Pedersen has also been the Otis Lecturer in Japan (1988). In 1989 he was honored as the Herbert S. Greenward Distinguished Professor in Architecture at the University of Illinois in Chicago. Mr. Pedersen is a Director of the Architectural League in New York City, a member of the New York State Association of Architects, the Society of Architectural Historians, and an Honorary Member of the St. Paul Chapter of the American Institute of Architects. He is a Fellow of the A.I.A. and of the American Academy in Rome.

Sheldon Fox

Sheldon Fox was born in New York City in 1930. He received a Bachelor of Architecture degree in 1953 from the University of Pennsylvania, where he graduated with high honors. From 1953 to 1955 he served in Korea as a first lieutenant in the United States Army.

Prior to joining in the founding of Kohn Pedersen Fox in 1976, Mr. Fox was a Senior Vice-President of John Carl Warnecke and Associates (1972–76) and a Partner in the firm of Kahn and Jacobs, Architects (1955–72), both in New York City.

Mr. Fox has been practicing architecture for over thirty-seven years and is registered in sixteen states. In addition to his duties as Managing Partner for all financial and administrative affairs of the firm, he has served as Partner-in-Charge for many of the firm's projects throughout the United States.

Mr. Fox is a Fellow of the American Institute of Architects, an associate member of Building Officials and Code Administrators International, and an active member of the New York Building Congress, for which he has served as Director. He has also been a Director of the Lighthouse Business Council and of the Architectural League of New York City. He is active in civic affairs and has served as Chairman of the Design Review Board and as Director of the Mid-Range Civic Association, both in Stamford, Connecticut. Mr. Fox is a founding member of the Large Firm Roundtable and a member of the Practice Management Committee of the A.I.A. He has lectured on architectural management and served on several academic and professional juries.

Robert L. Cioppa

Robert L. Cioppa was born in Mount Vernon, New York, in 1942. Mr. Cioppa was a liberal arts honors student at Boston College before receiving his Bachelor of Architecture degree from Pratt Institute in 1967. That same year, he was the recipient of the New York Society of Architects Alpha Ro Chi Medal. He is also a graduate of the Stanford University Graduate School of Business Executive Program, which he attended in 1983.

Prior to joining Kohn Pedersen Fox in 1977, Mr. Cioppa was an Associate at John Carl Warnecke and Associates (1973–76) in New York City. He also worked at Hobart Betts Associates (1968–73) and at Unimark Associates (1967–68). As a Partner at KPF, he is responsible for the management of major projects across the United States and for the administration and operations of the firm.

Mr. Cioppa is a Fellow of the American Institute of Architects and a member of the A.I.A.-sponsored Large Firm Roundtable of Human Resources. He is also a member of the Construction Specifications Institute, the Urban Land Institute, and the Design Professional Management Association. Mr. Cioppa was Director of the New York State Society of Architects and Chairman of the Budget and Finance Committee for the 1988 A.I:A. National Convention New York Chapter activities. He has served on design juries and has lectured on architecture, career planning, construction, and high-technology buildings.

William C. Louie

William C. Louie was born in New York City in 1942. Mr. Louie began working as an architect in 1961, and he received a Bachelor of Science in Architecture degree from the City College of New York in 1974. Prior to joining Kohn Pedersen Fox in 1977, Mr. Louie was a Senior Associate with John Carl Warnecke and Associates (1969–77). At KPF, he has served as Job Captain, Project Manager, and Project Designer on numerous buildings and projects throughout the United States and in Australia, New Zealand, Indonesia, Japan, and Singapore.

Mr. Louie is a member of the American Institute of Architects and the New York State Association of Architects and is a registered architect in New York State. Mr. Louie's awards include three Prestressed Concrete Institute Professional Awards, in 1984, 1986, and 1990, for Goldome Bank, Arbor Circle North and South, and Shearson Lehman Hutton Plaza, respectively. He also received two awards from the New York State A.I.A., one Merit Award in 1986 for General Re Headquarters and one Excellence in Design Award in 1990 for 1325 Avenue of the Americas. In addition, in 1991, he was the recipient of two awards from the New York Association of Consulting Engineers, for Mellon Bank and for Shearson Lehman Hutton Plaza.

Lee A. Polisano

Lee A. Polisano was born in Atlantic City, New Jersey, in 1952. He received a Bachelor of Arts degree from LaSalle College in 1974 and, in 1977, a Master of Architecture degree from Virginia Polytechnic Institute. Prior to joining Kohn Pedersen Fox in 1981, Mr. Polisano worked at Kevin Roche–John Dinkeloo & Associates (1977–80) in New Haven, Connecticut. In 1985, Mr. Polisano was honored by *Engineering News Record* and the U.S. Construction Industry as one of the year's "Men Who Made Marks in 1984," for his building design and development of construction techniques using architectural concrete. He has won numerous other awards for this application as well. Two of Mr. Polisano's buildings have received awards: one Honor Award from the National A.I.A. in 1987 for the Procter & Gamble Corporate Headquarters and another from *Progressive Architecture* in 1988 for Mainzer Landstrasse 58. He has delivered papers to the Urban Design Institute in the United Kingdom and the Stockholm School of Economics in Sweden. In addition, he has served as a visiting critic at a number of universities. Mr. Polisano is a member of the American Institute of Architects and the Royal Institute of British Architects. Since 1989, he has assumed Partner-in-Charge responsibilities for Kohn Pedersen Fox International in London.

David M. Leventhal

David M. Leventhal was born in Boston, Massachusetts, in 1949. He received his Bachelor of Arts degree in 1971 and a Master of Architecture degree in 1978, both from Harvard University. Prior to joining Kohn Pedersen Fox in 1979, Mr. Leventhal worked at the Metropolitan Museum of Art (1972–73) in New York City and at Cain, Farrell & Bell (1978–79), the successor firm to McKim, Mead & White, also in New York City. He is a member of the American Institute of Architects and, in 1988, he received the New York A.I.A. Chapter Design Award for 70 East 55th Street in Manhattan. The same building received the Tucker Award for Design Excellence in 1989. Since 1989, Mr. Leventhal has assumed Design Partner responsibilities for Kohn Pedersen Fox International in London.

Gregory Clement

Gregory Clement was born in Providence, Rhode Island in 1950. He received a Bachelor of Arts degree in 1973 and a Master of Architecture degree in 1975, both from the University of Pennsylvania in Philadelphia. He was also the recipient of the Dales Travelling Fellowship in 1974 as well as other merit scholarships. Prior to joining Kohn Pedersen Fox in 1984, Mr. Clement was a Senior Designer at I.M. Pei & Partners (1982–84) in New York City and an Associate at Cathers, Lukens, Thompson (1980–82) in Philadelphia, where he was responsible for the Philadelphia College of Art expansion and restoration, which received an Honorable Mention from the Philadelphia chapter of the A.I.A. in 1982. He was also affiliated with Geddes Brecher Qualls Cunningham (1976–78) in Princeton, New Jersey. Since 1993, as a Partner at Kohn Pedersen Fox, Mr. Clement has been responsible for the management of major projects across the United States, Europe, and Asia as well as for the administration and operations of the firm in New York. He is a member of the American Institute of Architects and a registered architect in Pennsylvania, Delaware, Connecticut, and New York state and has served on numerous architectural design juries. Two of the buildings he has worked on have received awards: Rockefeller Plaza West received the *Progressive Architecture* Design Citation in 1989, and the Capital Cities/ABC Headquarters in New York City won the A.I.A./B.I.A. Brick in Architecture Award in 1993.

Senior Associate Partners

Charles P. Alexander was born in Bangor, Maine in 1947. Mr. Alexander was educated at Cornell University, where he received both his Bachelor of Architecture degree in 1971 and his Master of Architecture degree in 1973. Prior to joining Kohn Pedersen Fox in 1980, Mr. Alexander was a Designer at Hellmuth, Obata & Kassabaum, P.C. (1979) in New York City. He also worked at Mandala International (1977–78) and Perry Dean Stahl & Rogers (1975–76), both in Boston, Massachusetts. Mr. Alexander was also in private practice (1977) in Cambridge, Massachusetts. He has held architectural faculty positions at the Department of Visual Studies at Harvard University, the College of Art, Architecture & Planning at Cornell University, and at the Boston Architectural Center. Mr. Alexander is a member of the American Institute of Architects and has represented KPF at the A.I.A. Large Firm Roundtable and the A.I.A. Professional Development Program. Since 1989, in addition to his responsibilities as Project Manager for numerous projects across the United States, including Hawaii, Mr. Alexander is in charge of all the project staffing and personnel needs of the firm.

Richard H. Clarke was born in Northfield, Illinois in 1952. Mr. Clarke was educated at Dartmouth College, where he graduated *magna cum laude* and Phi Beta Kappa with a Bachelor of Arts in 1974 and, in 1979, he received his Master of Architecture degree with honors from Yale University, and was awarded the Feldman Thesis Prize. Prior to joining Kohn Pedersen Fox, he was a Project Architect at Gwathmey Siegel & Associates (1980–82) and at Eisenman/Robertson Architects (1982–83) both in New York City. He has taught and served on architectural juries at Yale, Cooper Union, Parsons School of Design, University of Pennsylvania, and Columbia. Mr. Clarke is a member of the American Institute of Architects and a registered architect in New York state. His designs for 1250 Boulevard René-Levésque in Montreal, Canada, won the 1993 Citation for Distinguished Architecture from the New York Chapter of the A.I.A. and the Prix Orange from Save Montreal in 1992, and his design for the Federal Reserve Bank of Dallas received the 1993 Design Award for Distinguished Architecture from the Houston Chapter of the A.I.A.

Peter Schubert was born in Evanston, Illinois in 1955. Mr. Schubert received his Bachelor of Science in Architecture degree from Ohio State University in 1978, where he graduated *cum laude* and received the Alpha Rho Chi Medal. He continued his studies at Columbia University, where he received his Master of Architecture degree in 1981 and the A.I.A. Award/Certificate for Outstanding Future Professionals. Prior to joining Kohn Pedersen Fox in 1984, Mr. Schubert was a staff architect at Skidmore, Owings & Merrill (1983–84), Peterson Littenberg (1982–83) and at Michael Schwarting and Associates (1981–82), all in New York City. He has taught at Columbia University, Catholic University in Washington, D.C., and Rome, Italy; and at the City College of New York. Mr. Schubert is a member of the American Institute of Architects and a registered architect in New York state. He was a Senior Designer for the winning entry in the World Bank Headquarters Competition, now nearing completion in Washington, D.C., in addition to designing many of the firm's projects in the United States, including Hawaii, as well as in Singapore.

Jerri K. Smith was born in Manhattan, Kansas in 1949. Ms. Smith received her Bachelor of Science in Architecture degree from Ohio State University in 1977, where she graduated *summa cum laude* and received several A.I.A. scholarships and fellowships. She continued her studies at Cornell University where she received her Master of Architecture degree in Urban Design in 1981. Prior to her studies in architecture she was a Vista volunteer (1970–73) in Columbus, Ohio. Later, Ms. Smith was an Urban Designer at Koetter Kim Associates (1990–91) in London, England. She has taught at the Catholic University of America, the Institute for Architecture and Urban Studies, New Jersey Institute of Technology, Cornell, and has lectured in Italy. She is a member of the American Institute of Architects and a registered architect in New York state. Working at Kohn Pedersen Fox since 1981, she has been a Designer for award-winning projects such as the gardens at the Procter & Gamble General Offices Complex in Cincinnati, the Mellon Bank Center in Philadelphia, and 500 E Street S.W. in Washington, D.C.

Associate Partners

Michael D. Greene, A.I.A.
Bachelor of Environmental Design, honors, North Carolina State University, 1976
Master of Architecture, honors, Virginia Polytechnic Institute, 1978

Thomas Holzmann
Bachelor of Science in Architecture, University of Illinois, 1976

Paul Katz, A.I.A.
Bachelor of Architecture and Planning, Israel Institute of Technology, 1982
Master of Architecture, Princeton University, 1984

Christopher S. Keeny, A.I.A.
Bachelor of Arts, *magna cum laude*, Yale University, 1976
Master of Architecture, Harvard University, 1981

Paul S. King, A.I.A.
Bachelor of Science in Architecture, University of Virginia, 1978
Master of Architecture, University of Virginia, 1982

James A. von Klemperer, A.I.A.
Bachelor of Architecture, *magna cum laude*, Harvard University, 1979
Master of Art, Trinity College, Cambridge University, 1980
Master of Architecture, *magna cum laude*, Princeton University, 1983

John T. Koga, A.I.A.
Bachelor of Architecture, Cornell University, 1983
Master of Architecture, Harvard University, 1985

John M. Lucas, A.I.A.
Bachelor of Arts, Yale University, 1963
Master of Architecture, University of Pennsylvania, 1968

Craig Benton Nealy, A.I.A.
Bachelor of Architecture, Cornell University, 1980
Master of Architecture, Urban Design, Cornell University, 1981

Bun-Wah Nip, A.I.A.
Bachelor of Science in Architecture, Taiwan National Cheng Kung University, 1963
Master of Architecture, Kansas State University, 1966

James E. Outen, A.I.A.
Bachelor of Science in Architecture, The City College, 1976

William I. Schweber, A.I.A.
Bachelor of Architecture, Massachusetts Institute of Technology, 1969

Collaborators

The people listed here are among those who have worked in the offices of Kohn Pedersen Fox and assisted on the building and projects in this book.

New York
1976–1992
Scott Aagre
Saunichi Abe
Lidia Abello
Stephanie Adolph
Juan Alayo
Margaret Albanese
Howard Albert
Dimitri Alexandrakis
Giancarlo Alhadeff
Robert Allen
Izai Amorim
Robin Andrade
Hiroyuki Aoshima
Alan Aranoff
Traci Aronoff
Robert Ashton
Theresa Atkin
Isabelle Autones
Christine Awad
Robert Aydlette
Dayo Babalola
Steven Bach
Veena Bali
Paval Balla
Vladimir Balla
Gretchen Bank
Victoria Baran
Robert Barbach
Maura Barbour
Christopher Bardt
Anthony Barnaba
Joseph Barnes
Mark Barnhouse
Roger Barrett
Kevin Batchelor
Elias Batinjaneh
Terry Bell
Ann Benz
Richard Berdan
Sanford Berger
Susan Berger-Jones
David Bergman
Alexander Bergo
Scott Berry
Beth Bethea
Nathan Bibliowicz
Clarinda Bisceglia
Gabrielle Blackman
Dvora Blay
Gale Blocker
Joan Blumenfeld
Joe Bodkin
Deborah Booher
James Borchard
Roberta Boston-Ross
Robert Bostwick
Stephanie Bradie
Madaline Brady
Vicky Braun
Alexis Briski
Glenn Brode
Barry Bronfman
Bridget Brown
Darlene Brown
Duncan Brown
Gary Brown
Philip Brown

Jeffrey Bucholtz
Stephen Buck
Gae Buckley
Tamara Budecz
Carol Buhrmann
Jacob Buksbaum
Dawn Burcaw
Barbara Bures
Andrus Burr
David Bushnell
Stephen Byrns
Garnes Byron
James Cali
Delva Cameron
Vicky Cameron
Judy Cammer
Carmine Cappadona
Maximo Cardillo
Christian Carlson
Rebecca Carpenter
Daniel Castor
Peter Catalano
Greer Celestin
Walter Chabla
Joshua Chaiken
Benny Chan
Soo K. Chan
Tat Chan
Mark Chaney
Carol Chang
Celia Chang
Dean Chavooshian
Dan Cheetham
Hsueh Jane Chen
Grace Cheng
Anna Cherington
Benjamin Cherner
Nancy Cheung
Peter Ching
Du Choi
Tae K. Choi
Michael Chren
Carey Chu
Larry Cohen
Yolanda Cole
Jerry Conduff
Jeanne Constantin
Patricia Conway
Karen Cook
Roger Cooner
Enrico Cordice
Nathan Corser
Perry Cortell
Marc Costandi
Dawn Couch
Rustom Cowasjee
Courtney Coyne
Angela Crawford
Suzanne Cregan
John Crellin
Cynthia Crier
Roger Crowley
Marjorie Cruz
William Cunningham
Ben Curatolo
Milton Curry
Glen DaCosta
Elizabeth Daly
Karen Dauler

Eric Daum
Beverly Davis
William Davis
Susan Davis-McCarter
Kathryn Dean
Crane DeCamp
Raul de Carvalho
Anthony DeGrazia
Paul Deibert
Linda Delaney-Mazzarelli
Annabel Delgado
Deborah Delnevo
Robert Demel
François de Menil
Thomas Demetrion
Anthony Desnick
Joseph Devlin
Mary DeVries
David Diamond
Michael Dichiaro
James Dicker
Anthony Digisaza
Judith DiMaio
Joseph DiMonda
Lucinda Dip
Peter Dixon
Miriana Doneva
Velma Dortch
Kenneth Drucker
Marjann Dumoulein
Timothy Dunlap
Daashan Dunn
Dominic Dunn
John Duvall
Valerie Edozian
Christopher Egan
Bruce Eisenberg
Tzadik Eliakim
Reade Elliott
Meggan Engelke-Ros
John Fahy
Salima Farid
Jean Farrell
Curtis Fentress
John Fernandez
Kathleen Ferrara
Mark Fiedler
Deborah Finkelstein
Benjamin Firestine
Veronica Fischer
Almet Fitzgerald
Kevin Flanagan
Michael Fontaine
Howe Keen Foong
Rune Forberg
Michael Forstl
Alicia Foussats
Dania Francis
Arthur Freed
Paul Freitag
Barbara Friedman
Joe Furio
Robert Furno
John Michael Gabellini
Mary Sue Gaffney
Shannon Gallagher
Byron Garnes
Glenn Garrison
Noah Garrison

Mimi Garza
Anthony Gelia
Mark George
Maria Geronimo
Gerrit Geurs
Emil Gewirtzman
Sonia Gilbert
Leslie Gill
Sarah Gilliland
Paola Giurgola
Irvin Glassman
Jan Gleysteen
Laurence Goldberg
Robert Goldberg
Robin Goldberg
Georgia Goldstein
Frank Goode
Robert Goodwin
Michael Gordon
Jan Gorlach
Alexander Gorlin
Winifred Gorman
Genevieve Gormley
Alex Gotz
Susan Green
Michael Greene
Carolyn Grenier
Peter Gross
Barbara Guarrera
Ernest Guenzberger
Gail Guevara
Charles Gustina
Armando Gutierrez
Jonathan Halper
Cleveland Harp
John Harris
Timothy Hartley
Yukio Hasegawa
George Hauner
Andreas Hausler
Tami Hausman
David Hawkins
J. Deveraux Hawley
Laura Heim
Susanne Hein
Fia Hekmat
Anne Hendricks
Robert Henry
Marianne Hensky
Horst Herrmann
Tomas Hernandez Jr.
Anna Hill
Robin Hill
Natalie Hlavna
Angeline Ho
Douglas Wyatt Hocking
Julie Holm
Alison Holt
Klaus Hornell
Monique Houston
George How
David Howard
Herman Howard
Nancy Huertas
Beat Huesler
Virginia Incremona
Koichiro Ishiguro
Nobua Iwashita
Rama Iyengar

Margaret Jacobs
Akiko Jacobson
Michele Jankosky
Warren James
Raul Jara
Christopher Jarrett
Dowestant Jarrett
Thomas Jin
James Johnson
H. Creighton Jones
Todd Jones
Vincent Jordan
James Jorganson
Leonard Kady
Robert Kahn
James Kalsbeek
Michael Kao
Martin Kapell
David Kaplan
Joel Karr
Angie Katselianos
Marsha Kaufman
Cheryl Kaufmann
Lucien Keldany
Katherine Kennedy
Sharon Kennedy
Paul Kevin Kennon
Celina Kersh
Laura Kesten
Geraldine Kierse
Heegom Kim
Myoung Kim
Therese King
Peter Kirby
Samuel Klatskin
John Koga
Sulan Kolatan
Arthur Korenstein
Terry Kornblum
Thea Kosar
Michael Kostow
Michael Kronick
Vivian Kuan
Kunio Kudo
Nicola Kuhlo
Jeffrey Kusmick
Joseph Kusnick
Gail LaCava
Sharon Lahr
Malvina Lampietti
Robert Landsman
Amy Langer
Amy Lann
William LaPatra
Carmen Laracuente
Janis Learner
Fred Lebart
Judy Lee
Susan Lee
Vincent Lee
Young Lee
Ming Leung
Samuel Lewis
Gale Limansky
Barbara Lincoln
Tzen-Ying Ling
Betty Liu
Nora Lobosco
John Locke

Frank Lombardo
Donald London
Walter Lorenzut
John Lowery
Leslie Lu
Michael Mallardi
Plato Marinakos
Eloise Marinos
Michael Martin
Georgina Martinez
Marsha Martinez
Suzanne Martinson
Connie Maxwell
Arthur May
Martha Mazeika
David McAdams
Delroy McBarnett
George McBarnett
Raymond McCaskill
Carrol McCutchen
Ann McDonald
William McGilvray
Molly McGowan
Kathryn McGraw
Leon Meeks
Peter Menderson
Carlos Menendez
Hugh Mercer
Eugenia Merkulova
Willis Messiah
Stephen Mihailos
Kristen Minor
Jose Molina
Jose Monge
Gail Morrell
Anthony Mosellie
Marcie Moss
Jimmy Moustafellos
Nicole Mronz
Jane Murphy
Annette Naalund
Paul Naecker
George Nakamora
Alexandra Naoum
Saradendu Narayan
Thomas Navin
Lisa Negri
Kathryn Nesbitt
Wolfgang Neumüeller
Stephen Newbold
Elaine Newman
Jeffrey Ng
Beth Niemi
Mark Nosky
Vicky Novak
Susan Now
Ichiro Oda
Hun-Song Oh
Shin Ohnishi
Patrick O'Malley
Loretta Ost
Dex Ott
Sharon Paige
Christo Paitakis
William Palmore
Christine Panebianco
Demetrios Pantazis
James Papoutsis
Aaron Parker

Judy Parker
Russell Patterson
Kia Pedersen
Anthony Pellecchia
Robin Pendleton
Shi Foo Peng
Anne Perl de Pal
Josephine Perpall
Gordon Peterson
Catherine Phal-Colavecchio
Cheryl Phillips
Paul Pichardo
Vernon Pickette
Anna Pieczara-Blanchfield
Josephine Piro
Katherine Platis
Andrew Pollack
Geraldine Pontius
Hoi Yung Poon
Manuel Quijano
Rene David Quinlan
Toni Racana
Darcy Rathjan
Anne Reeve
Paul Regan
Duncan Reid
Thomas Reistetter
Francisco Rencoret
Glenn Rescalvo
Katherine Retelas
Rita Reynolds
Russell Riccardi
Margaret Rice
Charlene Richards
Marie Richter
Ilona Rider
Sonia Riley
Donna Robertson
Sheryl Robinson
Marjorie Rodney
Victor Rodriguez
Harold Rolls
Kenneth Rose
Michael Rose
Paul Rosen
Cordula Roser
Sandor Rott
Scott Rudenstein
Joseph Ruocco
John Sabolchak
Taal Safdie
Joel Sanders
Nicholas Santos
Keiko Sasaki-Spade
Jody Sayler
August Schaefer
Charles Schmitt
Erika Schmitt
Hilde Schneider
Alan Schwabenland
Laura Schwartz
Samantha Schweitzer
Susan Seastone
James Seger
Alexander Seniuk
Esmatollah Seraj
Thomas Shafer
Marybeth Shaw
John Sheffield

Audrey Shen
Frank Shenton
Chris Shoemaker
Lloyd Sigal
Myron Sigal
Andrea Simitch
Gillian Skeen
Charles Eric Slavin
John Smart
Charles Smith
Dawn Smith
Jerri Smith
Warren Smith
Ann Soochet
Richard Sowinski
Joe Spada
William Spade
Scott Specht
Stephanie Spoto
Laurie Stavrand
Susan Steakin
Ilene Steingut
Ralph Stern
Gary Stluka
Emil Stojakovic
John Stoltze
Gregory Straub
Christopher Strom
Christine Sudduth
Hisaya Sugiyama
Joseph Sullivan
Mary Sue Sutton
Edward Tachibana
Peter Tao
Lillian Tay
Amanda Taylor
Scott Teman
LuAnne Tepes
David Terrien
John Thomas
Mark Thometz
David Thompson
Charlotte Thomsen
Kimberly Thrower
Ernesto Trindade
Anthony Tsirantonakis
Cynthia Turner
Stephen Valentine
Tom Vandenbout
William Van Horn
Luis Vasquez
Andrew Vines
Vivian Volz
James von Klemperer
Jeff Wagenbach
Megan Walker
Alexander Ward
Gregory Waugh
Jane Webster
Peter Weed
Greta Weil
Eileen Weingarten
Benita Welch
Christine Wentz
Robert Whitlock
Benjamin Wilkes
Jeri Wilkins
Michael Wilkinson
Shane Williams

Katherine Willson
Elaine Wolf
Jann Wolfe
Amy Wollman
Chao-Ming Wu
Christopher Wynn
Masami Yamada
Shinichiro Yorita
Vladislav Zacek
Leah Zennario
Melissa Zicht
Fredric Zonsius
Birgit Zwankhuizen

London
1989–1992
Tomas Alvarez
Fabio Barry
Shirley Barton
Sabine Begemann
Margaret Berry
Elise Bloss
Pat Bryan
Craig Burns
Karl Clos
Stephen Collier
Karen Cook
Mark Costandi
Courtney Coyne
Bill Davis
Barry Docker
Brigitte Duperray
Kevin Flanagan
Grant Garner
Susanne Geiger
Graham Goymour
Alan Grant
Tracy Green
Annette Gröhmann
Lindsay Gwilliam
Andreas Hausler
Lars Hesselgren
Jonathan Jacobs
David Jensen
Mark Johnston
Katherina Kanzler
Ursula Klein
Sorina Kopp
Cecilia Kramer
Martha Lagess
Edwin Hock Thong Low
Patrick Lynch
Cindy Marshall
Melody Mason
Chris McDonald
John McFarland
Michael McNamara
Alberto Miceli
Suzanne Middleton
Evelyn Neumann
Wolfgang Neumüller
Natalie Newey
Larissa Olufs
Paul Pichardo
Erik Prochnik
Eliseo Rabbi
Brigit Rathouse
Francisco Rencoret

Dara Rigal
Gerhard Rinkens
Howard Rosenberg
Pablo Seggiaro
Andrew Shields
Lloyd Sigal
Thomas Sontheimer
Marcus Springer
Alexander Strub
John Stuart
Randal Suttle
Stephen Taylor
Peter Tao
Juan Vieira-Pardo
Sally Webb
Scott Wilson
Suzanne Woods
Des Wright
Klaus Zahn

Building Credits

This list of credits for the buildings and projects presented in this monograph appears in the same sequence of presentation; for a chronological sequence refer to Complete Chronology. First year indicates year of commission, followed by year of completion when the building was completed prior to 1992; estimated year of completion if the project is going ahead or under construction as of May 1992; or year design work was completed on an unbuilt project or competition. Area of construction, given in either square feet or square meters, is always approximate. Number of floors given in the built buildings may vary with the actual building due to mechanical floors, parking levels above and below ground, etc. In unbuilt projects or projects under construction, the number of floors given may vary from final number of floors for similar reasons.

712 Fifth Avenue
New York, New York
1985–1991
Partner-in-Charge: A. Eugene Kohn. Design Partner: William Pedersen. Senior Designer: Chao-Ming Wu. Project Manager, Associate Partner: Robert H. Busler. Project Team: Annabel Delgado, Barbara Friedman, Thomas Shafer. Client: 712 Fifth Avenue Associates. Associate Architect: Schuman Lichtenstein Claman & Efron, New York. Structure: Steel and concrete. Major Exterior Materials: Indiana limestone, Vermont marble, aluminum curtain wall. Major Interior Materials: Granite, marble, wood, glass. Gross Square Feet: 472,000. Number of Floors: 52.

Mellon Bank Center
Philadelphia, Pennsylvania
1984–1990
Partner-in-Charge: A. Eugene Kohn. Design Partner: William C. Louie. Senior Designer, Associate Partner: Peter Schubert. Project Managers: Jan Gleysteen, Myron Sigal. Job Captain: Deborah Booher. Project Team: Christine Awad, Anthony Barnaba, Annabel Delgado, Miriana Doneva, Michael Fontaine, James Jorganson, Carlos Menendez, Shi Foo Peng, Audrey Shen, Jerri Smith, James von Klemperer, Chao-Ming Wu, Vladislav Zacek. Client: Richard I. Rubin & Company, Inc., and Equitable Life Assurance Society of the United States. Structure: Steel frame. Major Exterior Materials: Granite and marble at podium, aluminum panels and glass curtain wall at tower. Major Interior Materials: Marble and granite walls with structural steel details, patterned terrazzo floors, aluminum leaf ceiling. Gross Square Feet: 1,200,000. Number of Floors: 53.

1325 Avenue of the Americas
New York, New York
1987–1990
Partner-in-Charge: A. Eugene Kohn. Design Partner: William C. Louie. Senior Designer, Associate Partner: Christopher Keeny. Senior Designer: Michael Gabellini. Project Manager, Associate Partner: Charles Alexander. Job Captain: Russell Patterson. Project Team: Jeffrey Bucholtz, Jacob Buksbaum, Miriana Doneva, Mark Fiedler, Kevin Flanagan, Genevieve Gormley, Peter Gross, Armando Gutierrez, Angeline Ho, Lucien Keldany, John Locke, John Lowery, Andrew Pollack, Frank Shenton. Client: Edward J. Minskoff Equities, Inc., and The Taubman Company. Structure: Steel frame. Major Exterior Materials: Granite, aluminum-and-glass curtain wall. Major Interior Materials: Marble walls, terrazzo floors, vaulted plaster ceilings. Gross Square Feet: 735,000. Number of Floors: 34.

225 West Wacker Drive
Chicago, Illinois
1985–1989
Partner-in-Charge: A. Eugene Kohn. Design, Senior Associate Partner: Gary Handel. Project Manager, Associate Partner: James E. Outen. Project Team: Robert D. Henry, Catherine Phal-Colavecchio, August Schaefer. Client: The Palmer Group, Ltd. Associate Architect: Perkins & Will, Chicago. Structure: Reinforced concrete. Major Exterior Materials: Gray granite, impala black granite, verde antique marble, glass curtain wall, stainless steel. Major Interior Materials: Ulano venato marble, verde issorie marble, stainless steel. Gross Square Feet: 800,000. Number of Floors: 31.

Capital Cities/ABC Headquarters
New York, New York
1986–1989
Partner-in-Charge: Sheldon Fox. Design Partner: Robert Evans. Senior Designers: Yolanda Cole, Christian Carlson. Project Manager, Associate Partner: Gregory Clement. Job Captain, Associate Partner: Thomas Holzmann. Project Team: Lydia Abello, Vladimir Balla, John Crellin, Susan Davis-McCarter, Lucien Keldany, John Locke, Loretta Ost, Robert Whitlock. Client: Capital Cities/ABC, Inc. Structure: Steel superstructure, concrete-on-metal-deck floors. Major Exterior Materials: Brick, limestone trim, granite, aluminum-and-glass windows. Major Interior Materials: Marble walls, terrazzo floors, stainless-steel trim. Gross Square Feet: 400,000. Number of Floors: 23.

United States Courthouse/Foley Square
New York, New York
1991–1994
Partners-in-Charge: A. Eugene Kohn, Robert Cioppa. Design Partner: William C. Louie. Senior Designer: James von Klemperer. Project Manager, Associate Partner: Christopher Keeny. Job Captain: Greg Waugh. Project Team: Izai Amorim, Vladimir Balla, Richard Berdan, Alexis Briski, Duncan Brown, Robert Busler, Richard del Monte, Deborah Delnevo, Lucinda Dip, Mark Fiedler, Robert Goodwin, Peter Gross, Armando Gutierrez, Tomas Hernandez, Anthony Mosellie, Russell Patterson, Margaret Rice, Michael Rose, Erika Schmitt, Susan Seastone, Audrey Shen, Stephanie Spoto, Scott Teman, David Thompson, Jeffrey Wagenbach, Robert Whitlock. Client: B.P.T. Properties Foley Square, L.P. Structure: Steel frame, concrete mat foundation. Major Exterior Materials: Granite, marble, aluminum, glass. Major Interior Materials: Marble, terrazzo, stainless steel, wood. Gross Square Feet: 750,000. Number of Floors: 27.

383 Madison Avenue/Scheme III
New York, New York
1987
Partners-in-Charge: A. Eugene Kohn, Robert Cioppa. Design Partner: William Pedersen. Senior Designer, Associate Partner: Richard del Monte. Project Manager, Associate Partner: James Outen. Project Team: Karen Cook, Sulan Kolatan, Katherine Willson. Client: First Boston Realty and Development Corp. Structure: Steel frame. Major Exterior Materials: Clear reflective glass, white metal panels. Major Interior Materials: Stone, terrazzo. Gross Square Feet: 1,150,000. Number of Floors: 48.

Canary Wharf Tower
London, England
1986–1987
Partners-in-Charge: A. Eugene Kohn, Robert Cioppa. Design Partner: William Pedersen. Senior Designer, Associate Partner: Craig B. Nealy. Project Manager, Associate Partner: Mark Strauss. Job Captain: Katherine Willson. Project Team: Stephanie Bradie, Annabel Delgado, Masami Yamada. Client: The Canary Wharf Development Co. Ltd. Associate Architect: YRM Architects and Planners, London. Structure: Composite steel and concrete-frame system. Major Exterior Materials: Brushed metal mullion system with tinted vision glass and metalized-stone infill panels. Gross Square Meters: 242,000. Number of Floors: 47.

311 South Wacker Drive
Chicago, Illinois
1985–1990
Partners-in-Charge: A. Eugene Kohn, Robert Cioppa. Design Partner: William Pedersen. Senior Designer, Associate Partner: Richard del Monte. Job Captain: Terry Kornblum. Project Team: Joshua Chaiken, William Davis, Jim Papoutsis, Jody Sayler, Andrew Vines, Vladislav Zacek. Client: Lincoln Property Co. Associate Architect: Hardwood K. Smith & Partners, Chicago. Structure: Concrete. Major Exterior Materials: Pink, gray, and black granite, green marble, silver glass in clear anodized aluminum mullions (walls); translucent glass in clear aluminum mullions, back lit (roof). Major Interior Materials: Light gray, dark gray, white and red marble (floors); dark gray and light gray marble with mahogany trim (walls); clear glass skylight above winter garden, plaster ceilings elsewhere (ceilings). Gross Square Feet: 1,400,000. Number of Floors: 65.

Chicago Title and Trust Center
Chicago, Illinois
1986–1992
Partners-in-Charge: Sheldon Fox, Robert Cioppa. Design Partner: David Leventhal. Project Planner, Associate Partner: Mark Strauss. Senior Designer: Kevin Flanagan. Project Manager: John Lowery, Robert Goldberg. Job Captain, Associate Partner: Bun-Wah Nip. Project Team: Scott Aagre, Robert Allen, Barbara Bures, Daniel Castor, Dan Cheetham, Kenneth Drucker, Barbara Friedman, Sarah Gilliland, Armando Gutierrez, Beat Huesler, Dow Jarrett, Tom Jin, Ilona Rider, Peter Schubert, Robert Whitlock. Client: The Linpro Company. Structure: Steel, concrete core. Major Exterior Materials: Sardinian white granite, painted metal, glass. Major Interior Materials: Marble. Gross Square Feet: 1,000,000. Number of Floors: 50.

One Fountain Place
Cincinnati, Ohio
1985–1988
Partner-in-Charge: A. Eugene Kohn. Design Partner: William Pedersen. Senior Designer, Associate Partner: Craig B. Nealy. Senior Designers: Thomas Shafer, Christian Carlson. Project Team: Marie Richter, Peter Weed, Robert Whitlock. Client: JMB/ Federated Realty. Associate Architect: RTKL, Baltimore. Structure: Concrete, steel. Major Exterior Materials: Metal-and-glass curtain wall, metal-and-granite infill panels. Gross Square Feet: 1,200,000. Number of Floors: 50.

Station Center
White Plains, New York
1986–1988
Partners-in-Charge: A. Eugene Kohn, Robert Cioppa. Design Partner: William Pedersen. Senior Designer, Associate Partner: Paul Gates. Project Team: Robert Aydlette. Client: The Penn Central Corporation. Structure: Concrete-steel hybrid. Major Exterior Materials: Limestone, aluminum, glass. Gross Square Feet: 710,000. Number of Floors: 12–14.

Goldman Sachs European Headquarters
London, England
1987–1991
Partners-in-Charge: A. Eugene Kohn, Lee Polisano. Design Partner: William Pedersen. Senior Designer, Associate Partner: Craig B. Nealy. Project Manager, Associate Partner: James E. Outen. Job Captain: Peter Tao. Project Team: Robin Andrade, Carol Buhrmann, Joshua Chaiken, Karen Cook, Roger Cooner, John Crellin, Susan Davis-McCarter, Miriana Doneva, Angeline Ho, Jane Murphy, Mark Nosky, Stephanie Spoto, Meghan Walker. Client: LDT Partners. Associate Architect: EPR Architects Limited, London. Structure: Steel frame. Major Exterior Materials: Granite, aluminum, glass. Major Interior Materials: Polished black granite, anigre veneer, sandblasted glass. Gross Square Meters: 41,800. Number of Floors: 10.

St. Paul Companies Headquarters
St. Paul, Minnesota
1987–1991
Partner-in-Charge: Robert Cioppa. Design Partner: William Pedersen. Senior Designer, Associate Partner: Richard del Monte. Project Manager: Glenn Garrison. Job Captain: Walter Chabla. Project Team: Lidia Abello, Robin Andrade, Mark Chaney, Deborah Delnevo, Armando Gutierrez, James Jorganson, Lucien Keldany, Paul Kevin Kennon, Audrey Shen. Client: St. Paul Companies. Structure: Concrete. Major Exterior Materials: Granite and limestone with punched windows, reflective glass (walls); aluminum panel system with metallic paint finish (roof). Major Interior Materials: Terrazzo at entrance, lobbies, and cafeteria (floors); marble, stainless steel, gypsum board with stainless-steel divider strips (walls); gypsum board (ceiling). Gross Square Feet: 500,000. Number of Floors: 2–17.

Canary Wharf
London, England
1987–1991
Partner-in-Charge: Lee Polisano. Design Partners: William Pedersen, David Leventhal. Senior Designer: Sulan Kolatan. Project Manager, Associate Partner: William Schweber. Project Manager: Michael Greene. Job Captains: Anthony Mosellie, Don London, Michael Martin. Project Team: Lidia Abello, Robert Allen, Tomas Alvarez, Christine Awad, Mark Barnhouse, Susan Berger-Jones, Duncan Brown, Robert Busler, Vicky Cameron, Walter Chabla, Karen Cook, Roger Cooner, Susan Cregan, John Crellin, Cynthia Crier, William Davis, Richard del Monte, François de Menil, Bruce Eisenberg, John Fernandez, Mark Fiedler, Rune Forberg, Georgia Goldstein, Armando Gutierrez, George Hauner, Tomas Hernandez, Chris Jarrett, Lucien Keldany, Sue Kim, Alex Klatskin, John Koga, William LaPatra, John Locke, Nora Lobosco, Marie Richter, Marjorie Rodney, Taal Safdie, Keiko Sasaki-Spade, Lloyd Sigal, Laurie Stavrand, John Stuart, Joseph Sullivan, Lillian Tay, Cindy Turner, Andrew Vines, Jann Wolfe. Client: Olympia & York Development Ltd. Associate Architect: EPR Partnership, London. Structure: Steel. Major Exterior Materials: Vermont marble and painted metal, glass. Major Interior Materials: Statuary venato and gray bardiglio marble, stucco, glass, metal. Gross Square Meters: 67,000 and 46,500. Number of Floors: 10.

Mainzer Landstrasse 58
Frankfurt am Main, Germany
1986–1993
Partners-in-Charge: A. Eugene Kohn, Lee Polisano. Design Partner: William Pedersen. Senior Designer, Associate Partner: Paul King. Project Manager: Andreas Hausler. Project Team: William Davis, Robert Demel, Armando Gutierrez, George Hauner, Nicole Mronz, Jane Murphy, Evelyn Neumann, Beth Niemi, Wolfgang Neumüller, James Papoutsis, Klaus Zahn, Birgit Zwankhuizen. Client: Agima Aktiengesellschaft für Immobilien-anlage. Associate Architect: Nägele Hofmann Tiedemann und Partner, Frankfurt. Structure: Reinforced concrete. Major Exterior Materials: Glass, painted aluminum, painted steel, celtic gray flamed and honed granite. Major Interior Materials: Statuario venato marble, blue lanhelin granite, brushed stainless steel. Gross Square Meters: 77,000. Number of Floors: 52.

1250 Boulevard René-Lévesque Ouest
Montreal, Canada
1988–1992
Partner-in-Charge: A. Eugene Kohn. Design Partner: William Pedersen. Senior Designer, Associate Partner: Richard Clarke. Project Manager, Senior Associate Partner: Sudhir Jambhekar. Job Captain: Glen DaCosta. Project Team: Carol Buhrmann, Miriana Doneva, Bruce Eisenberg, John Koga, Carlos Menendez, Stephanie Spoto. Client: Marathon Real Estate, Ltd., and IBM Canada, Ltd. Associate Architect: LaRose Petrucci & Associés, Montreal. Structure: Reinforced concrete, earthquake resistant. Major Exterior Materials: Rockville white granite, low-e vision and back-painted spandrel glass, aluminum and stainless steel. Major Interior Materials: Canadian black granite, fiore di pesce marble, anigre veneer, stainless steel, sandblasted glass and plaster. Gross Square Meters: 152,000. Number of Floors: 47.

Rockefeller Plaza West
New York, New York
1987–1991
Partner-in-Charge: Robert Cioppa. Design Partner: William Pedersen. Senior Designer, Associate Partner: Paul Gates. Senior Designer, Public Spaces: Paul Kevin Kennon. Project Manager, Associate Partner: Gregory Clement. Job Captain: George Hauner. Project Team: Kevin Batchelor, Alex Bergo, Alexis Briski, Max Cardillo, Mark Chaney, Ben Cherner, Mark Costandi, John Crellin, Marjann Dumoulein, Dominic Dunn, Valerie Edozien, Robert Furno, Robert Goodwin, Peter Gross, Armando Gutierrez, Tomas Hernandez, Eloise Marinos, Darcy Rathjen, Francisco Rencoret, Erika Schmitt, John Stoltze, Hisaya Sugiyama, Ed Tachibana, Andrew Vines. Client: Rockefeller Center Development Corporation. Structure: Structural steel. Major Exterior Materials: Limestone, granite, glass curtain wall, ornamental metal. Major Interior Materials: Marble, terrazzo, ornamental metal. Gross Square Feet: 1,600,000. Number of Floors: 55.

Three Bellevue Center
Bellevue, Washington
1988–1994
Partner-in-Charge: A. Eugene Kohn. Design Partner: William Pedersen. Senior Designer, Associate Partner: Peter Schubert. Project Manager, Senior Associate Partner: Sudhir Jambhekar. Project Team: Milton Curry, Marjorie Cruz, Angeline Ho, Eugenia Merkulova, Duncan Reid. Client: Wright Runstad & Company. Associate Architect: Callison Partnership, Seattle. Structure: Steel frame. Major Exterior Materials: Stone, aluminum, blue-gray glass. Major Interior Materials: Stone, metal, wood. Gross Square Feet: 568,000. Number of Floors: 30.

Chifley Tower
Sydney, Australia
1987–1992
Partner-in-Charge: A. Eugene Kohn. Design Partner: William C. Louie. Senior Designer, Associate Partner: Christopher Keeney. Senior Designer: Yolanda Cole. Project Manager, Associate Partner: Robert Busler. Project Team: Vladimir Balla, Mark Barnhouse, Roger Cooner, John Duvall, Reade Elliott, Michael Fontaine, Joe Furio, Robert Goodwin, Genevieve Gormley, William LaPatra, Eugenia Merkulova, Beth Niemi, Andrew Pollack, Hilde Schneider, August Schaefer, Scott Specht, Emil Stojakovic, Lillian Tay, Vivian Volz,

Gregory Waugh. Client: Kumagai (NSW) Pty., Ltd. (Original client: Bond Corporation.) Associate Architect: Travis Partners Pty., Ltd., Sydney. Structure: Steel frame. Major Exterior Materials: Granite and marble, aluminum-and-glass curtain wall, stainless-steel details. Major Interior Materials: Marble and granite walls, patterned terrazzo floors, coffered plaster ceiling. Gross Square Meters: 116,280. Number of Floors: 42.

Bank Niaga Headquarters
Jakarta, Indonesia
1989–1993
Partner-in-Charge: Robert Cioppa. Design Partner: William C. Louie. Senior Designer: James von Klemperer. Job Captain: Roger Cooner. Project Team: Joseph Barnes, Cynthia Crier, Marjann Dumoulein, Valerie Edozien, Tzadik Eliakim, Howe Keen Foong, Joseph Furio, Joel Karr, Lucien Keldany, Sharon Lahr, Scott Specht, Scott Teman. Client: Bank Niaga. Associate Architect: P.T. Wiratman & Associates, Jakarta. Structure: Cast-in-place concrete frame and precast double-tee floors. Major Exterior Materials: Granite, aluminum-and-glass curtain wall with aluminum brise-soleil details. Major Interior Materials: Marble, granite, and wood-panel walls, marble floor, wood coffer ceiling. Gross Square Meters: 64,000. Number of Floors: 27.

550 South Hope Street
Los Angeles, California
1988–1992
Partners-in-Charge: A. Eugene Kohn, Robert Cioppa. Design Partner: William Pedersen. Senior Designer, Associate Partner: Paul Gates. Project Team: Shunichi Abe, Kevin Batchelor, Angeline Ho, Francisco Rencoret. Client: Obayashi America Corporation and The Koll Company. Associate Architect: Langdon Wilson Architects, Los Angeles. Structure: Concrete for parking, steel for tower high-rise. Major Exterior Materials: Granite, aluminum, glass. Major Interior Materials: Travertine, granite, glass. Gross Square Feet: 610,000. Number of Floors: 27.

Tobishima Headquarters
Tokyo, Japan
1990
Partner-in-Charge: A. Eugene Kohn. Design Partner: Robert Evans. Senior Designer, Associate Partner: Paul Gates. Project Team: Robert Demel, Nicole Mronz, Hisaya Sugiyama. Client: Tobishima Corporation. Associate Architect: Tobishima Corporation, Tokyo. Structure: Steel and concrete. Major Exterior Materials: Stone, glass, aluminum. Major Interior Materials: Stone walls and floors, luminous glass ceiling. Gross Square Meters: 63,000. Number of Floors: 24.

Morrison Tower
Portland, Oregon
1989–1994
Partner-in-Charge: A. Eugene Kohn. Design Partner: William Pedersen. Senior Designer, Associate Partner: Peter Schubert. Project Manager, Senior Associate Partner: Sudhir Jambhekar. Project Team: Milton Curry, Angeline Ho, Duncan Reid. Client: Wright Runstad & Company. Associate Architect: McKinnely Architects, Portland. Structure: Steel. Major Exterior Materials: Stone, metal, glass. Major Interior Materials: Stone, metal, wood. Gross Square Feet: 585,000. Number of Floors: 30.

Ameritrust Center
Cleveland, Ohio
1988–1995
Partner-in-Charge: A. Eugene Kohn. Design Partners: Robert Evans, William Pedersen. Senior Designer: Christian Carlson. Project Manager: Robert Barbach. Job Captain: Gregory Waugh. Project Team: Gabrielle Blackman, Duncan Brown, David Bushnell, Kathryn Dean, Reade Elliott, Rune Forberg, Tomas Hernandez, Rama Iyengar, Eugenia Merkulova, Elaine Newman, Beth Niemi, Susan Seastone, Audrey Shen, Eric Slavin, Yung Sun-Lee. Client: The Richard & David Jacobs Group. Structure: Steel superstructure. Major Exterior Materials: Granite, aluminum-and-glass curtain wall. Major Interior Materials: Marble and wood walls, terrazzo floors, luminous glass ceiling. Gross Square Feet: 1,880,000. Number of Floors: 63.

World Bank Headquarters
Washington, D.C.
1989–1996
Partners-in-Charge: A. Eugene Kohn, Sheldon Fox. Design Partner: William Pedersen. Senior Designer, Associate Partner: Craig B. Nealy. Project Manager: William H. Cunningham. Job Captain: Joseph P. Ruocco. Project Team: Isabelle Autones, Dayo Babalola, Vladimir Balla, Joseph Barnes, Suzanne Cregan, Eric Daum, Dominic Dunn, Valerie Edozien, Armando Gutierrez, Fia Hekmat, Michael Martin, Hun Oh, Paul Regan, Duncan Reid, James Seger, Frank Shenton, David Thompson, Thomas Vandenbout. Contributors: Robin Andrade, Pavel Balla, Mark Barnhouse, Gabrielle Blackman, Larry Cohen, Cynthia Crier, Glen DaCosta, Anthony DiGrazia, Mark Fiedler, Robin Goldberg, Koichiro Ishiguro, Sulan Kolatan, Judy Lee, Ming Leung, Jenny Ling, Kristen Minor, Nicole Mronz, Beth Niemi, Esmatollah Seraj, Audrey Shen, Emil Stojakovitch, John Stoltze, Hisaya Sugiyama. Client: The International Bank for Reconstruction & Development (The World Bank). Associate Architect: Kress Cox Associates, Washington D.C. Structure: Slurry wall foundation, poured-in-place concrete superstructure, poured-in-place post-tensioned concrete superstructure. Major Exterior Materials: Glass, aluminum, painted-and-precast-concrete curtain wall. Major Interior Materials: Precast concrete, patterned glass, terrazzo, wood. Gross Square Feet: 1,200,000 new; 800,000 renovated. Number of Floors: 13.

Federal Reserve Bank of Dallas
Dallas, Texas
1989–1992
Partner-in-Charge: A. Eugene Kohn. Design Partner: William Pedersen. Senior Designer, Associate Partner: Richard Clarke. Job Captain: Glen DaCosta. Project Team: Tat Chan, Marjann Dumoulein, Alex Gotz, Joel Karr, Ming Leung, Tzen-Ying Ling, Nicole Mronz, Ryoichi Nakamura, Susan Seastone, John Sheffield, Thomas Vandenbout, Robert Whitlock. Client: Federal Reserve Bank of Dallas. Associate Architect: Sikes Jennings Kelly & Brewer, Houston. Structure: Reinforced concrete frame, lightweight steel deck roofs. Major Exterior Materials: Limestone, aluminum, lightly reflective glass, painted steel, exposed concrete. Major Interior Materials: Travertine, limestone, granite, aluminum, stainless steel, bronze, wood veneer, carpet. Gross Square Feet: 1,050,000. Number of Floors: 2–14.

Meydenbauer Convention Center
Bellevue, Washington
1989–1993
Partner-in-Charge: A. Eugene Kohn. Design Partner: William Pedersen. Senior Designer: John Koga. Project Manager, Senior Associate Partner: Sudhir Jambhekar. Job Captain: Miriana Doneva. Project Team: Milton Curry, Mary Sue Gaffney, Duncan Reid. Client: Bellevue Convention Center Authority and the City of Bellevue, Washington. Associate Architect: Howard Needles Tammen & Bergendoff, Bellevue. Structure: Concrete and steel. Major Exterior Materials: Precast concrete, stucco, metal, glass. Major Interior Materials: Wood panels, terrazzo and carpet flooring, painted gypsum board, acoustical panels. Gross Square Feet: 280,000. Number of Floors: 6.

147 Columbus Avenue
New York, New York
1990–1992
Partner-in-Charge: Sheldon Fox. Design Partner: William Pedersen. Senior Designer: James Papoutsis. Project Manager, Associate Partner: Thomas Holzmann. Job Captains: Scott Aagre, Nathan Corser. Project Team: Tae Choi, Sarah Gilliland, Joel Karr, Annette Naalund, Lillain Tae, Vivian Volz. Client: Capital Cities/ ABC, Inc. Structure: Steel frame, concrete foundation. Major Exterior Materials: Brick, cast stone, aluminum, glass, granite, limestone, patterned art glass. Major Interior Materials: Encaustic, terrazzo, aluminum, patterned art glass. Gross Square Feet: 160,000. Number of Floors: 10.

Milton Keynes Warehouse
Milton Keynes, England
1990
Partner-in-Charge: Lee Polisano. Design Partner: David Leventhal. Senior Designer, Associate Partner: Paul King. Senior Designer: Sulan Kolatan. Project Team: John Fernandez, Marie Richter. Client: Kumagai Gumi and

Ranelagh Developments. Structure: Steel columns, steel cables. Major Exterior Materials: Painted metal, Kalwall, glass. Major Interior Materials: Painted metal, Kalwall, glass. Gross Square Meters: 18,000. Number of Floors: 1–2.

State House/58–71 High Holborn
London, England
1989–1994
Partner-in-Charge: Lee Polisano. Design, Senior Associate Partner: Gary Handel. Senior Designer: Tomas Alvarez. Project Manager: Peter Tao. Job Captain: Alan Grant. Project Team: Isabelle Autones, Alex Klatsakin, Amy Lann, Francisco Rencoret, Glenn Rescalvo, Miguel Rodriguez (New York); Barry Docker, John McFarland, Eliseo Rabbi, Suzanne Woods (London). Client: High Holborn Estates. Structure: Reinforced concrete. Major Exterior Materials: Marquis gray marble, jet-mist granite, glass curtain wall. Major Interior Materials: Marquis gray marble, jet-mist granite, glass. Gross Square Meters: 40,400. Number of Floors: 9.

St. Paul Companies South Building
St. Paul, Minnesota
1990–1992
Partner-in-Charge: Robert Cioppa. Design Partner: William Pedersen. Senior Designer, Associate Partner: Richard del Monte. Project Manager: Glenn Garrison. Job Captain: Walter Chabla. Project Team: Alexis Briski, Tamara Budecz, Max Cardillo, Roger Cooner, Gerritt Geurs, Marie Richter. Client: St. Paul Companies. Structure: Existing. Major Exterior Materials: Limestone, granite, precast ribs, clear reflective glass, aluminum mullions. Major Interior Materials: Existing. Gross Square Feet: 500,000. Number of Floors: 5.

Carwill House I
Stratton Mountain, Vermont
1988–1989
Design Partner: William Pedersen. Senior Designer: Joshua Chaiken. Project Architect: Alex Bergo. Project Team: Mariana Doneva, John Fernandez, Gerritt Geurs, George Hauner, Chiou He Ko, Cynthia Turner. Client: Mr. and Mrs. William and Carolyn Stutt. Structure: Wood frame. Major Exterior Materials: Lead-coated copper, cedar siding, Vermont slate. Major Interior Materials: Fir cabinets and trim, cherry floors, slate floors and countertops, plastered gypsum-board walls and ceilings. Gross Square Feet: 9,500. Number of Floors: 2 1/2.

Carwill House II
Stratton Mountain, Vermont
1989–1991
Design Partner: William Pedersen. Senior Designer: Joshua Chaiken. Project Architect: Alex Bergo. Project Team: Tzadik Eliakim, John Fernandez, Armando Gutierrez, Cecelia Kramer, Anthony Mosellie, Kia Pedersen, Denise Vanderlind, Susan Seastone. Client: Mr. and Mrs. William and Carolyn Stutt. Structure: Wood frame. Major Exterior Materials: Lead-coated copper, cedar siding, Vermont slate. Major Interior Materials: Fir cabinets and trim, cherry floors, slate floors and countertops, plastered gypsum-board walls and ceilings. Gross Square Feet: 6,500. Number of Floors: 3.

Mills House
Shelter Island, New York
1990–1993
Design Partner: William Pedersen. Project Architect: Malvina Lampietti. Client: Mr. Michael Mills and Ms. Laureen Bedell. Structure: Wood frame. Major Exterior Materials: Cedar siding, lead-coated copper roofing, teak windows, bluestone block chimney and base. Major Interior Materials: Fir and maple floors, painted wood trim, plaster, kirk stone. Gross Square Feet: 4,500. Number of Floors: 2.

Hanseatic Trade Center
Hamburg, Germany
1990–1993
Partner-in-Charge: Lee Polisano. Design, Senior Associate Partner: Gary Handel. Senior Designers: Glenn Rescalvo, Karen Cook, Francisco Rencoret. Project Manager: Wolfgang Neumüller. Project Team: Richard Berdan, Dawn Burcaw, Carey Chu, Mary Ann Hensler, Douglas Wyatt Hocking, Nicole Mronz (New York); Karl Clos, Graham Goymour, Cecilia Kramer, Martha Lagess,

Michael McNamara, Paul Pichardo, Erik Prochnik, Pablo Seggiaro (London). Client: HTC. Structure: Reinforced concrete. Major Exterior Materials: Brick, stainless-steel curtain wall. Major Interior Materials: Stone, precast concrete, metal. Gross Square Meters: 92,900. Number of Floors: 6–15.

Platz der Akademie/Block 30
Berlin, Germany
1991–1992
Partner-in-Charge: Lee Polisano. Design Partner: David Leventhal. Senior Designer: Kevin Flanagan. Project Team: Lars Hesselgren, Katharina Kanzler, Andrew Shields, John Stuart. Client: The Landmarks Group and DG Bank. Structure: Concrete. Major Exterior Materials: Limestone, painted metal. Gross Square Meters: 23,300. Number of Floors: 8.

University of Pennsylvania/Revlon Campus Center
Philadelphia, Pennsylvania
1990–1995
Partners-in-Charge: A. Eugene Kohn, Sheldon Fox. Design Partner: William Pedersen. Senior Designer: Joshua Chaiken. Project Manager, Associate Partner: Gregory Clement. Job Captain: Glen DaCosta. Project Team: John Fernandez, Tomas Hernandez, Nobua Iwashita, Kristen Minor, Edward Tachibana. Client: University of Pennsylvania. Structure: Steel. Major Exterior Materials: Brick, limestone, granite, metal, glass skylights. Major Interior Materials: Stone, wood, gypsum board, carpet. Gross Square Feet: 205,000. Number of Floors: 5.

Newport Harbor Art Museum
Newport Beach, California
1990–1991
Partners-in-Charge: A. Eugene Kohn, Robert Cioppa. Design Partner: William Pedersen. Senior Designer: Sulan Kolatan. Project Manager, Associate Partner: Christopher Keeney. Job Captain: Joshua Chaiken. Project Team: Kevin Batchelor, Mary Sue Gaffney, Paul Katz, Malvina Lampietti, Esmatollah Seraj, Thomas Vandenbout. Client: Newport Harbor Art Museum. Associate Architect: Gruen Associates, Los Angeles. Structure: Concrete. Major Exterior Materials: Stucco, stone, lead-coated copper. Major Interior Materials: Plaster, stone, wood. Gross Square Feet: 75,000. Number of Floors: 1.

Disney Institute and Town Center
Osceola, Florida
1991
Partner-in-Charge: A. Eugene Kohn. Design Partner: William Pedersen. Senior Designer, Associate Partner: Peter Schubert. Senior Designer: Paul Kevin Kennon. Project Team: Mark Chaney, Jerry Conduff, Marjorie Cruz, Katherine Dean, Tomas Hernandez, George Howe, Eugenia Merkulova. Rendering: Thomas Schaller. Client: Disney Development Company. Structure: Steel, wood. Major Exterior Materials: Wood, stucco, metal, glass. Major Interior Materials: Wood, stucco, metal, glass. Gross Square Feet: 1,000,000. Number of Floors: 2–7.

Hamm Plaza
St. Paul, Minnesota
1989–1992
Partner-in-Charge: Robert Cioppa. Design Partner: William Pedersen. Senior Designer: Stephanie Spoto. Project Manager: Glenn Garrison. Job Captain: Walter Chabla. Project Team: Alex Bergo, Grace Cheng, Richard del Monte, Deborah Delnevo, August Schaefer. Collaborating Artist: Jackie Ferrara. Client: St. Paul Companies and The City of St. Paul. Structure: Concrete. Major Exterior Materials: Granite, stainless steel. Gross Square Feet: 10,000.

Niagara Toll Station
Niagara Falls, New York
1990
Partner-in-Charge: A. Eugene Kohn. Design Partner: William Pedersen. Senior Designer, Associate Partner: Peter Schubert. Project Team: John Fernandez. Client: Niagara Falls Bridge Commission. Associate Architect: William Nicholas Bodouva Associates, New York City. Structure: Steel. Major Exterior Materials: Metal, glass. Major Interior Materials: Metal, glass, wood. Gross Square Feet: 80,000. Number of Floors: 1–2.

Tokyo Marriott
Tokyo Bay, Japan
1990
Partners-in-Charge: A. Eugene Kohn, Robert Cioppa. Design Partner: William Pedersen. Senior Designer, Associate Partner: Paul Katz. Project Manager: Tom Demetrion. Job Captain: Robert Whitlock. Project Team: Carey Chu, Mary Sue Gaffney, Malvina Lampietti, Ryoichi Nakamora. Client: Withheld at client's request. Associate Architects: Nikken Sekkei, Tokyo, and Taisei Corporation, Tokyo. Structure: Steel towers, reinforced concrete base and lower structure. Major Exterior Materials: Granite, precast concrete, painted aluminum. Gross Square Meters: 127,000. Number of Floors: 35.

Nagoya Station Building
Nagoya, Japan
1990–1999
Partner-in-Charge: A. Eugene Kohn. Design Partner: William Pedersen. Associate Partners: Paul Katz, John Lucas. Senior Designer: John Koga. Project Manager: Michael Greene. Job Captain: Roger Cooner. Project Team: Christine Awad, Dawn Burcaw, Carey Chu, Jerry Conduff, Thomas Demetrion, Lucinda Dip, Mary Sue Gaffney, Tomas Hernandez, Douglas Wyatt Hocking, Paul Kevin Kennon, Kristen Minor, James Moustafelos, Glenn Rescalvo, Erika Schmitt, Lloyd Sigal, Emil Stojakovic, Hisaya Sugiyama, Edward Tachibana, Shinichiro Yorita. Client: Central Japan Railway Co., Ltd. Associate Architects: Seizo Sakata, Master Architect, Tokyo, and Nagoya Station Building Design Joint Venture (Taisei Corporation, Tokyo, and Sakakura Associates, Tokyo). Structure: Steel, reinforced concrete. Major Exterior Materials: Granite, architectural precast concrete, ceramic tile. Major Interior Materials: Granite, stainless steel. Gross Square Meters: 416,610. Number of Floors: 51 and 53.

JFK Terminal One
Queens, New York
1992
Partner-in-Charge: A. Eugene Kohn. Senior Designer, Associate Partner: Craig Nealy. Project Team: Gabrielle Blackman, Valerie Edozian, Irvin Glassman, Elaine Newman. Client: Terminal One Association. Associate Architects: DMJM Architects and Engineers, New York, and Frederic R. Harris, Inc., New York. Structure: Steel frame. Major Exterior Materials: Aluminum, glass, concrete. Major Interior Materials: Aluminum, glass, terrazzo, glass block, pattern glass, drywall, metal laminate panels, plastic laminate panels, stainless-steel trim. Gross Square Feet: 670,000. Number of Floors: 2–4.

M. Project
Machida, Japan
1991–1992
Partner-in-Charge: A. Eugene Kohn. Associate Partners: Paul Katz, John Lucas. Design, Associate Partner: Craig B. Nealy. Project Team: Valerie Edozian, Deborah Finkelstein, Beth Niemi, Paul Regan. Client: Withheld at client's request. Associate Architect: Mitsubishi Estate Company, Ltd., Tokyo. Structure: Steel frame. Major Exterior Materials: Board-formed precast concrete, thermal-finished granite and cleft slate with painted aluminum curtain wall. Gross Square Meters: 102,000. Number of Floors: 20.

Concert Tower
Honolulu, Hawaii
1991–1994
Partner-in-Charge: Sheldon Fox. Design Partner: William Pedersen. Senior Designer, Associate Partner: Peter Schubert. Project Manager, Associate Partner: Charles Alexander. Project Team: Ming Leung, Ichiro Oda, Kia Pedersen, Marie Richter. Client: The Myers Corporation. Structure: Concrete. Major Exterior Materials: Stone, glass, metal brises-soleils. Major Interior Materials: Stone, wood. Gross Square Feet: 250,000. Number of Floors: 30.

Warsaw Bank Center
Warsaw, Poland
1991–1995
Partner-in-Charge: A. Eugene Kohn. Senior Designer, Associate Partner: Richard Clarke. Project Manager, Associate Partner: Gregory Clement. Project Team: Vladimir Balla, Valerie Edozian, Trish Fleming, Ming Leung, Jenny Ling, Kristen Minor, Beth Niemi, Erika Schmitt. Client: EP Partners, Ltd.,

National Bank of Poland, and Golub Epstein Partnership. Associate Architects: Biuro Projekty Architektury J & J, Warsaw, and A. Epstein and Sons International, Chicago. Structure: Reinforced concrete. Major Exterior Materials: Granite, aluminum, insulated glass. Major Interior Materials: Granite, marble, wood veneer, bronze, stainless steel, glass. Gross Square Meters: 66,000. Number of Floors: 32.

Coraceros Complex
Viña del Mar, Chile
1992
Partner-in-Charge: A. Eugene Kohn. Design, Senior Associate Partner: Gary Handel. Senior Designers: Gabrielle Blackman, John Fernandez. Project Coordinator: Francisco Rencoret. Project Team: Philip Brown, Dawn Burcaw, Carol Chang, Robin Goldberg, Molly McGowen, Chris Strom, Edward Tachibana, Trent Tesch. Client: Manso de Velasco, S.A. Associate Architects: Dominguez Arquitectos & Asociados, Santiago. Structure: Concrete. Major Exterior Materials: Concrete, stucco, curtain wall. Major Interior Materials: Tile, plaster, wood, marble. Gross Square Meters: 303,000. Number of Floors: 2–27.

First Hawaiian Center
Honolulu, Hawaii
1991–1995
Partner-in-Charge: Sheldon Fox. Design Partner: William Pedersen. Senior Designer, Associate Partner: Peter Schubert. Project Manager, Associate Partner: Charles Alexander. Job Captain, Associate Partner: Bun-Wah Nip. Project Team: Robert Goodwin, Tomas Hernandez, Marcie Moss, Ichiro Oda, Glenn Rescalvo. Client: First Hawaiian Bank and The Myers Corporation. Structure: Steel and concrete. Major Exterior Materials: French limestone, stone, metal, glass. Major Interior Materials: Stone, wood. Gross Square Feet: 420,000. Number of Floors: 30.

Singapore Arts Center
Singapore
1992
Partner-in-Charge: A. Eugene Kohn. Design Partner: William Pedersen. Senior Designer, Associate Partner: Peter Schubert. Project Manager, Associate Partner: Robert Busler. Project Team: Juan Alayo, Isabelle Autones, Carol Chang, Irvin Glassman, Robert Goodwin, Vivian Kuan, Plato Marinakos, Tom Reistetter, Chris Strom. Client: City of Singapore. Associate Architects: RSP & Associates, Singapore, and Heisel & Associates, New York. Structure: Steel and concrete. Major Exterior Materials: Wood, glass, stone. Major Interior Materials: Wood, glass, stone. Gross Square Meters: 165,000. Number of Floors: 2–22.

Complete Chronology

This comprehensive list of buildings and projects is arranged in strict chronological order within each given year, according to the date when first commissioned. It includes buildings and projects designed in the New York and London offices. Those featured in this monograph are indicated by their page number. Buildings and projects featured in the book, but not listed, were commissioned prior to 1986.

1986

Federal Home Loan Bank Headquarters
San Francisco, California
Bank Headquarters, Completed 1991

Rockaway 80
Rockaway, New Jersey
Office Buildings

Chicago Title and Trust Center   *page 104*
Chicago, Illinois
Office Building, Completed 1992

Linpro San Diego
San Diego, California
Planning Study

45 West 18th Street
New York, New York
Office Building and Renovation, Feasibility Study

Hillman San Francisco
San Francisco, California
Planning Study

Canary Wharf Tower   *page 96*
London, England
Office Buildings

Kingswood Corporate Center
North Castle, New York
Office Buildings, Master Plan

AT&T Corporate Center Competition
Atlanta, Georgia
Mixed-use Complex, Hotel and Office Facilities

Ritz-Carlton Kansas City
Kansas City, Missouri
Hotel, Feasibility Study

Station Center   *page 112*
White Plains, New York
Mixed-use Complex, Office and Residential

B.A.R.T. Pleasant Hill
Pasadena, California
Planning Study, Feasibility Study

Bank of America Office Center
Pasadena, California
Planning Study, Feasibility Study

Glasgow World Trade Center
Glasgow, Scotland
Mixed-use Complex, Master Plan

Kip's Bay
New York, New York
Residential Complex, Feasibility Study

Santa Monica Common Competition
Santa Monica, California
Mixed-use Complex

AARP Headquarters
Washington, D.C.
Office Building, Completed 1991

Capital Cities/ABC Headquarters   *page 86*
New York, New York
Corporate Headquarters, Completed 1989

Grand Central Tower Competition
New York, New York
Office Building and Renovation

Brooklyn Museum Master Plan Competition
Brooklyn, New York
Museum Expansion, Galleries, Support Facilities

Hyatt Regency Stanford
Palo Alto, California
Hotel

Hyatt Tysons Corner
Tysons Corner, Virginia
Hotel, Feasibility Study

London Bridge City Competition
London, England
Office Building, Recreational Facilities

Reston Town Center Competition
Reston, Virginia
Mixed-use Complex

Westchester Corporate Center
Yonkers, New York
Planning Study

The Market Street Project
San Antonio, Texas
Planning Study

Interstate Tower
Charlotte, North Carolina
Office Building, Completed 1990

Fidelity Las Colinas
Irving, Texas
Regional Corporate Headquarters

Bellevue Master Plan
Bellevue, Washington
Planning Study

Lansburgh Competition
Washington, D.C.
Mixed-use Complex

Chase Stone Center
Colorado Springs, Colorado
Mixed-use Complex, Completed 1990

Atlanta Office Tower
Atlanta, Georgia
Office Building, Feasibility Study

Mainzer Landstrasse 58 *page 148*
Frankfurt am Main, Germany
Mixed-use Complex, Completed 1993

Richmond Competition
Richmond, Virginia
Office Building, Feasibility Study

Judiciary Office Building Competition
Washington, D.C.
Institutional Building

1987

15 William Street
New York, New York
Office Building

Financial Plaza
New York, New York
Public Plaza, Feasibilty Study

383 Madison Avenue/Scheme III *page 94*
New York, New York
Office Building and Corporate Headquarters

Ninth Avenue Tower, Scheme II
New York, New York
Office Building

Commonwealth Center
Boston, Massachusetts
Mixed-use Complex

Goldman Sachs European Headquarters *page 116*
London, England
Corporate Headquarters, Completed 1991

191 Peachtree Tower Competition
Atlanta, Georgia
Office Building

Motorola Toronto
Toronto, Canada
Planning Study

Madison Square Garden Competition
New York, New York
Mixed-use Complex, Office Building

King's Reach Office Building Competition
London, England
Mixed-use Complex, Offices and Residential Renovation

Union Planters National Bank
Memphis, Tennessee
Bank Headquarters, Mixed-use Complex

1325 Avenue of the Americas *page 78*
New York, New York
Office Building, Exhibition Facilities, Completed 1990

125 West 55th Street Competition
New York, New York
Office Building, Trading Facilities

CIGNA Office Building
Philadelphia, Pennsylvania
Office Building

Sun Trust Headquarters
Atlanta, Georgia
Corporate Headquarters

Canary Wharf *page 142*
London, England
Office Buildings, Completed 1991

Gallery Place
Washington, D.C.
Planning Study

660 Madison Avenue
New York, New York
Office Building Renovation, Under Construction

400

Broadcast Center Development
Toronto, Canada
Residential Tower and Hotel

Franklin Court
Washington, D.C.
Office Building, Completed 1992

Federal Triangle Competition
Washington, D.C.
Mixed-use Complex

Corporate Center II
San Diego, California
Feasibility Study

International Square
Washington, D.C.
Office Building Renovation

First Citizens Bank & Trust Company Headquarters
Raleigh, North Carolina
Corporate Headquarters

Foley Square Courthouse Competition
New York, New York
Courthouse Building

Friedrich-Ebert-Anlage 39–45
Frankfurt am Main, Germany
Office Buildings

Federal Reserve Bank of Dallas   *page 244*
Dallas, Texas
Bank Headquarters, Completed 1992

Chicago Tribune
Chicago, Illinois
Office Building, Feasibility Study

Marriott Acapulco Resort Hotel
Acapulco, Mexico
Hotel

Crestline Office Park
Atlanta, Georgia
Master Plan

The Broomielaw Development
Glasgow, Scotland
Mixed-use Development

Grand Bay Hotel Competition
Tokyo, Japan
Hotel

Sacramento Competition
Sacramento, California
Mixed-use Complex

Chao Phraya River Complex
Bangkok, Thailand
Mixed-use Complex, Feasibility Study

World Bank   *page 234*
Washington, D.C.
Bank Headquarters, Under Construction

Meydenbauer Convention Center   *page 260*
Bellevue, Washington
Convention Center, Under Construction

Irvine Center II/Parcel 9
Irvine, California
Office Buildings, Master Plan, Completed 1991

State House/58–71 High Holborn   *page 272*
London, England
Office Building

Two Oxford Center
Pittsburgh, Pennsylvania
Office Building

Pactel
San Diego, California
Office Building

Two Independence Square
Washington, D.C.
Office Building, Completed 1992

Carnegie-Mellon University
Pittsburgh, Pennsylvania
Research Laboratories

Windsor Station
Montreal, Canada
Planning Study, Feasibility Study

Carwill House II   *page 282*
Stratton Mountain, Vermont
Private Residence, Completed 1991

Bank Niaga Headquarters   *page 204*
Jakarta, Indonesia
Bank Headquarters, Completed 1993

Sudirman Development Competition
Jakarta, Indonesia
Mixed-use Complex

1990

Port Authority–Bus Terminal Tower Competition
New York, New York
Office Building

147 Columbus Avenue   *page 266*
New York, New York
Office and Support Facilities, Completed 1992

4 Great St. Helen's
London, England
Office Building

Columbia University East Campus Redevelopment
New York, New York
Master Plan, Design Study

Winter Garden Theater Hotel
New York, New York
Hotel and Residential, Feasibility Study

Marriott at Tower Oaks Competition
Rockville, Maryland
Warehouse and Office Building

Ambassador Site
Los Angeles, California
Feasibility Study

Cambridge Center Master Plan
Cambridge, Massachusetts
Mixed-use Complex, Master Plan

Navy Pier Competition
Chicago, Illinois
Mixed-use Development

Imperial Oil Headquarters Competition
Toronto, Canada
Mixed-use Complex, Corporate Headquarters

Orix Headquarters
Makuhari, Japan
Mixed-use Complex, Corporate Headquarters

1991

Friedrichstrasse Competition
Berlin, Germany
Mixed-use Complex

Disney Institute and Town Center Competition   *page 316*
Osceola, Florida
New Town Master Plan

Russelsheim
Rhein-Main Valley, Germany
Mixed-use Complex, Master Plan

Cleveland Indians Baseball Stadium
Cleveland, Ohio
Sports Stadium, Feasibility Study

Bennelong Center
Sydney, Australia
Office Building

Roppongi Towers
Tokyo, Japan
Office Buildings

Teluk Betung Headquarters
Singapore
Corporate Headquarters, Feasibility Study

Gatot Subroto Master Plan
Jakarta, Indonesia
Mixed-use Complex, Master Plan

Georgia Place Limited
Vancouver, Canada
Mixed-use Complex, Feasibility Study

United States Courthouse/Foley Square   *page 90*
New York, New York
Courthouse, Support Facilities

Westchester Place
White Plains, New York
Mixed-use Complex, Master Plan

Kuala Lumpur City Center Competition
Kuala Lumpur, Malaysia
Mixed-use Complex

Cooper-Hewitt Museum
New York, New York
Museum Exhibition Design, Feasibility Study

Warsaw Bank Center   *page 354*
Warsaw, Poland
Bank Headquarters

Orix-Makuhari/Scheme II
Makuhari, Japan
Office Building

Morgan Stanley Regional Headquarters
Stamford, Connecticut
Corporate Headquarters

Texas Rangers Stadium Competition
Arlington, Texas
Sports Stadium, Feasibility Study

Concert Tower   *page 350*
Honolulu, Hawaii
Office Building, Musician's Union Offices

Osaka South Sea-Port Development
Osaka, Japan
Office Building

Colgate Project
Jersey City, New Jersey
Mixed-use Complex, Offices and Retail

White Plains Federal Courthouse Competition
White Plains, New York
Courthouse, Support Facilities

Hotel Pierre
New York, New York
Hotel Renovation

Platz der Akademie/Block 30   *page 304*
Berlin, Germany
Office Buildings and Residential

The Grand Metropolitan at Lincoln Center
New York, New York
Mixed-use Complex, Residential and Commercial

ABC-TV Studios 25/26
New York, New York
Residential and Technical Facilities, Feasibility Study

BDNI Office Complex
Jakarta, Indonesia
Bank Headquarters

Halle Competition
Halle, Germany
Mixed-use Complex, Master Plan

Waterfront Place
Honolulu, Hawaii
Residential Complex

180 Maiden Lane
New York, New York
Office Building, Feasibility Study

M. Project   *page 346*
Machida, Japan
Mixed-use Complex, Office and Residential

First Hawaiian Center   *page 364*
Honolulu, Hawaii
Office Building, Bank Headquarters

The Hague Office Building
The Hague, The Netherlands
Office Building, Feasibility Study

1992

Bismarkstrasse
Berlin, Germany
Office Building

IRS Prince Georges County Competition
New Carrolton, Maryland
Institutional Headquarters

1625 I Street Competition
Washington, D.C.
Office Building

Dongbu
Seoul, Korea
Office Building, Feasibility Study

Cleveland Indians Stadium
Cleveland, Ohio
Consultants

UNICEF Headquarters
Westchester, New York
Corporate Headquarters

Portland Federal Courthouse Competition
Portland, Oregon
Courthouse, Support Facilities

Greater Orlando Airport Administration
Orlando, Florida
Airport Facility

Coraceros Complex Competition   *page 358*
Viña del Mar, Chile
Mixed-use Complex

SONY Center Competition
Berlin, Germany
Office Complex, Master Plan

Giddings & Lewis Headquarters
Fond du Lac, Wisconsin
Corporate Headquarters

Amtrak
Philadelphia, Pennsylvania
Master Plan, Feasibility Study

Federal Energy Regulatory Commission
Washington, D.C.
Office Building

Synergy Center
Atlanta, Georgia
Mixed-use Complex

Hainan/West Island Resorts
Hainan Island, China
Resort Hotel, Casino

Costanera Center
Santiago, Chile
Mixed-use Complex

Singapore Arts Center Competition   *page 368*
Singapore
Mixed-use Complex

Taichung Tower
Taichung, Taiwan
Master Plan, Office Building

Brooklyn Academy of Music
Brooklyn, New York
Lobby, Feasibility Study

JFK Terminal One Competition   *page 340*
Queens, New York
Airport Facility

Kowloon Mass Transit Railway Development
Kowloon, Hong Kong
Transportation

La Torre del Angel/Paseo de la Reforma 347
Mexico City, Mexico
Office Building, Hotel

Lloyd's Register of Shipping Competition
London, England
Office Facilities

Dusseldorf Derendorf Competition
Dusseldorf, Germany
Mixed-use Complex

Block 209A
Berlin, Germany
Feasibility Study

Amtrak 30th Street Station
Philadelphia, Pennsylvania
Master Plan, Air Rights Development

Central Reclamation Project
Hong Kong
Master Plan, Mixed-use Urban Design

GTA/GTC
Jakarta, Indonesia
Residential Complex

Wachovia Headquarters
Winston-Salem, North Carolina
Corporate Headquarters

Hong Kong Station Competition
Hong Kong
Master Plan, Transportation Center

Norfolk R-8 Planning Study
Norfolk, Virginia
Master Plan

Puerto Madero, Dock 4
Buenos Aires, Argentina
Office Building

Bull Wharf
London, England
Office Building

Manhattan Day School
New York, New York
School Addition

Selected Bibliography
1986–1992

For a selected bibliography covering the years 1976 through 1986, refer to the monograph on the firm edited by Sonia R. Cháo and Trevor D. Abramson, published by Rizzoli in 1987. Complete material, including newspaper articles from the United States, Europe, Asia, and Japan, covering the years 1986 to 1992 and 1976 to 1986 is located in the archives of Kohn Pedersen Fox in New York.

General

"The AD 100 Architects: An Exclusive Guide to the World's Foremost Architects." *Architectural Digest*, August 15, 1991, pp. 174–176.

Allen, Linn. "Sure, They Look Great, But . . ." *Chicago Tribune*, March 31, 1991, np.

Anderson, Grace M. "Five by KPF." *Architectural Record*, February 1987, pp. 126–135.

"Architectonics." *Process: Architecture* (Japan), January 1986, p. 7.

"Architects of the Year." *New York Observer*, March 5, 1990, np.

Arcidi, Philip. "Inquiry: What Becomes a Lobby Most?" *Progressive Architecture*, April 1991, pp. 84–91.

Bachmann, Wolfgang. "Chicago—Besuch bei den alten Damen." *Bauwelt* (Germany), October 27, 1989, pp. 1920–1955.

Bednar, Michael J. *The New Atrium.* New York: McGraw-Hill, 1987.

Birnbach, Lisa. *Going to Work.* New York: Villard Books, 1988.

Blomstedt, Ansii, dir., with Christian Laine and Ioannis Karalais, exec. prods. *New Chicago Skyscrapers.* Metropolitan Films and The Chicago Athenaeum, 1990, color, 30 min.

Branch, Mark A. "Formal Axis in Weekend Clothes." *Progressive Architecture*, November 1990, pp. 86–89.

Cháo, Sonia R., and Trevor D. Abramson, eds. *Kohn Pedersen Fox: Buildings and Projects 1976–1986.* New York: Rizzoli International Publications, 1987.

Curtis, William J. R. *Modern Architecture Since 1900*, 2nd ed. Englewood Cliffs: Prentice Hall, 1987.

———. "Contemporary Transformations of Modern Architecture." *Architectural Record*, June 1989, pp. 108–117.

Dean, Andrea Oppenheimer. "Breaking Into New Markets." *Architecture*, August 1991, pp. 91–94.

Decker, Howard. "Chicago on the Rise." *Architecture*, February 1990, pp. 78–83.

Dixon, John Morris. "10 On 10." New York Chapter/American Institute of Architects (exhibition catalogue), May 1988, np.

———. "P/A Portfolio: On the Sidewalks of New York." *Progressive Architecture*, July 1988, p. 76.

Doyle, Margaret. "Kohn Pedersen Fox: Designers on a Fast Track." *Building Design & Construction*, October 1988, p. 96.

Dumaine, Brian. "Architects for the '90s." *Fortune*, June 22, 1987, pp. 152–163.

Dunlap, David. "A $234.6 Million Mixed-Use Tower For the West Side." *New York Times*, July 5, 1992, Real Estate section, pp. 1, 3.

Edwards, Joanna. "Architect's Survey Reveals How Practitioners Envision Their Profession." *Architecture*, September 1991, pp. 91–94.

Ellis, William S. "Skyscrapers: Above the Crowd." *National Geographic*, February 1989, pp. 145–173.

Fletcher, Sir Bannister. *A History of Architecture*, 19th ed. Edited by John Musgrove. London: Butterworths, 1987, pp. 1433–1434.

Freeman, Allen. "AIA Honor Awards 1987." *Architecture*, May 1987, pp. 122–127.

Futagawa, Yukio, ed. "Kohn Pedersen Fox." *GA Document* (Japan), April 1987, pp. 88–95.

Gapp, Paul. "Building Tension." *Chicago Tribune*, April 9, 1989, Arts section, p. 4.

———. "The Eminent Domain." *Chicago Tribune*, March 8, 1992, sec. 13, pp. 18–19.

Geibel, Victoria. "Television Romance." *Architecture*, December 1990, pp. 56–59.

Gill, Brendan. "The Skyline: The Death of the Skyscraper?" *The New Yorker*, March 4, 1991, pp. 90–94.

Giovannini, Joseph. "Kohn Pedersen Fox." *Process: Architecture* (Japan), November 15, 1989, pp. 10–13.

Goff, Lisa. "Chicago Builds a New Skyline." *Progressive Architecture*, January 1987, pp. 46–53.

Goldberger, Paul. "Architecture that Pays Off Handsomely." *New York Times Magazine*, March 16, 1986, pp. 48–54, 74, 78.

———. "A Tempered Skyline Strengthens a City of Steel." *New York Times*, January 3, 1988, sec. 2, p. 28.

———. "Breaking the Rules to Make a Corner an Urban Event." *New York Times*, October 9, 1988, sec. 2, p. 31.

———. "Proud of Its Height, A New Tower Rules Over Seattle." *New York*

Times, November 27, 1988, sec. 2, p. 38.

———. "Fashions in Brick and Mortar Make Room for Conscience." *New York Times,* December 25, 1988, sec. 2, p. 32.

———. "Corporate Design that Stays on the Safe Side." *New York Times,* May 13, 1990, sec. 2, p. 37.

———. "A New York Firm Sets the Style in Chicago." *New York Times,* September 30, 1990, sec. 2, p. 34.

Grant, Mario. "How Floor Plates Shape the Corporation." *Corporate Design and Realty,* February 1986, pp. 32–35.

Greenwood, Douglas. "Corporations Shape Skylines with Signature Buildings." *Valley Vintage* (Northridge, California), April 19, 1990, np.

Greer, Nora Richter. "Americans Abroad: Some Coming Attractions." *Architecture,* January 1989, pp. 64–71.

Harriman, Marc S. "Practice: Government as Client." *Architecture,* April 1991, pp. 97–101.

Harrington, Kevin. "Urban Update: Chicago." *The Society of Architectural Historians Newsletter,* December 1987, pp. 1–3.

Heery, George, and Laura Heery. "How Do They Get Those Commissions?" *Architectural Record,* January 1990, pp. 37–41.

Horsley, Carter B. "Touch of the Poets." *New York Post,* May 12, 1988.

Hoyt, Charles K. "Making It in a Changing Economy." *Architectural Record,* September 1991, pp. 47–48.

Hume, Christopher. "Firm's Style Towers Over Mediocre Rivals." *Toronto Star,* November 19, 1987.

James, Warren A. "Architecture: William Pedersen." *Architectural Digest,* November 1988, pp. 238–245.

Jencks, Charles. *Post-Modernism: The New Classicism in Art and Architecture.* New York: Rizzoli International Publications, 1987.

———. *Architecture Today.* New York: Harry N. Abrams, 1988.

Kamin, Blair. "The Town's Top 10." *Chicago Tribune,* March 2, 1992, sec. 2, p. 3.

Kennedy, Shawn G. "Elegant Lobbies to Lure Office Tenants." *New York Times,* August 5, 1990, np.

Klotz, Heinrich, and Luminita Sabau, eds. *New York Architecture 1970–1990.* New York: Rizzoli International Publications, 1989.

Kohn, A. Eugene. "Statement." *Process: Architecture* (Japan), November 15, 1989, pp. 6–9.

———. "A Richer Architecture." In *African-American Architects in Current Practice,* edited by Jack Travis. New York: Princeton Architectural Press, 1991, pp. 16–17.

———. "Global Architecture in a Fractured World." *The Tokyo Report/The Nikkei Weekly* (Japan), May 1992, p. 1.

"Kohn Pedersen Fox Associates." *Process: Architecture* (Japan), November 15, 1989.

Kudo, Kunio. "Introduction: Recent High Rise Projects by Kohn Pedersen Fox." *Architecture + Urbanism* (Japan), April 1988, pp. 19–21.

Levy, Matthys P. "Structures that Combine Concrete and Steel." *Architecture,* June 1989, pp. 102–104.

Lewis, Rogo K. "Three Buildings Succeed in Erecting 'Great Wall.'" *Washington Post,* January 25, 1992, p. E4.

Linn, Charles. "Daylighting Analysis Critical for Successful Atrium Design." *Architectural Lighting,* June 1987, pp. 21–27.

London, Donald. "An Affinity for Ornament." *Architectural Record,* May 1990, pp. 121–125.

Markoutsas, Elaine. "Between Traditional and Modern, Chicago Carves a Unique Architectural Niche." *Contract,* May 1990, p. 160.

Maschal, Richard. "Charlotte Ups the Ante." *Architectural Record,* July 1988, pp. 104–110.

———. "Touch of Class." *Charlotte Observer,* October 14, 1990, pp. F1, F3.

McQuade, Walter. "The High Rise of Kohn Pedersen Fox." *Architecture,* May 1989, pp. 122–127.

Mosca, Basile. "Le Gratte-Ciel, Toujours: 3e Salon International de l'Architecture." *Techniques & Architecture* (France), October 1990, pp. 60–62.

Murphy, Jim. "Marketing Architectural Services." *Progressive Architecture,* July 1988, p. 88.

"1989 Tucker Award Winners." *Building Stone Magazine,* May/June 1989, pp. 29–30.

Norton, Bettina. "An Interview with Ross Gorin." *Boston Preservation Alliance Letter,* January 1989, p. 5.

Panizza, Mario. *Mister Grattacielo.* Rome: Editori Laterza, 1987.

Pedersen, William. "Method and Intentions 1976–1989." *Process: Architecture* (Japan), November 15, 1989, pp. 14–18.

Phillips, Cheryl. "Creativity: Designers Envision More than a Ballpark." *Morning Star-Telegram* (Fort Worth, Texas), August 10, 1991, np.

Rothman, Andrea. "He Changed the Skyline. Now, He's Changing." *Business Week,* January 28, 1991, pp. 50–51.

Saliga, Pauline, ed. *The Sky's The Limit: A Century of Chicago Skyscrapers.* New York: Rizzoli International Publications, 1990.

Schmertz, Mildred F. "Japanese Imports." *Architecture,* September 1990, pp. 72–75.

Schreiber, Mathias. "Das neue New York." *Frankfurter Allgemeine* (Germany), June 7, 1989, np.

Scully, Vincent. *American Architecture and Urbanism,* rev. ed. New York: Holt, 1988.

Strong, Ann L., and George E. Thones. *The Book of the School: 100 Years of the Graduate School of Fine Arts of the University of Pennsylvania.* Philadelphia, 1990.

"38th Annual P/A Awards." *Progressive Architecture,* January 1991, pp. 106–107.

Tindall, Susan. "Chicago: A World in a City." *The Construction Specifier,* May 1990, np.

Wiseman, Carter. "Fall Preview: Architecture." *New York,* September 11, 1989, np.

Zeaman, John. "A Classic in Modern Suburbia." *Bergen Record* (Bergen County, New Jersey), June 19, 1986, np.

712 Fifth Avenue

Gaskie, Margaret. "Double Play." *Architectural Record,* June 1992, pp. 90–95.

Gill, Brendan. "The Skyline: 712 Fifth." *The New Yorker,* June 10, 1991, pp. 97–102.

Goldberger, Paul. "Has Fifth Avenue Become Beside the Point?" *New York Times,* January 7, 1990, sec. 2, p. 31.

———. "A Shot of Adrenaline for Fifth Avenue." *New York Times,* March 10, 1991, sec. 2, p. 34.

———. "The Year in the Arts: Architecture 1991." *New York Times,* December 29, 1991, sec. 2, p. 38.

Harriman, Marc S. "Set in Stone." *Architecture,* February 1991, pp. 79–83.

Nesmith, Lynn. "Unlimited Vision." *Architecture,* December 1990, pp. 66–73.

"On the Avenue." *Architectural Record,* September 1988, p. 55.

Russell, James S. "Designing the Super-Thin New Buildings." *Architectural Record,* October 1990, pp. 105–109.

Mellon Bank Center

Binzen, Peter. "Promoting Mellon Center as the Height of Quality." *Philadelphia Inquirer,* March 13, 1989, p. D3.

Dorris, Virginia Kent. "Concrete and Steel Unite." *Engineering News Record,* July 19, 1990, pp. 30–32.

Futagawa, Yukio, ed. "Kohn Pedersen Fox." *GA Document* (Japan), April 1987, pp. 88–95.

Goldberger, Paul. "City's Skyline Is Looking Up, for the Most Part." *Philadelphia Inquirer,* July 9, 1990, p. A7.

"Mellon Bank, Philadelphia, Pennsylvania, 1990." *Process: Architecture* (Japan), November 15, 1989, pp. 74–77.

"Plans Revealed for Philadelphia's Tallest Office Building." *Architectural Record,* November 1986, p. 32.

Solomon, Nancy. "Women in Corporate Firms." *Architecture,* October 1991, pp. 79–87.

1325 Avenue of the Americas

Arcidi, Philip. "Inquiry: What Becomes a Lobby Most?" *Progressive Architecture,* April 1991, pp. 84–91.

"A Special Commitment to Architectural Integrity." *Real Estate Forum,* November 1990, np.

225 West Wacker Drive

"Another Chicago Job For Kohn Pedersen Fox." *Inland Architect,* November/December 1987, p. 19.

Bachmann, Wolfgang. "Chicago—Besuch bei den alten Damen." *Bauwelt*

(Germany), October 27, 1989, pp. 1920–1955.

Decker, Howard. "Chicago on the Rise." *Architecture*, February 1990, pp. 78–83.

Gapp, Paul. "Two on Wacker: 225 West, a Shorter, Kinder, Downtown Design." *Chicago Tribune*, July 21, 1991, Arts section, p. 14.

Goff, Lisa. "Chicago Builds a New Skyline." *Progressive Architecture*, January 1987, pp. 46–53.

Hadley, Candice. "Aspiring Spires." *Inside Chicago*, November 1989, pp. 72–73.

Kent, Cheryl. "Chicago Looks Up & Back." *Progressive Architecture*, July 1989, pp. 31–34.

"Portland Cement Association's 1990 Concrete Building Awards." *Architectural Record*, February 1991, p. 23.

Sachner, Paul M. "High-Risk High Rises." *Architectural Record*, October 1990, pp. 87–89.

"Sky's the Limit." *Chicago Tribune*, March 18, 1990, np.

"Two Chicago Buildings Selected as PCA Award of Excellence Winners." *Construction Digest*, February 4, 1991, np.

Capital Cities/ABC Headquarters
Dixon, John Morris. "P/A Portfolio: On the Sidewalks of New York." *Progressive Architecture*, July 1988, p. 76.

Geibel, Victoria. "Television Romance." *Architecture*, December 1990, pp. 56–59.

Gill, Brendan. "The Skyline: The Death of the Skyscraper?" *The New Yorker*, March 4, 1991, pp. 90–94.

Goldberger, Paul. "ABC Versus Neighbors: Stand-Off on West 67th Street." *New York Times*, January 17, 1988, sec. 2, p. 28.

United States Courthouse/Foley Square
Cohen, Ted. "Feds Take Shortcut to Foley Square." *Metropolis* (New York), December 1991, pp. 13–14.

Oser, Alan. "A Spur to Slow Construction." *New York Times*, April 28, 1991, sec. 10, pp. 5, 15.

Wolff, Craig. "Building Plans for Foley Square Are Unveiled." *New York Times*, March 30, 1991, pp. 21–22.

383 Madison Avenue/Scheme III
Anderson, Grace M. "Five by KPF." *Architectural Record*, February 1987, p. 126.

Futagawa, Yukio, ed. "Kohn Pedersen Fox." *GA Document* (Japan), April 1987, pp. 88–95.

"383 Madison Avenue Scheme III." *Architecture + Urbanism* (Japan), April 1988, pp. 34–37.

Canary Wharf Tower
"Canary Wharf Tower." *Architecture + Urbanism* (Japan), April 1988, pp. 42–45.

Chão, Sonia R., and Trevor D. Abramson, eds. *Kohn Pedersen Fox: Buildings and Projects 1976–1986*. New York: Rizzoli International Publications, 1987, pp. 278–285.

311 South Wacker Drive
Anderson, Grace M. "Five by KPF." *Architectural Record*, February 1987, p. 126.

Bachmann, Wolfgang. "Chicago—Besuch bei den alten Damen." *Bauwelt* (Germany), October 27, 1989, pp. 1920–1955.

"Case History Report." *Concrete Reinforcing Steel Institute*, 1991, np.

Davis, Jerry C. "Best of the '90s Nominees Make a Classy Final 40." *Chicago Sun-Times*, December 31, 1990, np.

Fisher, John, and William Michalenya. "Building Blocks for the Future." *Civil Engineering*, October 1990, p. 83.

Gapp, Paul. "Two on Wacker: 311 South: Beauty at the Base, A Beast On Top." *Chicago Tribune*, July 21, 1991, Arts section, p. 15.

Goff, Lisa. "Chicago Builds a New Skyline." *Progressive Architecture*, January 1987, pp. 46–53.

Harriman, Marc S. "High Strength." *Architecture*, October 1990, pp. 85–92.

Markoutsas, Elaine. "Building, Rehabs Pump Up Wacker." *Crain's Chicago Business*, October 21, 1990, np.

"1991 Design Awards Program." *New York Architecture Volume 4*. New York

Chapter/American Institute of Architects, 1991, pp. 11–12.

"Un nuovo grattacielo a Chicago: il 311 South Wacker Drive." *L'industria italiana del cemento* (Italy), October 1992, pp. 628–639.

Ridout, Graham. "High on Concrete: Concrete USA." *Building*, September 30, 1988, p. 43.

"Tall Concrete Buildings Come of Age." *Engineering News Record*, November 30, 1989, pp. 25–28.

"311 South Wacker Drive." *Architecture + Urbanism* (Japan), April 1988, pp. 38–41.

"311 South Wacker Drive, Chicago, Illinois, 1990." *Process: Architecture* (Japan), November 1989, pp. 116–121.

Wright, Gordon. "'Up/Down' Sequence Speeds Construction of Tallest Concrete Building." *Building Design & Construction*, January 1989, pp. 23–24.

———. "Chicago Tower Sets Concrete Height Record." *Building Design & Construction*, April 1991, pp. 56–59.

Chicago Title and Trust Center
Kamin, Blair. "Chicago Development Moves Out of the Loop." *Architecture*, October 1992, pp. 26–27.

Kent, Cheryl. "The New Towers Boost Chicago's Theater District." *Inland Architect*, May/June 1989, p. 5.

Masello, David. "KPF Twin Peaks to Rise in Chicago." *Architectural Record*, October 1990, p. 15.

Sachner, Paul M. "High-Risk High Rises." *Architectural Record*, October 1990, pp. 87–89.

One Fountain Place
"Fountain Place." *Architecture + Urbanism* (Japan), April 1988, pp. 50–53.

Merkel, Jayne. "Fountain Place, Cincinnati." *Inland Architect*, September/October 1986, p. 7.

"One Fountain Place, Cincinnati, Ohio." *Process: Architecture* (Japan), November 1989, pp. 82–85.

Station Center
"35th Annual P/A Awards: Station Center." *Progressive Architecture*, January 1987, pp. 98–100.

Goldman Sachs European Headquarters
"Architect-Designed Lighting." *Architecture*, June 1992, pp. 108–109.

Bussel, Abby. "(In)visible Giant." *Progressive Architecture*, March 1992, pp. 96–102.

"Goldman Sachs International Headquarters, London, U.K., 1990." *Process: Architecture* (Japan), November 1989, pp. 98–101.

"Goldman Sachs U.K. Headquarters." *Architecture + Urbanism* (Japan), April 1988, pp. 54–58.

Lydall, Sutherland. "Americans in London." *Progressive Architecture*, January 1989, pp. 37–38.

Mallett, Lee. "Imprint on Fleet Street." *Building Design*, February 19, 1988, p. 10.

Pawley, Martin. "Essay: Peterborough Court and Siblings." *Progressive Architecture*, March 1992, p. 103.

Powell, Kenneth. "Telegraph Topped Out." *Daily Telegraph* (London), March 3, 1990, p. 15.

Sala, Delia. "Goldman Sachs U.K. Headquarters." *Habitat Ufficio* (Italy), August/September 1992, pp. 68–77.

"A Welcome Invasion from the Other Side of the Atlantic." *Daily Telegraph* (London), March 13, 1990, np.

St. Paul Companies Headquarters
Mack, Linda. "They Leave a Bit of Themselves in What They Build." *Minneapolis Star Tribune*, February 7, 1991, pp. E1, E8.

———. "St. Paul Companies Building Has Just The Right Feel To It." *Minneapolis Star Tribune*, June 24, 1991, p. F1.

Meryhew, Richard. "St. Paul Companies' New Building a Boost For City." *Minneapolis Star Tribune*, July 24, 1990, np.

Millett, Larry. "Modernism Reaches Out to St. Paul." *St. Paul Pioneer Press Dispatch*, August 14, 1988, np.

———. "St. Paul's Designer Tower." *Inland Architect*, November/December 1988, p. 18.

———. "St. Paul Civility." *Architecture Minnesota*, July/August 1992, pp. 38–43.

Monson, Christopher. "Looming Large." *City Business Minneapolis*, October 28, 1990, pp. 17–21.

Nesmith, Lynn. "Modern Homecoming." *Architecture*, November 1992, pp. 76–83.

Peterson, Susan E. "The St. Paul Expansion Called 'Thing of Beauty.'" *Minneapolis Star Tribune*, August 4, 1988, np.

"St. Paul Companies Corporate Headquarters, St. Paul, Minnesota, 1991." *Process: Architecture* (Japan), November 1989, pp. 106–110.

Canary Wharf

Aldersey-Williams, Hugh. "Americans in London Docklands." *Progressive Architecture*, June 1988, pp. 27–28.

Davies, Colin. "Critique: On the Waterfront." *Progressive Architecture*, April 1992, pp. 122–125. Reprinted from *The Architects Journal*, London, December 1991.

"The Developer Who Looks a Decade Ahead." *London Times*, January 15, 1990, np.

Dietsch, Deborah K. "Americans in London." *Architecture*, September 1990, pp. 64–71.

Dixon, John Morris. "Isle of Dogs: An American Perspective." *Progressive Architecture*, April 1992, p. 126.

Futagawa, Yukio, ed. "Kohn Pedersen Fox." *GA Document* (Japan), April 1987, pp. 88–95.

Greer, Nora Richter. "Americans Abroad: Some Coming Attractions." *Architecture*, January 1989, pp. 64–71.

Joffroy, Pascale. "Londres a Bon Port." *Architectes et Architecture* (France), July/August 1988, p. 23.

Latham, Ian. "Tower Power." *Building Design* (London), November 21, 1986, p. 2.

Longworth, R. C. "London Constructs a European Gateway." *Chicago Tribune*, February 19, 1990, np.

Lydall, Sutherland. "Americans in London." *Progressive Architecture*, January 1989, pp. 37–40.

"Olympia & York—Canary Wharf." *Process: Architecture* (Japan), November 1989, pp. 102–105.

Piomella, Rosario Angrisano. "Office Complex, Canary Wharf, London 1984–1990." *Zodiac* 5, Editrice Abitare, 1988, pp. 116–159.

Mainzer Landstrasse 58

Dean, Andrea Oppenheimer. "European Forecast." *Architecture*, September 1990, p. 58.

Dietsch, Deborah K. "Americans in London." *Architecture*, September 1990, pp. 64–71.

Futagawa, Yukio, ed. "Kohn Pedersen Fox." *GA Document* (Japan), April 1987, pp. 88–95.

Greer, Nora Richter. "Americans Abroad: Some Coming Attractions." *Architecture*, January 1989, pp. 64–71.

Horsley, Carter B. "Touch of the Poets." *New York Post*, May 12, 1988, np.

Jonak, Ulf. *Die Frankfurter Skyline*. Frankfurt: Fisher Taschenbuck Verlag, 1991.

"Mainzer Landstrasse 58." *Architecture + Urbanism* (Japan), April 1988, pp. 46–49.

"Mainzer Landstrasse 58, Frankfurt, Germany, 1992." *Process: Architecture* (Japan), November 1989, pp. 90–94.

Metz, Tracy. "The New Downtown." *Architectural Record*, June 1992, pp. 80–85.

"35th Annual P/A Awards: Frankfurt Mixed-Use Complex." *Progressive Architecture*, January 1988, pp. 96–98.

1250 Boulevard René-Lévesque Ouest

Bronson, Susan. "'Superstar' Explains How to Build Skyscrapers that Work." *Montreal Gazette*, February 25, 1989, np.

Freedman, Adele. "Montreal's Newest and Finest Rises Above the Skyline." *Globe and Mail* (Montreal), May 16, 1992, p. C13.

Hustak, Alan. "View Masters." *Montreal Gazette*, January 2, 1992, pp. D1, D3.

Phillips, Rhys. "Montreal Skyscraper Awe-inspiring." *Ottawa Citizen*, February 29, 1992, p. 16.

"1250 Boulevard René-Lévesque Ouest, Montreal, Canada." *Process: Architecture* (Japan), November 1989, pp. 128–133.

Wagner, Michael. "Breaking Ground." *Interiors*, August 1989, p. 144.

Rockefeller Plaza West

Dunlap, David. "Rockefeller Center: The Labyrinthian Path to Building a 55-Story Tower." *New York Times*, September 9, 1990, sec. 10, p. 23.

Goldberger, Paul. "A Gesture to the 'Good' Rockefeller Center." *New York Times*, May 21, 1989, sec. 2, p. 32.

———. "Mute in Manhattan: A Politically Correct Building." *New York Times*, June 9, 1991, sec. 2, p. 38.

Huxtable, Ada Louise. "Rockefeller Plaza West." *Center: The Magazine of Rockefeller Center*, March/April 1991, pp. 4–9.

"Rockefeller Plaza West, New York, New York, 1993." *Process: Architecture* (Japan), November 1989, pp. 122–125.

"36th Annual P/A Awards." *Progressive Architecture*, January 1989, pp. 90–92.

White, Andrew. "The Center Moves West." *Metropolis* (New York), October 1990, pp. 26–29.

Three Bellevue Center

"First Interstate Plaza, Bellevue, Washington, 1991." *Process: Architecture* (Japan), November 1989, pp. 78–81.

"A Tower of Crystal Majesty." *Seattle Daily Journal of Commerce*, April 6, 1989, p. 1.

Chifley Tower

"The Bond Building, Sydney, Australia, 1992." *Process: Architecture* (Japan), November 1989, pp. 111–115.

Normile, Dennis, with Nadine Post. "Going Circles in Sydney." *Engineering News Record*, January 20, 1992, pp. 22–23.

———, with David B. Rosenbaum. "Sydney Tower Tests Australians." *Engineering News Record*, June 17, 1991, pp. 28C1–28C2.

550 South Hope Street

Canty, Don. "Core Concerns." *Architectural Record*, June 1990, pp. 58–65.

Newman, Morris. "L.A. Towers That Don't Forget the Pedestrians." *Progressive Architecture*, December 1992, pp. 13–14.

Morrison Tower

Brenneman, Kristina. "Office Tower Designer Wins Prestigious AIA Award." *Portland Daily Journal of Commerce* (Oregon), February 20, 1990, np.

Johnson, Angela P. "An Obstacle or an Oracle?" *Oregon Business*, July 1990, p. 69.

Ameritrust Center

"Ameritrust Center, Cleveland, Ohio, 1993." *Process: Architecture* (Japan), November 1989, pp. 126–127.

Barnett, Jonathan. "In Cleveland, Of All Places." *Architecture*, December 1988, pp. 88–91.

"Cleveland Office Boom to Add 6 Million Sq. Feet." *Building Design & Construction*, October 1990, p. 34.

Johnston, Christopher. "Three Towers to Peak in Cleveland." *Progressive Architecture*, May 1989, p. 26.

Miller, Carol Poh. " . . . And Cleveland's Designer Tower." *Inland Architect*, November/December 1988, p. 21.

"New Towers for Atlanta, Cleveland." *Building Design & Construction*, October 1988, p. 28.

Salisbury, Wilma. "Design for Essence of an Area." *Plain Dealer* (Cleveland), December 18, 1988, Arts section, p. 1.

Wagner, Michael. "Breaking Ground." *Interiors*, September 1989, p. 144.

"A Work of Art . . . Symbolic of the City: Ameritrust Center Envisioned as Mediator Among Towers." *Plain Dealer* (Cleveland), December 18, 1988, np.

World Bank Headquarters

Forgey, Benjamin. "Banking on the Past." *Washington Post*, April 28, 1990, np.

Rensbarger, Fran. "Washington: World Bank is Upgrading." *New York Times*, November 22, 1992, Real Estate section, p. 11.

Russell, James. "Middle-Age Makeovers." *Architectural Record*, March 1991, pp. 156–163.

"38th Annual P/A Awards." *Progressive Architecture*, January 1991, pp. 106–107.

Vonier, Thomas. "World Bank Report." *Progressive Architecture*, July 1990, pp. 23–24.

Federal Reserve Bank of Dallas

Barna, Joel Warren. "New Federal Reserve Bank in Dallas." *Progressive Architecture*, November 1990, p. 25.

Brown, Steve. "City Making Strides to Return to Boom Years." *Southwest Real Estate News*, May/June 1990, pp. 10–16.

————. "Work Underway on Fed Complex." *Dallas News*, June 15, 1990, np.

Dillon, David. "The Fed's New Home Provides an Instant Landmark." *Dallas Morning News*, September 8, 1992, pp. C1, C4.

Fisher, Daniel. "Federal Reserve Shows First Peek at New Headquarters in Dallas." *Dallas Times-Herald*, June 15, 1990, np.

Hampton, Jeff. "Fed Builds New Bank in Dallas." *New York Times*, September 4, 1991, p. D17.

Harriman, Marc S. "Government as Client." *Architecture*, April 1991, pp. 97–101.

Meydenbauer Convention Center

Adamson, Loch. "Art & Architecture." *Journal-American* (Bellevue, Washington), February 13, 1991, p. B1.

Enlow, Clair. "Bellevue Center Proceeding." *Seattle Daily Journal of Commerce*, June 20, 1990, sec. A, np.

Gantenbein, Douglas. "Bringing Up Bellevue." *Architectural Record*, July 1988, pp. 108–111.

Carwill House I

"Carwill House, Stratton Mountain, Vermont." *Process: Architecture* (Japan), November 1989, pp. 134–136.

Carwill House II

"The AD 100 Architects: An Exclusive Guide to the World's Foremost Architects." *Architectural Digest*, August 15, 1991, pp. 174–176.

Dixon, John Morris. "Viewing Angles." *Progressive Architecture*, November 1992, pp. 80–83.

"Pedersen Moonlights in Vermont." *Architectural Record*, May 1991, p. 19.

Mills House

"The AD 100 Architects: An Exclusive Guide to the World's Foremost Architects." *Architectural Digest*, August 15, 1991, pp. 174–176.

Hanseatic Trade Center

Waterfront: Una Nuova Frontiera Urbana. Venice: Centro Internazionale Città D'Acqua (exhibition catalogue), 1991.

University of Pennsylvania/Revlon Campus Center

Jung, Helen. "Architect is Selected for Campus Center Plan." *Daily Pennsylvanian* (University of Pennsylvania, Philadelphia), September 12, 1990, p. 1.

Newport Harbor Art Museum

Curtis, Cathy. "Local Architects Honor School Designs, 'On-the-Boards' Projects." *Los Angeles Times*, July 24, 1990, np.

————. "A New Epoch for Art Museum." *Los Angeles Times*, January 12, 1991, pp. F1, F19.

Vanderknyff, Rick. "Plans for New Home Put on Hold." *Los Angeles Times*, January 25, 1992, pp. F1, F18.

Awards

1986

New York State A.I.A.
Merit Award
General Re Corporate Headquarters
Stamford, Connecticut

New York City A.I.A.
What Might Be Award
Station Center
White Plains, New York

Precast/Prestressed Concrete Institute
Professional Design Award
Hyatt Regency
Greenwich, Connecticut

Precast/Prestressed Concrete Institute
Professional Design Award
Arbor Circle North and South
Parsippany, New Jersey

Friends of Downtown Chicago
Best New Building Design
333 Wacker Drive
Chicago, Illinois

Portland Cement Association
Award for Excellence
Tabor Center
Denver, Colorado

1987

Progressive Architecture
Design Award
Station Center
White Plains, New York

National A.I.A
Honor Award
Procter & Gamble Corporate Headquarters
Cincinnati, Ohio

New York State A.I.A.
Design Award of Merit
Hyatt Regency
Greenwich, Connecticut

1988

New York State A.I.A.
Design Award
70 East 55th Street
New York, New York

Progressive Architecture
Design Award
Mainzer Landstrasse 58
Frankfurt, Germany

Architectural Precast Association
Carl E. Shawver Award for Design Excellence
Third National Bank Tower
Nashville, Tennessee

National Association of Industrial and Office Parks
Best High-Rise Urban Design
500 E Street S.W.
Washington, D.C.

National Association of Industrial and Office Parks
Grand Award
Arbor Circle North and South
Parsippany, New Jersey

1989

New York City A.I.A.
Medal of Honor
Kohn Pedersen Fox Associates P.C.

New York City A.I.A.
Design Award Citation
Carwill House I
Stratton Mountain, Vermont

Progressive Architecture
Design Award
Rockefeller Plaza West
New York, New York

National A.I.A.
Brick in Architecture Award
ABC-TV Studio 23/24
New York, New York

Building Stone Institute
Tucker Award for Design Excellence
70 East 55th Street
New York, New York

1990

National A.I.A.
Architectural Firm of the Year Award
Kohn Pedersen Fox Associates P.C.

New York State A.I.A.
Excellence of Design Award
1325 Avenue of the Americas
New York, New York

Building Stone Institute
Tucker Award for Design Excellence
Lincoln Center
Minneapolis, Minnesota

Architectural Precast Association
Award of Merit in Design and Manufacturing Excellence
500 E Street S.W.
Washington, D.C.

Concrete Industry Board
Award for Excellence in Design and Construction
712 Fifth Avenue
New York, New York

Portland Cement Association
Concrete Building Award of Excellence
225 West Wacker Drive
Chicago, Illinois

Precast/Prestressed Concrete Institute
Honorable Mention
Shearson Lehman Hutton Plaza
New York, New York

Architectural Review Committee of Greenwich
William P. Deluca Award
Hyatt Regency
Greenwich, Connecticut

Architectural Review Committee of Greenwich
Cooperation Award
200 Greenwich
Greenwich, Connecticut

1991

New York City A.I.A.
Distinguished Architecture Citation
311 South Wacker Drive
Chicago, Illinois

Progressive Architecture
Design Citation
The World Bank
Washington, D.C.

New York Association of Consulting Engineers
First Prize for Engineering Excellence
712 Fifth Avenue
New York, New York

New York Association of Consulting Engineers
Certificate of Engineering Excellence
Mellon Bank Center
Philadelphia, Pennsylvania

New York Association of Consulting Engineers
Certificate of Engineering Excellence
Shearson Lehman Hutton Plaza
New York, New York

Precast/Prestressed Concrete Institute
Design Award
American Association of Retired Persons Headquarters
Washington, D.C.

Precast/Prestressed Concrete Institute
Special Recognition Award
125 Summer Street
Boston, Massachusetts

Concrete Industry Board
Award of Merit for Out of Area Citation
St. Paul Companies Headquarters
St. Paul, Minnesota

1992

Commerce Bank/Philadelphia Business Journal
Building Excellence Award
Mellon Bank Center
Philadelphia, Pennsylvania

Save Montreal
Le Prix Orange
1250 Boulevard René-Lévesque Ouest
Montreal, Canada

Significant Exhibitions

1986

Lieux de Travail
Centre Georges Pompidou, Centre de Creation Industrielle
Paris, France

Modern Redux: Critical Alternatives for Architecture in the Next Decade
The Grey Art Gallery and Study Center, New York University
New York, New York

South Ferry Plans and Proposals
The Urban Center Gallery, Municipal Art Society
New York, New York

New York City A.I.A. Unbuilt Awards Exhibition
The National Academy of Design
New York, New York

The Architecture of Kohn Pedersen Fox
The School of Design, North Carolina State University
Raleigh, North Carolina

Architectural Heritage Preservation
The Urban Center, New York City A.I.A.
New York, New York

1987

Portals: Points of Entry
Valencia Community College
Orlando, Florida

New New York
The Queens Museum
New York, New York

GA International '87
GA Gallery
Tokyo, Japan

Sketches–Ink Drawings–Renderings
Ballenford Architectural Books and Gallery
Toronto, Canada

New York City A.I.A. Awards Exhibition
The National Academy of Design
New York, New York

Special Recognition Award: Hyatt Regency Hotel
The Concrete Industry Board of New York
New York, New York

1988

Dessins sur Montréal 2
Complexe Guy Farreau, International Biennial in Urban Design
Montreal, Canada

New Chicago Skyscrapers
ArchiCenter Gallery, Chicago Architectural Foundation
Chicago, Illinois; Prague, Czechoslovakia

10 on 10: The Critics Choice
The Urban Center Gallery, New York City A.I.A.
New York, New York

100 Years—100 Architects
Gallery Ma
Tokyo, Japan; Osaka, Japan

The Current Architecture of Kohn Pedersen Fox
The Gallery of Design, The Merchandise Mart
Chicago, Illinois

Architecture Exhibit
A + U Gallery
Tokyo, Japan

Architecture
The Collegiate School
New York, New York

Excellence in Design: Heron Tower
New York State A.I.A.
New York, New York

135 Years and Still Growing
St. Paul Companies Headquarters
St. Paul, Minnesota

Experimental Skytowers
Water Tower Place, Rizzoli International Bookstore and Gallery
Chicago, Illinois

1989

New York Architecture 1970–1990
Traveling Exhibition, The Architecture Museum
Frankfurt, Germany; Madrid, Spain; Seville, Spain; Taipei, Taiwan

Design USA
Traveling Exhibition, United States Information Agency
The U.S.S.R: Moscow, St. Petersburg, Donetsk, Kishinev,
Dushanbe, Alma-Ata, Novosibirsk, Khbarovsk, Vladivostok

New Chicago Projects
The Chicago Athenaeum
Chicago, Illinois

Tall Buildings
Allendale Square
Perth, Australia

1990

Building by Design: Architecture at IBM
The National Building Museum
Washington, D.C.

1990 Salon International de l'Architecture
Grande Halle de la Villette
Paris, France

Architecture for the City: Kohn Pedersen Fox
Minnesota Museum of Fine Art
St. Paul, Minnesota

On the Waterfront: Site Sensitive Building by the Chicago River
ArchiCenter Gallery
Chicago, Illinois

Centennial Exhibition
The University of Pennsylvania
Philadelphia, Pennsylvania

Accent on Architecture
The American Institute of Architects
Washington, D.C.

Architecture in Boston 1975–1990
Bank of Boston, The Society of Architectural Historians Meeting
Boston, Massachusetts

Blueprints for Growth
Chapter Gallery, American Institute of Architects
Portland, Oregon

1990 Excellence in Design Awards
The Princess Hotel, New York State A.I.A. Convention
South Hampton, Bermuda

Kohn Pedersen Fox: Architectural Firm of the Year
George R. Brown Convention Center, National A.I.A. Convention
Houston, Texas

The New York City Panorama
The Queens Museum
New York, New York

New Chicago Architecture
Union Station
Washington, D.C.

Kohn Pedersen Fox Associates
YKK–Cupples Design Forum
Tokyo, Japan; Osaka, Japan

1991

Buenos Aires International Biennial of Architecture
Center of Art and Communication (CAYC), Cultural Center of the City
of Buenos Aires
Buenos Aires, Argentina

1991 Salon International de l'Architecture
Palazzo dell'Arte
Milan, Italy

Fukuoka Near Future Fair
Town Center and Art Gallery, United States Information Agency
Fukuoka, Japan

New York City A.I.A. Awards Exhibition
The New-York Historical Society
New York, New York

**The Art of Architectural Drawings and Photography in America
1956–1990**
The Rye Arts Center
Rye, New York

New Chicago Architecture
The Chicago Athenaeum
Chicago, Illinois

Celebrating the Architecture of Our New Home
The Mellon Bank Center, Ballard, Spahr, Andrews & Ingersoll
Philadelphia, Pennsylvania

Architektur und Aufzüge
Architektur Forum, Otis
Zürich, Switzerland

1992

**Entre la Lira y el Arco: Figura y Abstracción en el Trabajo de Kohn
Pedersen Fox**
Museo de Arte Contemporaneo, Universidad Central
Santiago, Chile

Manifeste: 30 Ans de Création en Perspective 1960–1990
Centre Georges Pompidou, Centre de Creation Industrielle
Paris, France

Illustration Credits

All photographs, renderings, and architectural models were provided by Kohn Pedersen Fox in New York and London except those noted below. Our gratitude to those listed for their contribution to making this monograph possible.

Photographs:
Aker Photography, 16 top left, 225, 226, 227, 228, 229, 230, 231, 232 lower middle, 232 bottom
Tom Bonner, 209, 210, 211, 212, 213, 214–15
The Buffalo and Erie County Historical Society, 24 top
CI&A Photography, 205, 206, 207
Cable Studios, 85 top
The Chicago Historical Society, 22 bottom right (photo by Hedrich-Blessing)
Chris Edgecombe, 273, 274, 275
Elliot Fine, 18 bottom
Wayne N. T. Fujii, 161, 165, 166, 167, 168–69, 173, 176–77, 180–81, 284, 285, 286–87, 288, 289, 290, 291
Galleria dell'Accademia, 36
Dennis Gilbert, 116 left, 118, 119, 120–21, 122, 123, 124, 125, 128, 129, 148 right, 149, 150, 152, 153, 154–55, 156, 157, 158, 159
Simon Hazelgrove, 305
George Heinrich, 141
Horner, 14, 15, 109
James F. Housel, 221, 222, 223, 262–263, 264, 265
Timothy Hursley, 56–57
Warren James & Associates, 42–43
Barbara Karant, 10, 48, 49, 53, 105, 106, 107
Balthazar Korab, 23 top
Chun Y. Lai, 25 bottom left
George Lambros, 84, 85 bottom, 102–3
Lenscape, Inc., 190, 191
Mark Lohman, 27 top right
Oren Makov, 30 top
Barbara Mathes Gallery, 38 top
The Metropolitan Museum of Art, 35: Greek. Vases, Red-Figured. Athenian. 5th C. B.C. ca. 450 B.C. Bell Krater: Dionysos, Satyrs and Maenads. Attributed to the Methyse Painter. Detail: full view of Kitharist. Rogers Fund, 1907. (07. 286.85)
Gregory Murphey, 55, 101
The Museum of Modern Art, 22 top right: Ludwig Mies van der Rohe. *Glass Skyscraper.* 1922. Project. Model. Photograph courtesy Mies van der Rohe Archive, The Museum of Modern Art, New York;
39 bottom: Constantin Brancusi. *Bird in Space.* (1928). Bronze (unique cast), 54 x 8 1/2 x 6 1/2". Collection, The Museum of Modern Art, New York. Given anonymously;
40 top: Umberto Boccioni. *Development of a Bottle in Space.* (1912). Silvered bronze (cast 1931), 15 x 23 3/4 x 12 7/8". Collection, The Museum of Modern Art, New York. Aristide Maillol Fund;
40 bottom: Umberto Boccioni. *Unique Forms of Continuity in Space.* (1913). Bronze (cast 1931), 43 7/8 x 34 7/8 x 15 3/4". Collection, The Museum of Modern Art, New York. Acquired through the Lillie P. Bliss Bequest;
41 top right: Franz Kline. *White Forms.* (1955). Oil on canvas, 6' 2 2/3" x 50 1/4". Collection, The Museum of Modern Art, New York. Gift of Philip Johnson;
44: Alexander Rodchenko. *Line Construction.* (1920). Colored ink on paper, 14 3/4 x 9". Collection, The Museum of Modern Art, New York. The Riklis Collection of McCrory Corporation (fractional gift);
45 top: Laszlo Moholy-Nagy. *Yellow Circle.* (1921). Oil on canvas, 53 1/8 x 45". Collection, The Museum of Modern Art, New York. The Riklis Collection of McCrory Corporation (fractional gift);
45 bottom: El Lissitzky (Lazar Markovich Lissitzky). *Proun 19D.* (1922?). Gesso, oil, collage, etc., on plywood, 38 3/8 x 38 1/4". Collection, The Museum of Modern Art, New York. Katherine S. Dreier Bequest
The New-York Historical Society, 28 top (photo by Irving Browning)
Brian Nolan, 79, 80 top left, 80 top right, 326–27
Claes Oldenburg, 39 top (photo by Geoffrey Clements)
Peter Olson, 73, 74, 75, 76, 77
Richard Payne, 164, 170, 172, 246–47, 248, 249, 250–51, 252, 253, 254–55, 256–57, 258, 259
© Jock Pottle/Esto Photographics, 12 bottom, 13, 16 top right, 16 bottom, 17, 18 top, 25 top, 25 bottom right, 27 top left, 27 middle right, 58–59, 62–63, 67, 69, 80 bottom left, 80 bottom right, 81, 87, 89 top left, 89 bottom left, 89 bottom right, 92, 93, 110, 111, 135, 136, 137, 138, 139, 183, 186, 187, 188, 189, 193, 194, 195, 217, 236–37, 240–41, 242–43, 267, 268, 269, 270–71, 281, 294, 295, 301, 302, 303, 308, 309, 314–15, 317, 318–19, 336, 337, 348,

349, 350 left, 351, 352, 353, 357, 362–63, 365, 366, 367, 368, 372–73, 374, 375, 380–81
Cervin Robinson, 20, 30 bottom, 68, 70, 71, 88, 89 top right
Kevin Roche John Dinkeloo Associates, 23 bottom
© The Rockefeller Group, Inc., 22 top left
Thomas L. Schumacher, 24 bottom, 25 middle right, 26, 27 middle left, 29 right
Eric Sierins, 197, 198–99, 200, 201, 202, 203
Timothy Soar, 142–43, 144–45, 146, 147
Sporting Pictures Ltd., 32
Steinkamp/Ballogg Photography, 83
© Ezra Stoller/Esto Photographics, 22 bottom left
The Tate Gallery Collection, 38 bottom
Tropical Studios, 41 left
The Trustees of the Sir John Soane Museum, 25 middle left
© Judith Turner, 29 left, 50–51, 52, 54, 60–61, 126–27, 132–33, 171, 174–75, 178, 179, 383
© Luca Vignelli, 384, 385, 386, 387, 388
The Whitney Museum of American Art, 41 bottom right: Franz Kline. *Mahoning.* 1956. Oil and paper collage on canvas. 80 x 100 inches. (203.2 cm x 254 cm). Collection of the Whitney Museum of American Art. Purchase, with funds from the Friends of the Whitney Museum of American Art. 57.10
Don F. Wong, 131, 140, 277, 278 top left, 278 bottom left, 278 bottom right, 279 top left, 325

Renderings:
Peter Matthews, 219, 298–99, 300
Thomas Schaller, 12 top, 232 top, 232 upper middle, 233, 310–11, 320, 321, 322, 323, 328–29, 330–31, 338 bottom, 342–43, 344–45 top, 355, 356, 376, 377, 378, 379
Lebbeus Woods, 114–15
Vladislav Yeliseyev, 338 top, 339

Models:
Awad Architectural Models, 13, 16 top right, 16 bottom, 17 top, 17 bottom, 27 top right, 27 middle right, 110, 111, 183, 189 bottom left, 190, 191, 217, 236–37, 240–41, 242–43, 270–71, 301, 302, 303, 326–27, 348, 349, 350 left, 351, 352, 353, 362–63, 365, 366, 367
Kenneth Champlain, 186, 187, 188, 189 top left, 189 top right, 189 bottom right, 357 (new building)
Exhibit Group, 16 top left, 225, 226, 227, 228, 229, 230, 231, 232 lower middle, 232 bottom
Patricia Fleming, 18 top
Dale Flick, 27 top left, 193, 194, 195
Kandor Modelmakers, 273, 274, 275, 305
Michael Kennedy, 294, 295
M.G. Modelmaking, 368, 372–73, 374, 375, 380–81
Kazem Naderi and Rick Bottino, 281
1-2-3 Architectural Models, 309 (new building)
Waldemar Sokolowski and Janusz Skalski, 357 (urban context)
Tenguerian Models, 221, 222, 223, 309 (urban context)
Roderick Weaver, 336, 337

Editor's Acknowledgments

A book of this scope requires vision, will, and patience. Bill Pedersen provided the first, Gene Kohn, the second, and Shelley Fox, the third.

My discussions at KPF with David Leventhal, Bill Louie, Lee Polisano, Bob Cioppa, and Bob Evans offered profound insights into the common ground they share: working for better design, better architecture, and better cities in which to live.

Also at KPF, there are important collaborators who made this entire process fascinating. My thanks to Maura Barbour, Delva Cameron, Peter Catalano, Nancy Cheung, Richard del Monte, Georgia Goldstein, Gail Guevara, Gary Handel, Tomas Hernandez, Natalie Hlavna, Carrol McCutchen, Craig Nealy, Francisco Rencoret, Ilona Rider, Marjorie Rodney, Peter Schubert, Chris Strom, and David Terrien.

At Rizzoli special thanks go to Gianfranco Monacelli, David Morton, and Andrea Monfried. To Massimo Vignelli, many thanks for his beautiful design of the book, and to Abigail Sturges, my gratitude for seeing it realized. To Judith Turner whose art never ceases to impress and delight us, thank you. Thanks to Joseph Giovannini whose laser-like insight made us aware of important moments in the architecture of KPF. Many thanks to Christian Norberg-Schulz who enlightened and inspired us. And to Tom Schumacher for his numerous and stimulating ideas.

Many thanks also to past and present collaborators who have worked at KPF since 1976.

Warren A. James
New York, 1992